THE OUTDOOR TRAVELER'S GUIDE
THE ALPS

THE OUTDOOR TRAVELER'S GUIDE
THE ALPS

TEXT BY
MARCIA R. LIEBERMAN

PRINCIPAL PHOTOGRAPHY BY
TIM THOMPSON

STEWART, TABORI & CHANG

NEW YORK

Published in 1991 by
Stewart, Tabori & Chang, Inc.
575 Broadway, New York, New York 10012

Library of Congress Cataloging-in-Publication Data

Lieberman, Marcia, 1936–
    The outdoor traveler's guide to the Alps / text by Marcia R.
Lieberman ; photographs by Tim Thompson.
      Includes index.
      ISBN 1-55670-177-2
      1. Hiking—Alps—Guide-books.   2. Outdoor recreation—Alps—Guide
-books.   3. Alps—Description and travel—Guide-books.
    I. Thompson, Tim, 1942–   II. Title.
    GV199.44.A4L54   1991
    914.94'7—dc20   91-3146
                                                CIP

Distributed in the U.S. by Workman Publishing,
708 Broadway, New York, New York 10003
Distributed in Canada by Canadian Manda Group,
P.O. Box 920 Station U, Toronto, Ontario M8Z 5P9
Distributed in all other territories by
Little, Brown and Company, International Division,
34 Beacon Street, Boston, Massachusetts 02108

Printed in Japan
10 9 8 7 6 5 4 3 2 1

Design: Lynn Pieroni and Paul Zakris
Maps: Guenter Vollath
Natural-history consultant: John Farrand, Jr.
Captions: Bettina Drew
Index: Pat Woodruff

Air transportation for the principal photographer
of this book was provided by

Contents

Author's Acknowledgments

THE WRITING OF A BOOK covering the entire alpine region, involving six countries and five languages (French, German, Italian, Slovenian, and Romansch), as well as numerous technical areas, was a daunting challenge. I wish to express my deepest appreciation to native speakers of these languages who assisted with translations and to the many experts in various fields who provided invaluable assistance in the preparation of this text.

Professor Bruno Giletti of the Department of Geological Sciences at Brown University was instrumental in guiding the section on geology. I will not forget his patience and good humor as I struggled with the complexities of this field. I would also like to acknowledge his colleague, Professor Tim Byrne, who advised me on this subject at an earlier stage of the manuscript. Gordon Binkhorst provided valuable research assistance.

Professor Johanna Schmitt of the Graduate Program in Ecology and Evolutionary Biology at Brown University Department was extremely generous with her time, reviewing and correcting my descriptions of alpine plants; during the course of several consultations she taught me a great deal about this subject. Marguerite Dorian graciously provided additional assistance. I also wish to express my gratitude to John Farrand, Jr., for carefully reviewing my texts on alpine geology, fauna, and flora.

Professor Heinrich Bülthoff of the Department of Cognitive and Linguistic Sciences at Brown University was an invaluable help with German translation; Heidi Smith, William Tecumseh Fitch, Edith Fabos, Monika Helmle, and Daniela Fenwick-Smith also provided welcome assistance. Linda Campani and Dr. Blossom S. Kirschenbaum graciously helped with Italian translation.

The staff of various national tourist offices were of great assistance in collecting much-needed information. Erika Lieben and Regula Pickel of the Swiss National Tourist Office were indefatigable in finding and sending me material about even the most remote corners of Switzerland, and pulled many a "rabbit out of the hat" at a moment's notice. They also assisted in obtaining Romansch translations. Marion Fourestier of the French Government Tourist Office helped greatly with research, and similarly found answers to difficult questions. I am also grateful to Silverio Nardoni of the Italian Government Travel Office, Hedy Wuerz of the German National Tourist Office, to Elizabeth Karba of the Austrian National Tourist Office, and to Vesna Lonay of the Yugoslav National Tourist Office. Within Slovenia, Dušan Blažin was an excellent, knowledgeable guide to the Julian Alps, providing very interesting information about the natural history and culture of the Mt. Triglav region. I am very grateful to Mladen Berginc, Janko Humar, and

Irena Zdovc: among the numerous ways they assisted was to find excellent material for me in English about Mt. Triglav National Park.

I wish to express my warmest thanks to my editor, Maureen Graney, whose dedication, sound judgment, and tireless attention played a very major role in the formation of this book. It has been a privilege to work with her. I was also very fortunate in having the assistance of a superb copy editor, Moira Duggan, who scrutinized every line of the text and checked altitudes, distances, foreign names, and accent marks; any remaining errors are mine, not hers.

Finally, I owe a debt of gratitude almost greater than I can express to Philip Lieberman: his encouragement and assistance in myriad ways carried me through a long and complex project.

Photographer's Acknowledgments

THE ALPS IN THEIR SPECTACULAR diversity are nearly inexhaustible for the hiker. From the Dolomites to the Matterhorn, the landscape is singular and strong. There are few places on earth more rewarding on a trek of a day or a month.

As the photographer for this book on the Alps I shot in six countries throughout a year's period, exposing nearly eight hundred rolls of 36-exposure film. The logistics for covering such a broad area in the various seasons was considerable, and I am in the debt of the national tourist boards of all the countries for their kind assistance. In particular I want to express my deep appreciation to Erika Lieben at the Swiss National Tourist Office; Gerhard Markus of the Austrian National Tourist Office; and Eve Peterson at the French Tourist Office. Their constant involvement in lining me up with the right people in the many locales was indispensable.

I also want to convey a special thank you to many throughout the Alps who put me on the best paths and enriched my understanding of this grand environment. Notable among these are: Andreas Lechner, Hans Moser, Toni Wurzrainer, Hubert Schwaerzler, Amade Perrig, Jrene Schmocker, Friedrich Kratzer, Hans Danuser, Myriam Imseng, Pascale Favre, C. Kuster, Jean Brissaud, Alain Galvez, and the Cogne Tourist Bureau.

I would also like to gratefully acknowledge the support of BRITISH AIRWAYS, which flies to the following destinations in and near the Alps: Zurich, Geneva, Basel, Munich, Vienna, Salzburg, Milan, Turin, Bergamo, and Marseilles.

Introduction

THE ALPS are an awesome sight. They manifest every fascinating feature of the landscape that is now called "alpine" throughout the world: snowcapped mountains and towering peaks of sheer rock buttressed by jagged, knife-edged ridges, dangerous ice walls, and a profusion of glaciers of every sort—valley glaciers and hanging glaciers torn by the force of gravity and the steepness of their beds into precipitous, wild, labyrinthine icefalls. This challenging terrain proved so irresistible to certain nineteenth-century men and women that they created the sport of alpinism. Trained with Alpine techniques and using equipment largely developed in the Alps, mountaineers then set forth to climb the peaks of the Himalayas, the Andes, and Antarctica. And although skiing was introduced to the Alps from Scandinavia only within the last hundred years, the Alpine countries have radically transformed the sport with new downhill, or "alpine," ski techniques and the equipment to make them possible.

The landscape of the Alps, however, is more than a monochromatic realm of rock, ice, and snow. Between tree line and the permanent snow line is a region of grasses and herbaceous plants, the alpine meadows with their profusion of astonishing, brilliant wildflowers. Owing to their geographical location (the highest peaks are near 46° of latitude) and the resulting low snow line, meadows are so close to glaciers in the Alps that the eye can see the dazzling contrast of green meadows and the brilliant white icing of the glaciers above them. In the Himalayas, much farther south, the permanent snow line is generally much higher so that often a great expanse of barren terrain separates pasture and glacier; the two can be seen together in the same view only from afar. In the Colorado Rockies, high grassland is abundant, but there are no great glaciers above it.

The Alps are also unusual in that they are near the centers of European civilization, and so are extraordinarily accessible. Major gateway cities include Geneva, Zurich, and Milan; there are also approaches from Grenoble, Nice, Vienna, Ljubljana, Munich, Bern, Salzburg, Innsbruck, Venice, and Turin.

Geographically, this great chain is composed of three sections: the western, central, and eastern Alps. The western Alps are the highest, with peaks in France, northwestern Italy, and Switzerland soaring over 4,000 m/13,000 ft; the easternmost Alpine peak over 4,000 meters is the Piz Bernina, in southeastern Switzerland. The central Alps, not quite as high but in places still plentifully surrounded by glaciers, extend between eastern Switzerland and central Austria, including the Alpine parts of Germany. The still lower eastern Alps are found in eastern Austria and Slovenia.

The only true wilderness in these mountains is in the zone of the glaciers, for many of the valleys have been settled since ancient times. As in other mountainous regions of the world with difficult terrain and climate, the people here formerly depended on milk and cheese derived from their herds and flocks, ensuring this supply by the strategy of dual pastures. In summer, the sheep, goats, and cattle are driven up from valley farms to the high-alpine meadows to graze; a summer farm, consisting of uncultivated mountain pastures and a simple hut where milk is turned into cheese, is called an *alp* (*alm* in much of Austria, *alpage* or *pâturage* in French, *malga* in Italian, and *planina* in Slovenian). While the animals graze on these high pastures, grass is mown in the valleys as many as three times in a summer, to prepare enough hay for winter fodder. Travelers in the Alps will see this economy still practiced nearly everywhere.

The Alps can be visited and enjoyed throughout the year, although not every activity can be practiced in every season. Conditions vary from year to year, of course, but snow generally falls in the high mountains by the end of October or early November, somewhat later in the lower mountains and hills. Most of the high roads over the Alpine passes and also many hiking trails are clear by June, though some roads may be open earlier. Serious hikers should wait until at least the end of June; the hiking season extends until October. The national tourist offices of the Alpine countries can advise you about conditions each season. Lower areas may be toured in early spring. Most of the alpine wildflowers bloom in June or July, with the greatest variety and brilliance of flowers in early summer, yet many continue to bloom through August. The alpine weather in late summer is generally at its finest and most settled.

Most visitors to the Alps need to acclimatize to the higher altitudes, though mountain resorts on average are lower here than some in Colorado and New Mexico. The body adapts to high altitude on its own, usually within a few days to a week. It is important to give this process time; physical activity should be light at first, then gradually increase.

Outdoor Activities in the Alps

Hiking. The classic Alpine activity is also the simplest: walking. A network of hiking routes extends to almost every corner of the mountains. There are trails up every valley, connecting one farm to another; up many slopes, leading to the summer farms and meadows; and over nearly every pass, some of which were once trod by Roman armies as well as by shepherds, hunters, traders, and even smugglers. (In German, *Fussweg* is a footpath, *Wanderweg* is a hiking trail, *Bergweg* is a more challenging mountain trail, and *Höhenweg* is a trail high above a valley. A trail is *sentier* in French, *sentiero* in Italian,

ALPINE COUNTRIES

F R A N C E

G E R

GER

Rhein

Basel

Boden See

LIECHTENSTEIN

Oberstdorf

ALLGÄ

Vaduz

Bludenz

Zurich See

Zurich

GLARUS ALPS

Rhein

RÄTIKON

SILVRET

SW

Bern

Vierwaldstätter See

Davos Platz

RHAETIAN A

Lac de
Neuchâtel

Thunersee

Brienzersee

St. Gotthard Pass

St.
Moritz

ENGADINE N

SWITZERLAND

Lac Léman

BERNESE ALPS

Jungfrau ▲

Rhône

ALPS

LEPONTINE

Lago di Como

Sion

Simplon
Pass

Genève

VALAISIAN ALPS

Matterhorn

PARCO
NAZIONALE
INCISIONE
RUPESTRI

Chamonix

Great St Bernard Pass

Lago
Maggiore

Lyons

Mont Blanc ▲

Aosta

Courmayeur

Peisey-
Nancroix

VAL D'AOSTA

Milan

VANOISE MASSIF

GRAN
PARADISO
N.P.

VANOISE N.P.

Grenoble

Po

ECRINS N.P.

Turin

ECRINS

HAUTES-
ALPES

QUEYRAS

Monte Viso ▲

QUEYRAS
REGIONAL
NATURAL
PARK

I T A

L

A

Genoa

Rhône

MARITIME

MER
CANTOUR N.P.

VALLÉE DES
MERVEILLES

ALPS

Gulf of
Genoa

di

Nice

MONACO

LIGURIAN SEA

Marseilles

| 0 | | 100 Mi |
| 0 | | 100 Km |

senda in Romansch, and *gorska pot* in Slovenian.) There are also many long-distance walking routes, some of which cross national borders. Many cable cars and chair lifts operate in summer, and hikers of all ages often use them for a boost up to the high slopes. Unlike a backpacking trip in Alaska or a trek in the Himalayas, a long-distance mountain walk in Switzerland has many escape points, where in case of poor conditions or bad weather you can cut short a trip by catching a bus or train out of a valley.

Alpine hikers do not need to carry sleeping bags, tents, or stoves. Camping out is not customary in the Alps, and is actually forbidden in many places. By concentrating overnight use in a few locations, the Alpine countries preserve fragile terrain that could be damaged by extensive camping. Hikers as well as climbers stay in huts, generally owned and operated by the national alpine club, or in mountain inns or villages. Huts are usually in very scenic locations, often as close to great glaciers and mountains as a hiker can get. Therefore, this book includes many outings which have a hut as their destination; many can be visited for lunch on a day hike. (The term for hut is *Hütte* in German; *refuge* or *cabane* in French; *rifugio, capanna,* or *baito* in Italian; *chamanna* in Romansch; and *koča* or *dom* in Slovenian.)

Though their accommodations vary somewhat in different countries, huts are essentially very simple. Dormitory sleeping is the general rule, often on long platforms shared by both sexes, with mattresses laid side by side, though some huts may have private rooms for four or two persons. Blankets and pillows are provided; a hiker may bring a sheet sack, though most Europeans do not. Showers and hot water on the whole are rare, and in some places toilets are outside the building. Huts provide hot meals, usually large portions of simple, hearty fare, though breakfast generally consists of bread and jam with tea or coffee. These provisions, as well as plentiful supplies of wine, beer, and soft drinks, are dropped by helicopter in some places, hoisted up by special lift lines in others, and occasionally still brought in on the backs of mules or men. In huts used often by climbers, guests are expected to retire by 9 or 10 P.M., as climbers must rise much earlier than hikers (sometimes at 2 or 3 A.M.). Most huts are open from the end of June or early July until the end of September. Many huts have radiotelephones, and it is advisable to phone ahead for reservations, especially on weekends or, in France and Italy, for the month of August. (A small number of huts have no guardian or food, though cooking pots and stove are available. These are indicated on regional maps.)

Anyone may stay at an alpine club hut, though members pay a reduced rate; by reciprocal agreements, national clubs give discounts to members of other clubs. Membership in the Swiss Alpine Club requires sponsors; membership in the other clubs is open to anyone.

Many Alpine hikers rent a vacation apartment or a hotel room in a village and take day trips in various directions, returning to the village at night. Some of these villages, once simple farming communities, are famous resorts today, transformed by tourism and especially by skiing. This book offers general descriptions of various walking routes, but it is not a detailed hiking guide. It is essential that hikers obtain regional topographic maps, which are commonly for sale in villages near the particular mountain areas. This book should also be supplemented when possible by a hiking guidebook with specific route instructions. Local tourist offices usually can supply information on routes and their present conditions. Route descriptions in this book follow the standard method for orienting stream directions: the source of a stream (or glacier) is its point of orientation; thus the right bank of a stream or glacier is to the right as you head downstream.

The Alpine hiker should be equipped with a pair of well-fitting, previously broken-in boots with Vibram soles. Leather is preferable to any of the treated fabrics, as it can be more effectively waterproofed. With these, wear a thin inner liner sock and a heavier outer sock. Gaiters, even short ones, help keep boots dry in snow or rain. Since mountain weather is changeable, you should always carry a full rain suit (parka and rain pants), as well as a sweater and gloves or mittens; a wool cap also is recommended. A good sunblock and lip sunscreen are very important; sunglasses and a sun hat are essential. (If you are planning to take a glacier excursion, bring glacier goggles and use a total sunblock on all exposed skin and lips.) You should also have a water bottle, lunch or snack food, and some first-aid supplies, including a few strips of moleskin. To carry this gear, a fairly lightweight pack with an internal frame is sufficient. A good pack should be comfortable and fit the back and shoulders properly; smaller packs with shoulder straps set closer together provide a better fit for many women and shorter men (they can be purchased in many Alpine locations). A pair of three-section, collapsible trekking poles is exceedingly useful on steep and slippery terrain.

Skiing. Skiing is another of the great Alpine sports, increasingly enjoyed now in summer as well as winter at the numerous resorts that maintain summer ski areas on their glaciers. Though mostly downhill skiing is practiced, cross-country skiing has become a specialty in selected areas like the Goms in the Rhone Valley of Switzerland, Austria's Otztal, or the villages of the French Queyras, to name only a few. With increased interest in this sport, many resorts in most Alpine valleys now offer cross-country skiing opportunities. Some of the smaller resorts and villages that do not have extensive lift systems and large, highly developed downhill areas offer especially attractive cross-country trails. (Inquire about local ski rental possibilities before you go.) Ski mountaineering is another favorite Alpine activity, done mostly in the spring and often on week-long tours from hut to hut; the Haute Route from Chamonix to Saas-Fee is a classic tour. Such ski tours should be undertaken only by people who are in good condition, accompanied by a licensed guide.

Climbing. Alpinism is synonymous with technical climbing on rock, snow, and ice. There are magnificent opportunities and challenges in these mountains, where the sport of climbing was born. Licensed guides may be found throughout the Alps, and there are numerous climbing schools, some run by guides' associations. It cannot be emphasized too greatly that inexperienced, ill-equipped climbers who are unaccompanied by guides risk injury and death. The presence of a licensed guide is the closest thing to a guarantee of safety that a climber can have.

Other Sports. A wide range of freshwater sports are enjoyed in the Alps, including swimming, sailing, and windsurfing in the large Alpine lakes, where the cleanliness of the water and the grandeur of the scenery enhance the experience. Kayaking and fishing in rivers and streams are also available. Hanggliding has been practiced for many years, and paragliding (a riskier sport) is increasingly popular. Many resorts also offer tennis, golf, and horseback riding. And of course botanists and bird watchers have a field day in the Alps (note, however, that many Alpine flowers are protected and may not be picked).

Safety

Alpine hiking involves unavoidable risks that every hiker assumes and must be aware of. Trails vary greatly in their degree of difficulty and the level of physical conditioning they require. Moreover, trail conditions may have deteriorated since this book was written. Rockslides caused by winter storms or avalanches may destroy bridges or sections of trail. Trail conditions can even change from one day to the next: though safe on a dry day, a trail may become dangerous in rain, snow, or fog. Steep slopes of wet grass are very slippery.

The hiker should never venture onto a glacier, whether or not it is snow-covered, unless roped and accompanied by a licensed guide.

Watch and listen for falling stones when you pass under or near a slope. These can sometimes be knocked down by animals grazing above, or by other hikers. Signs are sometimes posted warning of rockfall (*Steinschlag; chute des pierres; caduta di sassi*). Never choose a picnic spot under a cliff or on a steep slope strewn with loose rock.

Snow avalanches are a danger during the spring skiing season, especially in areas away from the *pistes* (monitored tracks). During summer they are a risk only on technical climbing routes. Skiers should not leave the monitored

A lateral moraine is part of the trail to the Schönbiel Hut in Switzerland's Valaisian Alps. The glacier that deposited this pile of rock debris and gravel has long since melted away.

tracks on glacier ski areas unless accompanied by a licensed guide, because of the danger of hidden crevasses.

It is advisable to get a weather report before starting on a long route. If the weather should suddenly look threatening, turn around if still possible. If a thunderstorm approaches, descend at once from high, exposed points or ridgelines. It is essential to carry warm and waterproof clothes in your pack, and wise to have some food.

Though an Alpine tarn may look irresistible on a hot day, glacier-fed water is ice cold, and it may be risky to plunge in.

Poisonous snakes are found in the Alps, although they are generally rare; it is wise to check a stone before you sit on it. There is also rabies in some parts of the Alps, and warning signs may be posted. Beware of animals that are unnaturally friendly or appear ill.

Persons who are not physically fit, who are middle-aged or older, or who have a chronic health problem should consult their doctors before engaging in hiking or skiing during an Alpine holiday.

Geology of the Alps

THE ALPS form a great arc that curves from the French Riviera to Yugoslavia. They are not, however, a single line of peaks with similar geological characteristics. There is no continuous ridge that stretches from one end of the Alps to the other. Rather, the Alps are a series of roughly parallel ridges that extend in a band nearly 1,000 km/600 mi long and about 200 km/120 mi wide. The Alps have as complex a geology as any mountain region on earth: different regions, ridges, and often adjacent mountains have different geological characteristics that reflect a complex series of collisions between tectonic plates and subsequent events including foldings, movement, metamorphism, erosion, and glaciations.

Though numerous types of rock can be found in the Alps, there are three basic forms. *Igneous rocks* such as basalt and granite derive from magma, the molten material within the earth that rises toward the surface, or erupts as a result of volcanic action. *Sedimentary rocks* such as limestone result from the compaction and cementation of particles of broken rock as well as the remains of marine animals that were deposited on the floors of ancient seas. *Metamorphic rocks* such as schist and gneiss are the result of heat and pressure acting on sedimentary or igneous rocks buried deep beneath the earth's surface and transforming their mineral constituents and texture. Both igneous and metamorphic rocks are classified as crystalline. The particular characteristics of rocks are determined by their chemical composition and by the temperatures and pressures to which they were subjected as well as the rate at which igneous rocks cooled (which affects their crystal structure).

Geologists hypothesize that there was once only one landmass on our planet, the great continent of Pangaea. Two hundred million years ago, Pangaea broke apart into a series of huge fragments or plates that have since drifted across the globe. The Alps were initiated about 100 to 130 million years later, when the Italian prong of the African plate moved north across the old Tethys Sea, of which the Mediterranean is a small remnant, and collided with the Eurasian plate. Many of the rocks that form the highest mountains in Switzerland moved more than 100 km/60 mi from their source and were buckled and deformed by the tremendous horizontal forces that resulted from the collision of continents. The resulting geology is extremely complex. Imagine a stack of carpets that has been rumpled by being forcefully pushed on one side. The layers of carpet will fold and even overturn. Then imagine the layers of carpet being worn away from the top in some places, leaving bottom layers on top of what were upper layers; in other places, fragments of top layers remain uppermost, but may be upside down.

Some areas are simply kneaded together. This is analogous to the formation of the Alps.

Layers of sedimentary rock were once deposited in the basin of the Tethys Sea, and these layers, along with igneous and metamorphic rocks from a much older mountain-building episode 300 million years ago, represent the carpets in our example. As the tectonic plates pushed against each other, the rock layers of the Italian plate thrust upward, overrode the European plate rocks, and all were folded or fractured over and over to varying degrees in different patterns in the various regions of the Alps. The remains of these layers—broad sheets of rock called *nappes*—were moved, squeezed, folded, fragmented, and even partially melted and then eroded, yielding a disorderly state in which nappes derived from older layers of rock are often found on top of younger rock. In many instances, the nappes were folded in extremely convoluted patterns. The detailed geology of the region thus varies for individual and even neighboring mountains. The Matterhorn, for example, is a fragment of Italy that was pushed on top of the mass of Switzerland, whereas the nappe that forms Monte Rosa, less than 16 km/10 mi south, is of a different origin; it is part of the European plate. The highest mountain entirely within Switzerland, the Dom, was formed when the Monte Rosa nappe moved on top of another nappe.

Although the birth of the Alps can be traced back to the Cretaceous period (between 135 and 70 million years ago), when the Italian tectonic plate collided with that of the rest of present-day Europe, the Alps as high mountains are a recent geological phenomenon. By the Pliocene epoch, about 5 million years ago, during which the first human-like animals (Australopithecines) appeared in Africa, the original mountains had been worn down to a chain of low hills. They were subsequently uplifted, due to the continued movement of the tectonic plates, at about the same time that the first modern human beings probably appeared—about 250,000 years ago in the Pleistocene epoch. The final form of the Alps, in which its valleys and peaks were sculpted and carved, derives from the great glaciations of the Pleistocene.

These glaciations account for the principal geological division of the Alps—the western versus the eastern Alps. The western division includes the Alps of France, Switzerland, and the northwest of Italy, the dividing line being roughly at the Austrian-Swiss border. In the western Alps, glacial activity caused extensive erosion of the surface sedimentary rock formations, exposing much of the inner igneous and highly metamorphosed rocks.

In general, the Alps can be divided into three structural zones. The northernmost is the Helvetic nappe, which consists of large granite intrusions surrounded by metamorphic schists and gneisses—traditionally characterized as crystalline. The Helvetic zone includes the Mont Blanc massif as well

"Pot holes" in the limestone beside the trail to the Refuge du Col de la Vanoise, in France's Vanoise National Park, were produced by the action of water. Facing page: Layers of sedimentary rock tilted upward in the Mont Blanc area are evidence of the great forces that formed the Alps.

as the Mercantour in southeastern France. In Switzerland, it includes the Diablerets, Wildhorn, and Gotthard, as well as the great peaks of the Bernese Oberland such as the Jungfrau, Eiger, and Mönch.

The Pennine nappe to the south consists of a number of smaller nappes including the St. Bernard, Monte Rosa, and Dent Blanche nappes, among many others. The overall structure of this zone is especially complex because the individual Pennine nappes are different in their structures; indeed, they are grouped in different ways by different scholars. The core of the Pennines is generally old Paleozoic crystalline rock covered in many places by highly metamorphosed sedimentary rocks, including the mica schist that characterizes much of the Pennine Alps. (The Paleozoic era extended from 570 to 225 million years ago.) The Gran Paradiso in Italy and part of the Vanoise in France belong to the Pennine zone.

The third zone is the Austro-Alpine, consisting of gneisses, granites, and other rocks altered by metamorphic processes; it forms a limited belt roughly to the east and south of the Gran Paradiso. The Briançonnais, an area of sedimentary and slightly metamorphosed sedimentary rock, occurs in France between the Mercantour and the Mont Blanc nappes (both Helvetic) and the Pennine nappes. The dolomite rock of the Col de l'Iseran in the Vanoise, for example, is part of the Briançonnais section. The eastern Alps have a somewhat simpler character. Their northern section consists of a band of sedimentary limestone mountains north of the Inn River. They include all the German Alps as well as the Dachstein massif, southeast of Salzburg. To the south, the Austro-Alpine zone sweeps in a wide band to Slovenia, with underlying Pennine rock formations exposed by erosion in several "windows" such as the Hohe Tauern and the Zillertal Alps, where underlying gneiss is exposed. For the most part the Austro-Alpine cover consists of slate (metamorphosed sedimentary rock); some igneous rocks are also present. The Dolomites in northeastern Italy consist of slightly metamorphosed sedimentary dolomite and limestone.

Glaciers. Besides tectonic movement, the other great factor that created the present Alpine landscape was glaciation. Geologists long believed that there were four great glacial episodes; recent theories hold that there have been many more, with a cyclicity of about 100,000 years—at least 20 major glacial advances. The glaciers were once far more extensive than they are today, extending far down into the lower valleys and covering all but the summits of the region. Though the glaciers have greatly receded since the last ice age, glaciers remain in many parts of the Alps and are one of the most distinctive features of this great chain. (The word for *glacier* is *Gletscher* or *Ferner* in German, *glacier* in French, *ghiacciaio* in Italian, *Vadret* in Romansch, and *ledenik* in Slovenian.)

A glacier is a mass of ice that flows over land. In an area where more snow falls than melts, the snow can reach a thickness so great that it recrystallizes into ice. Depending on the steepness of the underlying surface and the increasing mass of the ice, it will begin to move under its own weight, at which point it is considered to be a glacier.

Land elevation causes glaciers to form: at high altitude, snow falls instead of rain; northern-facing slopes receive less of the sun's light and warmth and retain even more snow through the summer. Thus glaciers form because of topography, but they also affect the topography: glacial action carves out both the valleys and their mountains.

There are several kinds of mountain glaciers: *valley glaciers* are broad rivers of ice flowing at a moderate gradient; *tributary glaciers* are higher and pitched at a steeper angle than the valley glaciers they feed; *cirque glaciers* are set against steep mountain walls or in hollows at their base.

A glacier may move from a few centimeters to a few meters per week, moving at a faster rate in its center than along its sides. Because the movement is slow, the ice exposed at the downstream end of a glacier (sometimes called its tongue, snout, or toe) may have traveled for hundreds or even thousands of years since it originated as fallen snow at the upstream part.

As a glacier flows from a bed of moderate grade down a steeper slope, the brittle upper surface of the ice cracks, forming the *crevasses* that are such a dangerous feature of these bodies of ice. Crevasses may be as deep as 50 to 60 m/160 to 200 ft. Glaciers are described as "covered" (that is, by snow) or "uncovered": on a covered glacier the crevasses are invisible, being hidden under snow, greatly increasing the danger to persons crossing the glacier. Some glaciers remain covered year-round. Many steep areas present the danger of icefalls: fracture of the ice creates huge blocks or towers of ice known as *séracs;* because of the underlying motion of the ice the séracs are unstable. Glaciers expand when the climate becomes cooler and more moist. They recede when it becomes warmer and drier; though the ice continues to flow in the same direction, the downstream section melts back faster than it can be resupplied with more ice flowing from the upstream section.

The landscape of the Alps was profoundly altered by glaciation. A moving glacier breaks off chunks, both large and small, of the rock over which it flows, carrying boulders, rock fragments, and also fine particles of sand or silt, as well as debris that falls onto the ice from nearby cliffs. The larger rocks gouge, scrape, and cut grooves in the underlying bedrock, while the finer particles, like sandpaper, polish the rock beneath. Glacial streams carrying this sand and silt (known as rock flour) often have a cloudy, milky appearance. The load deposited by a glacier along its sides is a *lateral moraine;* the load dumped by a glacier at the farthest point it reaches is a *terminal moraine.* As a glacier retreats from that point it may deposit *end moraines.* Material carried along the center of a glacier appears as a dark stripe, called a *medial moraine.*

Among the most characteristic features of a glaciated landscape are *cirques,* in which mountain walls are hollowed out by glaciers into cavities like half-bowls. When cirque glaciers pluck away at a ridge from both sides, the result is an *arête,* a jagged, knife-edge ridge. When the top of two cirques meet, a *gap, notch,* or *pass* is created. (In German the words for *pass* are *Pass, Joch,* or *Sattel,* and in some parts of Switzerland the words *Furgg* and *Furka* are used. In French, the term is *col;* in Italian, *passo;* in Romansch, *pass* or *fuorcla;* and in Slovenian, *sedlo.*) When cirque glaciers eat away at rock from three or more sides, the result is a *horn,* or pyramid-shaped peak, of which the Matterhorn is a classic example. Small lakes, such as the Schwarzsee below the Matterhorn, often are found in the basin of a cirque from which the glacier has disappeared. A large cirque at the head of a glaciated valley is often called an *amphitheater.*

The movement and erosive action of glaciers created the characteristic U-shaped valleys of the Alps (valleys created by the action of a river or stream are usually V-shaped). *Hanging valleys* are often a feature of glaciated landscapes: these result when the main valley glacier cuts faster and deeper than its tributaries can keep pace with; the tributary valleys remain "hanging" above the main valley.

The French Alps

The French Alps are in the southeastern part of France, extending along the Italian border. From the Prealps near the French Riviera they rise northward to the culminating peak of Mont Blanc near the Swiss border. The main alpine regions are the Mercantour, the Queyras, the Ecrins, the Vanoise, and the Mont Blanc massif. In all of these regions except the Mont Blanc massif there are national parks or regional natural parks protecting large scenic areas.

National Parks. The French national parks system is relatively new: the first one, the Parc National de la Vanoise, was established in 1963. The parks contain two zones, central and peripheral. In the central zone no permanent habitation or new construction is allowed, and hunting, fishing, and the gathering of plants is prohibited. In the peripheral zone, villages and resorts, including ski developments, are permitted.

Regional Natural Parks. These parks were created around inhabited zones. Their purpose is to protect not only the environment, wildlife, and sites of architectural and historic interest, but also to preserve the life and culture of the local people

Sheep graze in the high meadows of the Vanoise National Park, but ibex and other wild animals live here as well and are protected by park regulations.

23

and their traditional agricultural systems. Certain kinds of development are encouraged, such as the formation of agricultural cooperatives, the organizing of local artisans, and the creation of hiking trails and cross-country ski routes.

Ski Resorts. France is the European center of "purpose-built" Alpine ski resorts. Whereas in nearly all other parts of the Alps old villages have formed the basis for alpine ski development, the French have created entirely new resorts on virgin sites for the sole purpose of skiing. Modernity is the rule. The hotels and apartment buildings are often built of concrete in contemporary style, six or even eight or 10 stories high. The entire complex is designed to maximize skiing opportunities: lift systems are not only multiple but may also be so close to hotels that some can boast "door-to-door" skiing. The object is to make it possible to spend as many daylight hours as possible on the slopes. In considering a resort, skiers in France must weigh the advantages that these resorts provide in terms of sport against the charm of traditional village settings found elsewhere.

In most parts of the Alps, the old villages that have become alpine centers are all-season resorts. In France, however, most resorts are clearly favored in one season or another. Many villages that serve as a base for summer hiking into French Alpine areas are too modest to be called resorts at all and some are not accessible in winter. The great artificial ski resorts may have a few visitors in summer—cable cars operate and there are hiking trails—but winter is by far their most important season.

Les Grandes Randonnées. These are a series of French long-distance hiking routes, each with its own number. The GR 5, or Grande Randonnée Cinq, for example, extends from Metz, in northeastern France, to Nice on the Mediterranean coast. The routes are generally blazed or marked with their number. It is easy for day-hikers to pick up one segment of a GR. Routes within other Alpine countries are usually marked only with the next destination; long-distance European routes are marked by the letter E and a number (E 4, for example).

Refuges de Montagne and Gites d'Etape. The refuges are the huts of the CAF, the French Alpine Club. Gites d'Etape, found along the GR routes and in hamlets and some villages, are privately owned inns or private homes providing the plainest accommodations, often dormitory-style. Guests are expected to arrive on foot; some places allow guests to cook. Travelers to France should be aware that most of the French vacation during August. Advance booking for hotels and even alpine club huts is advisable during that month.

Addresses: For information on France, contact the French Government Tourist Office.

In the U.S., the public information number nationwide is 1-900-420-2003. Addresses in major cities are as follows: 610 Fifth Avenue, New York, NY 10020-2542. 645 North Michigan Avenue, Chicago, IL 60611-2836. 2305 Cedar Springs Road, Suite 205, Dallas, TX 75201. 9454 Wilshire Boulevard, Suite 303, Los Angeles, CA 90212-2967.

In Canada, the tourist office has two addresses: 1981 Avenue McGill College, Tour Esso No. 490, Montreal, QUE H3A 2W9; (514) 288-4264. 1 Dundas Street, West Suite 2405, Box 8, Toronto, ONT M5G 1Z3; (416) 593-4723.

In Great Britain, the tourist office address is: 178 Piccadilly, London WIV OAL; (44) 1 493-9232.

For information on joining the French Alpine Club, contact: Club Alpin Français (CAF), 24 Avenue de Laumière, 75019 Paris, France; (33) 1-42 02 68 44.

The Fédération Française de la Randonnée Pédestre (FFRP) publishes information on hiking in France. There is no individual membership in this federation; membership is obtained only by joining one of the many associations that belong to it. These include the Club Alpin Français. For a list of member associations or other information, contact: Fédération Française de la Randonnée Pédestre, Centre d'Information, 64, rue de Gergovie, 75014 Paris, France; (33) 1-45 45 31 02.

The Maritime Alps and the Mercantour National Park

AT THE SOUTHWESTERN TIP of the entire Alpine range are the Maritime Alps. The toe of the Alps is so close to the French Riviera that hikers coming down from the GR 5, one of the great trans-European hiking routes, can walk into Nice on their last day on the route. This is a transitional zone of mountains generally much lower than their cousins to the north, without glaciers and soaring peaks, but with the special charm that comes from a climate and vegetation still influenced by the Mediterranean. There are striking contrasts between the olive groves of the lower terrain, the larches and pines of the subalpine zone, and the alpine meadows above tree line.

In 1979 on the Mercantour massif, in the center of this region, the French created the Parc National du Mercantour. The highest mountains of this region are part of the same formation that produced the immense French Alps to the north, including the Mont Blanc group. The Maritimes are composed largely of granite, with areas of metamorphic schist and gneiss. At their western edge, however, mainly west of the Tinée River, the mountains are formed primarily of limestone.

Redstone in the Maritime Alps' Gorges du Cians was eroded over the centuries by rushing river waters. Facing page: The tributary streams of the Var River carved a series of canyons that lead into the Mercantour. The vegetation in the Gorges du Cians reflects the mild climate close to the Mediterranean.

This region shares the characteristic dryness of Provence. Snowfall is abundant in the higher mountains, but the region as a whole gets less rainfall than other Alpine areas.

The forest that once covered much of the Mercantour region was destroyed as land was cleared for grazing and farming. Reforestation is proceeding, however, and larch, fir, and pine once again cover much of the country. The tree line extends to the tops of the lower ridges, which as a result do not have a high-alpine appearance. The lower slopes are covered with forest containing a mixture of conifers and deciduous trees, including oak, chestnut, and hazelnut. In the higher, subalpine zone (up to 2,000 m/6,560 ft) the deciduous trees give way to conifers: larches, pines, fir. Above tree line is the recognizable alpine world of meadows, talus and scree slopes, and mountain walls and ridges.

Typical alpine fauna, including chamois, are found in these lower mountains, as in the higher Alps. Ibex, not native to this region, have been introduced here from Italy's Gran Paradiso National Park. Found at somewhat lower altitudes than chamois and ibex are mouflon (*Ovis musimon*), large, thickset wild sheep; the males have big, curved horns. They are also more timid than ibex, and much less tolerant of a human presence. This animal was introduced into the Mercantour from Corsica.

The villages on this southern flank of the Maritimes still have a Provençal appearance, with clusters of stone houses perched on ledges overlooking the slopes, rather like the hill towns seen farther south in Provence and Italy. The hillsides are frequently terraced for cultivation, another sight unusual in the Alps, and though many slopes are no longer farmed and have become overgrown with trees, the steps of the terracing are still visible.

The hill country and low mountains above the French coast comprise the Haute Provence. The southern part of this region is characterized by a series of impressive gorges—deep, narrow canyons that guard the approaches to the Mercantour. These were mainly formed by various tributaries of the Var, the biggest river along the eastern Riviera, which flows into the Mediterranean near Nice. One of the grandest of these canyons is the Gorges du Cians, formed by the Cians as it cuts its way south to reach the Var. The Cians originates in the Mercantour high country, and in a short distance sinks into a deep channel cut through dizzyingly steep walls of rock.

THE HAUTE VESUBIE

The Mercantour National Park extends in a somewhat narrow, horizontal band along the French-Italian border. The eastern part of the Mercantour is located in the district known as the Haute Vésubie, the upper reaches of the Vésubie River. Most of the highest mountains are in the Haute Vésubie, along the Italian border. The valley of the Vésubie, narrow and wooded, forms a main approach to the center of the park. Roquebillière and St.-Martin-Vésubie are two charming mountain villages near this entrance to the park.

From the Vallée de la Vésubie, the main course of the river, several tributary valleys descend from the Mercantour massif: the Boréon, Madone de Fenestre, and Gordolasque valleys.

Le Boréon

North of St.-Martin is the hamlet of Le Boréon with a hotel, a refuge, and several vacheries (mountain dairies). Le Boréon is a base for many hikes into the mountains and around the little lakes that lie within their folds and ridges. One trail from Le Boréon leads northward to the Lac du Mercantour, situated below a cirque hollowed out by an ancient glacier, long since vanished, from the Cime du Mercantour (2,772 m/9,094 ft). From the end of the small road that continues east of Le Boréon, you can hike northeastward to a junction, and then northwest to the twin Lacs Bessons on the steep, rugged slopes of the frontier ridge; there is an excellent view of the Tête de la Ruine (2,984 m/9,790 ft). The other trail from the junction leads northward to the Refuge de la Cougourde, sited below the Cime de l'Agnel (2,927 m/9,603 ft). From Le Boréon you can also pick up the GR 52 eastward to the Lac de Trecolpas. Le Boréon is a cross-country ski center.

Vallon de Madone de Fenestre

From St.-Martin-Vésubie, a small road leads northeast up the almost empty valley of Madone de Fenestre. Near the end of the road are several vacheries, a hotel, and a refuge. A trail climbs northward to the Lac de Fenestre, below the frontier ridge. Another walk leads eastward from Madone de Fenestre and then southeast to the Lacs de Prals, five pretty lakes in a fold below Mont Neiglier (2,786 m/9,140 ft).

Vallon de Gordolasque

This valley climbs northeast from Roquebillière toward the border. Past several vacheries and at the end of the road, a trail leads north to the Lac de la Fous, beneath the slopes of the biggest peak in the Mercantour park, the Cime du Gélas (3,143 m/10,311 ft). Near the lake is the Refuge de Nice.

SPRING GENTIAN
Gentiana verna
PURPLE GENTIAN
Gentiana purpurea

There are numerous species of gentians in the Alps of varying color and appearance. The purple gentian bears clusters of tubular reddish-purple flowers, with petals drawn together or slightly parted, like those of a barely-opened tulip. The inside of the petals is pale, and spotted with red. With its head of flowers, the plant reaches 20 to 60 cm/8 to 24 in. The leaves are large, long, and pointed.

This gentian flowers from July to August on alpine meadows and clearings in the woods, on lime-poor soil, from 1,600 to 2,700 m/5,249 to 8,858 ft. The Hungarian gentian *(Gentiana pannonica)*, found in the eastern Alps, is very similar, as is the spotted gentian *(Gentiana punctata)*, which has yellow flowers with purple spots.

Another flower, the spring gentian, is of distinctly different appearance. These little flowers are a brilliant electric blue, a color so saturated that this is perhaps the most vivid of all alpine flowers. Though each plant has only a single flower, the stalks grow in very close groups, creating the effect of small masses of vibrant color. The short stems grow out of a base surrounded by small olive leaves, and each plant is about 5 to 15 cm/2 to 6 in high.

The spring gentian blooms soon after the snow melts, generally in April, and remains into July or even August. It grows at altitudes between 800 and 3,000 m/2,600 and 9,800 ft in meadows and among boulders on almost any soil.

Spring gentian.

Purple gentian.

Facing page: Verdant hillsides and a backdrop of austere blue mountains follow France's highest car route, a steep and narrow road leading from the picturesque village of St.-Etienne-de-Tinée to the Col de la Bonette.

Another trail climbs northeast to Lac Autier, in a wild and lonely basin in the center of an ancient glacial cirque: crowning its jagged walls are the Tête du Lac Autier (2,740 m/8,990 ft), Tête Nord du Basto (2,794 m/9,167 ft), and Mont du Grand Capelet (2,935 m/9,629 ft). There is a small cross-country ski center in the Gordolasque valley.

LA VALLEE DES MERVEILLES

East of St.-Martin-Vésubie is a site known as la Vallée des Merveilles. Scattered here in an area of more than 12 km/7.5 mi near Mont Bégo are over 100,000 Bronze Age rock engravings, dating from 1800 to 1500 B.C. The marks include stylized animal and human forms and nonrepresentational shapes. Archaeologists believe that these early people made special journeys up into this high alpine valley to carve images into the great smooth slabs of schist so abundant here. The landscape is full of lakes and strewn with boulders; the rounded forms of ancient mountains create an undulating horizon and enhance the mysterious effect of these signs of a forgotten culture.

You must hike into the region to see la Vallée des Merveilles. There is access from three valleys. The easiest approach is from the Roya Valley, to the east. From St.-Dalmas-de-Tende a small road leads west to the Lac des Mesches, from which there is a path to the Refuge des Merveilles. (You can get a jeep ride from Mesches to the hut.) A much longer walk starts on a road between Roquebillière and Lantosque that leads eastward to the Col de Turini. From there a small road continues northeast to L'Authion, ending in a loop. From the northern edge of this loop you can pick up the GR 52, heading north to the Col de St.-Véran, which leads into the Merveilles area. A third route starts from the upper end of the Gordolasque valley, at the Pont du Countet, where a trail leads eastward over the Pas de l'Arpette into the Vallée des Merveilles.

The Vallée des Merveilles lies between the Mont du Grand Capelet on the west and Mont Bégo (2,872 m/9,422 ft) on the east. At the southern end of the valley, amid a group of lakes, is the Refuge des Merveilles, where a series of open-air tables present explanations of Bronze Age life. Guided tours are available in July and August. From the hut, a trail leads up the valley. At its northern end, beside another group of lakes, is the Refuge de Valmasque. At an altitude of over 2,000 m/6,560 ft, the valley is accessible only from the end of June to the end of October, depending on the earliness or lateness of that year's snowfall. The Valley of the Merveilles is a protected area within the national park; visitors must not step on or deface the stone engravings, or attempt to scratch new graffiti onto the rocks.

VAL DE LA TINEE

The Tinée Valley extends diagonally across the central section of the Mercantour. A series of gorges extends along much of the lower section of the Tinée and slightly north of the village of St.-Sauveur-sur-Tinée. The wild Val de la Tinée is very narrow and deep, winding through rock walls in the channel cut by the Tinée stream. High mountains such as Mont Giraud (2,606 m/8,550 ft) and the Cime des Lauses (2,651 m/8,697 ft) may be glimpsed through several side valleys. The Gorges de Valabres extend north of St.-Sauveur toward the Col de la Bonette.

Isola 2000

At the village of Isola in the Tinée Valley, a road climbs steeply northeastward to Isola 2000, one of France's completely modern ski resorts. Isola 2000, at the base of a cirque, is almost encircled by mountains that are steep and rocky, though none is above 3,000 m/9,842 ft. Fifteen km/9 mi from the nearest village, Isola has the feeling of being very remote. It is a ski community complete in itself, an artificial creation whose raison d'être is skiing. The many conveniences for skiers make intensive, all-day skiing possible; however, the buildings—stark, concrete boxes—look cold and impersonal.

Auron

Farther north up the Tinée Valley, this is a less artificial-looking little ski resort clustered around a square; the hotels are not uniformly concrete and contemporary, and a church with a stone steeple implies an existence outside of skiing.

Col de la Bonette

St.-Etienne-de-Tinée is a pretty village at the start of the approach to the Col de la Bonette (2,800 m/9,184 ft), the highest automobile route in France. It is narrow, has a steep grade, and there are sheer drops to the side in places. For a traveler driving north from the south of France, this is the first alpine-looking landscape to be seen from the road. Above tree line the country is wild and empty, resembling a high moor amid austere, stone-swept mountains. A few abandoned stone structures along the route are the remains of fortifications from World War II. At the top of the pass, a paved one-lane road in bad repair circles around the Cime de la Bonette (2,860 m/9,382 ft).

Queyras Regional Natural Park

THE QUEYRAS IS SPECIAL because it offers a great deal of alpine charm but has scarcely been discovered, even by the French, perhaps because it is remote from almost everything. The Mercantour park to the south is accessible from the eastern Riviera, but the Queyras, tucked off in a pocket where France seems to bulge into Italy (the region is enclosed on three sides by the Italian frontier), is near no major center and does not have any highly developed ski resorts. Geographically, this is the region of the Cottian Alps; its highest mountains, along the Italian border, are generally somewhat higher than the Mercantour peaks, and its valleys, though deep, are generally broader. It is mostly an upland, without the narrow gorges that distinguish the region of the most southerly French Alps. And its villages, pretty and unspoiled, no longer have the Provençal appearance found south of the Col de la Bonette. They have their own flavor, that of the Queyras.

A turquoise gem, Lac Ste.-Anne rests calmly above tree line. Most glacier-fed lakes are ice-cold, so plunging in may be risky for swimmers tempted by their beautiful water. Facing page: West of the fortified town of Château-Queyras rise the barren needle-like spires of the Casse Déserte, curious formations of limestone, dolomite, and gypsum.

A regional natural park was created in the Queyras in 1977 not only to protect the landscape and natural resources, but also to preserve cultural sites and to maintain the local economy.

The Haut (high) Queyras, east of the village of Château-Queyras, is part of the Pennine nappe and consists mainly of mica schist, while in the Bas (low) Queyras, limestone is found as well. Scarcely a glacier is left in the region, although the marks of former glaciation are abundant.

Though the Col de Vars, the pass at the southern entrance to the Queyras, is above tree line, the country here is soft, with rounded, gentle slopes. Just below the col on the northern side is the little ski resort of Les Claux, with a group of modern concrete apartment buildings—the only blemish on the landscape for many miles. The road descends to Guillestre near where the River Guil flows into the Durance; the Queyras is the basin of the River Guil.

Guillestre serves as the entry point for the central Queyras and can make a good base for exploring part of the countryside. A market town, it has an old castle tower and the remains of medieval ramparts. Guillestre sits in a big, open bowl of pastures and wheatfields, surrounded by low mountains, a lovely scene, though not high alpine. The finest excursions in the Queyras are in the mountains along its southeastern rim. Three main valleys provide access.

Vallon du Mélezet

East of Guillestre is a small gorge, and shortly beyond this is the junction for the road to Ceillac. A quiet village on a sloping terrace, Ceillac is a center for cross-country skiing and also has modest facilities for alpine skiing. South of Ceillac, the road enters the Vallon du Mélezet. The parking area near the end of the road is the starting point of several hiking routes.

Lac Ste.-Anne. The trail climbs the western slope of the Vallon du Mélezet, passes a lower lake set amid pine woods, and arrives at this turquoise lake above tree line. Behind the Lac Ste.-Anne is a cirque whose crest is serrated with sharp points—the Pics de la Font Sancte (3,385 m/ 11,105 ft). At its base is a steep névé, a permanent snowfield. A trail from this lake climbs east to the Col Girardin, a notch in the cirque (it is a pass to the Ubaye Valley to the south). East of the col is the Tête de Girardin (2,876 m/ 9,436 ft). A more direct but steeper trail from the bottom of the Mélezet Valley also leads to the Col Girardin.

Aigue Agnelle Valley

Between Guillestre and Château-Queyras, the narrow valley of the Guil is called the "Combe du Queyras." At Château-Queyras, and completely enclosed within its walls like a tiny Carcassonne, is a small fortified castle perched on top of a narrow, conical hill over the river. Ville-Vieille, a few kilometers still farther upstream, is at the head of the lovely, wide, and verdant valley of the Aigue Agnelle and its tributary stream, the Aigue Blanche. These two streams conjoin at the village of Molines, a pleasant place with traditional houses of stone and wood. Like the watercourses in the neighboring valleys, these streams originate in the high mountains to the south, along the Italian frontier. About 2 km/1.2 mi north of Molines are the "Demoiselles coiffées," a natural oddity easily seen from the road. These are several slender rock pillars, surmounted by large boulders balanced most improbably above them. The formations are the result of the erosion of sedimentary stone beneath boulders of rock more resistant to erosion; the same phenomenon can be seen at Euseigne in the Swiss Val d'Hérens.

St.-Véran. From Molines, the road climbs almost due south along the Aigue Blanche to St.-Véran (only residents may drive through the village; others can drive around it). At 2,040 m/6,693 ft, St.-Véran claims to be the highest community in Europe. This charming, unpretentious village hugs a fairly steep slope facing the Crête de Curlet, a long rock wall across the narrow valley. Among the village's old wooden houses is a fine church; a pair of sixteenth-century stone lions crouch below its porch columns. St.-Véran displays several examples of the curious and arresting old crucifixes found outdoors in certain mountain villages, a type of religious folk art. Simple, painted wooden objects, each representing an aspect of the crucifixion, are attached to the crosses—for example, a hand for those that beat Jesus, or a rooster for the apostasy of Peter.

St.-Véran, with several small ski lifts, is a center for downhill and cross-country skiing, ski mountaineering, and dogsledding. The absence of any big cable car surely helps preserve the quiet atmosphere.

Hikers have several choices. From St.-Véran, the GR 58 continues southeast up the valley. From the junction at the Chapelle de Clausis (you may drive this far before 9 A.M. or after 4 P.M.), a trail departs from the GR 58 to the right (southeast) and climbs to Lac de la Blanche for a close view of the Rocca Bianca (3,059 m/10,036 ft) and the Tête des Toillies (3,175 m/10,417 ft). If you remain on the GR 58 you can take a variant and climb to the Col de St.-Véran by bearing right (east) at a second junction. You can also walk from St.-Véran down to the river, from which the GR 58 climbs west and then south to the Col des Estronques; from the col, the GR 58 descends to Ceillac.

The Upper Valley of the Aigue Agnelle. East of Molines are the tiny villages of Pierre Grosse, Le Coin, and Fontgillarde, and these too are pretty and unspoiled. Like St.-Véran, these villages are centers for cross-country skiing, ski mountaineering, and dogsledding. Here, too, hikers will find sev-

At sunset, the serene peaks of the Queyras near the Col d'Izoard take on a rosy

eral possibilities. The unpaved road up this valley continues over the Col Agnel into Italy, but the pass is open only during good conditions, in the summer. A plaque commemorates all the armies that have supposedly marched along this route, starting with those of Hannibal and Julius Caesar. You can hike or drive to the Refuge Agnel above the end of the valley, between the Le Pain de Sucre (3,208 m/10,525 ft)—a French Sugarloaf—and the Pic de Caramantran (3,025 m/9,924 ft). The trail continues up to the Col Agnel. From the hut you can head east and north to the Lac Foréant, between Le Grand Queyras (3,114 m/10,216 ft) and Le Pain de Sucre. From the Pont de

glow while the pinnacles of the Casse Déserte catch the day's last golden light.

Lariane, east of Fontgillarde, a trail climbs southwest to the Col du Longet, below the Pic de Château Renard, for a view of the upper end of the valley.

Monte Viso

The biggest mountain in the Queyras region, Monte Viso (3,841 m/12,602 ft), is just over the Italian border, but there is a close view of its north face from a wonderful viewpoint on the French side, the Belvédère du Cirque. To reach this, continue along the valley of the Guil to Abriès, and then turn right (south) into the narrow valley of the Upper Guil, past Ristolas and L'Echalp. This valley is uninhabited, wooded, and wild. From L'Echalp, a trail next to a closed road in bad condition climbs to the Belvédère du Cirque. The Belvédère is a large grassy terrace facing a semicircle of mountains. At the center of this is a U-shaped saddle with the big, rugged wall of Monte Viso, flashing with snow, towering above it. There is plenty here to occupy the viewer: to the east is Monte Granero (3,166 m/10,387 ft) and, as the eye turns southward toward Monte Viso, the Pointe de Marte (3,152 m/10,341 ft), the Pointe Gastaldi (3,210 m/10,531 ft), and several more *pointes* of comparable height. The line of peaks snakes around to the west, reaching its highest point at L'Asti (Mont Aiguillette: 3,287 m/10,784 ft). Far below, along the valley floor, is the young stream of the Guil, issuing forth from the glaciers of Monte Viso. Hikers can continue up to the Refuge du Balif-Viso, on a superb site near the cirque and facing Mont Aiguillette. Big, furrowed cliffs, glistening with waterfalls, stand over the hut.

Val d'Ubaye

Between the northern edge of the Mercantour and the ridge of mountains along the southern edge of the Queyras is the valley of the Ubaye. The Ubaye is scenic, quite unknown, and thus unspoiled, with several pleasant hiking possibilities. The pretty hamlet of St.-Paul, south of the Col de Vars, is at the entrance of the valley. The small road continuing up the valley soon forks. To the right (southeast), a gravel road climbs to Fouillouse, a hamlet positioned on the GR 5 and 56. The Brec de Chambeyron (3,389 m/11,118 ft), topped by a big, square rock tower, dominates the scene. At Fouillouse you can take the GR 5/56 southeast as the route skirts the mountains along the Italian border. You can also follow the trail from Fouillouse north and then east to the Refuge de Chambeyron and a scattering of little lakes, also near the frontier chain.

Col d'Izoard

The route guarding the northern entrance to the Queyras is the dramatic Col d'Izoard (2,360 m/7,743 ft). The road departs from the valley of the Guil just west of Château-Queyras. The curious feature of this pass is the Casse Déserte, a bare, brown landscape like a nearly vertical desert, filled with clusters of gray-gold rock pinnacles. These needles were created by the pulverization of limestone and dolomite in the presence of gypsum, which cemented and consolidated the debris. From the pass there is a grand view of the Queyras mountains to the south and some of the Ecrins peaks to the north. The Tour de France bicycle race is sometimes routed over the Col d'Izoard.

Ecrins National Park

THE DAUPHINÉ ALPS ARE one of the three great French Alpine ranges, with a splendid cluster of glaciers and peaks, including the Barre des Ecrins, the highest mountain in France outside of the Mont Blanc group. This high alpine country is spread across the Ecrins (or Pelvoux) massif in a region called the Dauphiné, southeast of Grenoble. In the Middle Ages, the area belonged to a dauphin, who sold it to the kingdom of France. The highest mountains of the Dauphiné are found in the Parc National des Ecrins, which was created in 1973 and is today the largest French national park.

The grandest features of the Dauphiné Alps are found chiefly in the park's northern and central area. La Meije, one of the most famous mountains in the Alps, is close to the northern edge of the massif. Toward its center are the Barre des Ecrins (4,102 m/13,458 ft), which gave the park its name, and Mont Pelvoux (3,932 m/12,900 ft), the park's third highest peak. The rocks of the massif, part of the Helvetic nappe, are mainly crystalline: granite, gneiss, and metamorphic schist. The Ecrins is covered by approximately 12,000 hectares/ 29,651 acres of glacier, an expanse particularly remarkable because it is the southernmost area of substantial glaciation in the Alps. Some of the Ecrins glaciers are very extensive, but there are also numerous small glaciers—a sign of general glacier retreat. At a comparatively southern latitude and with a fairly dry climate, the Ecrins does not possess the best conditions for these ice sheets. Another curious feature of the park is the extraordinary difference in altitude (ranging from 800 m/2,625 ft to 4,102 m/13,458 ft) within its borders. The landscape is characterized by narrow valleys, enclosed between steep slopes and often blocked at the upper end by a glacier or mountain. The country here is fairly wild; you see almost no cattle or sheep grazing high in the mountains, and there are relatively few ski lifts.

La Meije and the Barre des Ecrins are only about 10 km/6 mi apart, but only an eagle or an expert climber could travel directly between them, as the way is filled with peaks and glaciers. The park is partly encircled by highways, and a few valleys with roads permit the motorist to draw near—and the hiker to enter—the high alpine magic circle.

Pages 42 and 43: Glaciers are slow-moving rivers of ice formed in places where more snow falls than melts: the snow packed below turns into ice and, on steep mountain slopes, begins to move under its own weight. Ice found downstream may have traveled many hundreds of years to get there. A dramatic example of this force is the Glacier de la Pilatte, which lies southeast of La Bérarde.

THE NORTHERN ECRINS:
THE ROMANCHE VALLEY

La Meije

The name La Meije comes from a local dialect word meaning "middle of the day," because the great peak is the only one that still reflects light after the other peaks have gone dark. The entire mountain group of which La Meije is a part hangs over the valley like a big, snowy apron, whitened by the glaciers frozen to this north wall. La Meije is a complex mountain with a big rocky crown above the Glacier de la Meije. Because of its serrated crest, this mountain is considered to have three summits: the western Grand Pic de la Meije (3,983 m/13,067 ft), the central Doigt de Dieu ("finger of God": 3,973 m/13,035 ft), and the eastern Meije Orientale (3,891 m/12,766 ft). It is connected by a deep, narrow notch to its neighboring peak to the west, Le Râteau (3,809 m/12,497 ft). The La Meije cable car from La Grave actually deposits tourists not on La Meije itself but at a point high on the northwest side of Le Râteau, at the ridge of the Col des Ruillans (3,211 m/10,534 ft). The glaciers directly below La Meije twist down precipitously toward the village of La Grave, but on the other side are broad glaciers with a gentler grade, and the La Meije cable car gives skiers access to these glaciers.

The first ascent of La Meije was made up the mountain's south face. It took more than a dozen attempts before climbers first ascended the north face, one of the few important "first ascents" achieved by local people rather than by the English.

Hikes from the La Meije Cable Car. From the intermediate station at Peyrou d'Amont you can walk west to a little lake, the Lac du Puy Vachier. A path loops around under the cable-car line and approaches the edges of the glaciers of Le Râteau and La Meije. You can walk down to La Grave.

La Grave

The easiest way to view La Meije is from the alpine village of La Grave, in the Romanche valley at the northern edge of the park. La Grave is sited below the north face of the mountain. It is an unpretentious place, an old-fashioned alpine village unlike modern high-rise ski resorts, with a guides' office and climbing school. There is cross-country skiing from La Grave along the valley floor, as well as alpine skiing and summer skiing on the glaciers.

Another celebrated view of La Meije and its entire complex is obtained across the valley from "les Hameaux des Traverses," the hamlets above La Grave—Les Terrasses, Ventelon, and Le Chazelet. The view from the terrace of the chapel in Le Chazelet is especially fine. (You can drive or walk to these hamlets.) The distance gained makes the great extent and grandeur of this north wall of the Ecrins more apparent. West of Le Râteau is the Pic de la Grave (3,669 m/12,037 ft); east of La Meije is the Pic Gaspard (3,883 m/ 12,739 ft) and the Bec de l'Homme (3,454 m/11,332 ft).

Lacs Lérié and Noir and Le Gros Têt. From Le Chazelet, you can follow the GR 54/50 westward past the Chalet de la Loge, turning south (left) at the first junction to reach these two little lakes for another excellent view of the Ecrins massif. For a higher viewpoint, walk partway on the GR 54/50 toward the Chalet de la Loge, but turn north (right) to climb to Le Gros Têt (also called the Cime du Rachas: 2,613 m/8,573 ft).

Les Deux Alpes and Alpe d'Huez

Two major ski resorts face each other across the western end of the Romanche Valley, in the Oisans district. Les Deux Alpes is a large resort on a high terrace above the western end of the Romanche Valley, at the far end of the north wall of the Ecrins. Les Deux Alpes is an artificial community, built for skiing, with dozens of big concrete hotels and apartment houses. The resort has a good view of many of the big Ecrins peaks, but unless you are on a top floor of a building facing south, you have to go to the parking lot at the end of town to see them. From there, you can see La Meije to the east, among other big peaks; the Jandri cable car connects skiers with the glaciers above La Grave. There is excellent skiing for all levels, and also cross-country skiing.

Alpe d'Huez is another "purpose-built" resort. Above it is the Pic du Lac Blanc (3,323 m/10,902 ft), a mountain at the edge of a group known as Les Grandes Rousses. A lift system rises to the summit; the view extends to Mont Blanc, the Gran Paradiso, and the towering peaks of the Ecrins including La Meije and the Barre des Ecrins. There is good skiing for all levels, and summer skiing on the Glacier de la Sarenne. This resort is linked by helicopter flights to Les Deux Alpes.

The Upper Romanche Valley

East of La Meije, trails above the Upper Romanche valley give excellent views of several other great mountains along the eastern side of the massif, including the Pic Gaspard and La Grande Ruine (3,765 m/12,352 ft). From La Grave drive eastward past Villar d'Arène to Le Pied du Col, where you can park. There pick up the GR 54 southeastward along the right bank of the Romanche. The route climbs in zigzags through a defile and reaches the Refuge de l'Alpe de Villar d'Arène.

Glacier d'Arsine. At the junction at the refuge, bear left (southeast) for the Col d'Arsine. Above is the Glacier d'Arsine, spread across a broad cirque between the Montagne des Agneaux (3,664 m/12,020 ft) and the Pic de Neige Cordier (3,613 m/11,854 ft).

Glacier de la Plate des Agneaux. At the junction at the Refuge de l'Alpe de Villar d'Arène, turn right (southwest) to Plan de Valfourche. At the junction there, turn left (south); the route contours along the edge of the Glacier de la Plate des Agneaux, then turns abruptly west to climb to the hut, superbly located below the summit of La Grande Ruine and overlooking the curving glacier.

Col du Lauteret and Col du Galibier

Two passes in the vicinity of La Grave, in close proximity to each other and to La Grave, also merit a trip. For travelers between La Grave and Briançon, the Col du Lauteret (2,057 m/6,749 ft) cannot be avoided, as it is positioned almost at the eastern entrance to the Romanche Valley. Above tree line, one looks southwest across sweeping green slopes to La Meije and also the massive tower of the Pic Gaspard.

Directly north of the Col du Lauteret is the much higher and more dramatic Col du Galibier (2,642 m/8,668 ft) on D 902; this is the most direct route from the Ecrins to the Vanoise massif via the district known as the Maurienne. From the pass, a little path climbs about 50 m/164 ft to a lookout point from which, to the south, the various peaks of the northern edge of the Ecrins massif resolve themselves into a broad wall, deeply furrowed and plastered with snow. The view is panoramic, and an orientation table identifies the various peaks you see from here as you slowly turn in a circle: besides many of the big Ecrins peaks, including the Barre and the Dôme des Ecrins, you can see Mont Blanc on a clear day.

THE CENTRAL ECRINS: VALLEE DU VENEON

The Vallée du Vénéon penetrates deeply into the center of the Ecrins. Excursions from La Bérarde take you into superb country in the heart of these mountains, with views of the south face of La Meije and many of the other big peaks. But there is no cable car here and you must walk to see the mountains.

La Bérarde

The road southeast to La Bérarde, D 530, departs from the Romanche Valley at Le Clapier, between Bourg d'Oisans and the Lac du Chambon, west of La Grave. Though the lower Vénéon Valley is alternately narrow and then some-

THE QUEYRAS AND THE ECRINS

- Main Roads
- Connecting Roads
- Points of Interest
- ▲ Peaks
- ⤬ Passes
- ⛫ Huts

15 Km

ITALY
FRANCE

Mt Granero ▲

Monte Viso ▲

Mt Cenero ▲

L'Echalp

Le Pain du Sucre ▲

QUEYRAS
REGIONAL
NATURAL PARK

L'Asti (Mt Aiguillette) ▲

Le Grand Queyras ▲

Abriès

Fontgillarde

Pic de Château Renaud ▲

St-Véran

Molines

Chapelle de Clausis

Tête de Toillies ▲

Brec de Chambeyron ▲

Fouillouse

Col des Estronques ⤬

Ville-Vieille

Guil

Casse Déserte

Pics de la Font Sancte ▲

Ceillac

Lac Ste-Anne

Tête de Girardin ▲

St-Paul

Col d'Izoard ⤬

Château-Queyras

Ubaye

Ubaye

Col de Vars ⤬

Briançon

Guillestre

Durance

Châteauroux

Pré de Mme.-Carle

L'Ailefroide

Col du Lauteret

Col du Galibier ⤬

Le Pied du Col ⤬

Bec de L'Homme ▲

La Grande Ruine ▲

REFUGE DU CHÂTELLERET ⛫

Vallouise

L'Argentière-la-Bessée

La Meije ▲

Le Rateau ▲

Pic de la Grave ▲

Les Bans ▲

REFUGE-HÔTEL DU GIOBERNEY ⛫

ECRINS
NATURAL PARK

Pic du Lac Blanc ▲

Le Chazelet

La Grave

Romanche

Lac du Chambon

Les Deux Alpes

Barre des Ecrins ▲

Mt Pelvoux ▲

La Bérarde

Orcières

Chorges

Lac de Serre-Ponçon

Allemont

Alpe d'Huez

Bourg d'Oisans

Le Clapier

Le Périer

L'Olan ▲

Le Désert

La Chapelle-en-Valgaudemar

Le Boreis

Gap

to
Grenoble

Entraignes

Valbonnais

St-Firmin

Corps

N

what wider, the upper valley contracts between rocky, nearly vertical walls; it seems only a deep crack as you near La Bérarde. Toward the upper end of the valley the road, cut high on the valley wall, is mainly wide enough for only one vehicle, but there are frequent "garages" or cutouts that enable vehicles to pass each other. Just before the end of the road the valley widens; there is a campground on the bank of the stream. A bridge leads to La Bérarde (1,720 m/5,643 ft), where the road ends. Beyond this the valley is once again deep and narrow, wild and beautiful.

As the country above La Bérarde is scarcely grazed by sheep, goats, or cows, there is varied vegetation on the valley floor, with occasional stands of very small trees such as birch and alder, instead of grassy meadows, giving the ground a rougher look.

La Bérarde is located near some of the finest scenery in the French Alps, but it has not been developed for skiing, and the road is closed during winter. It would be hard to find a place more unspoiled than this mere hamlet, with only a couple of extremely simple hotels and a tiny shop with a few modest provisions for the campers. There is also a French Alpine Club refuge, open to everyone (though members get a discount). There are, however, other villages and hamlets with accommodations along the road before La Bérarde. And despite the difficult condition of the road, there is bus service.

Despite its unassuming appearance, La Bérarde is a center for both alpinism and hiking. Its little chapel is full of plaques; one honors the party who left here in 1877 to achieve the first ascent of La Meije; others commemorate guides and alpinists who died on climbs in this area.

From La Bérarde, there are hikes in several directions as the hamlet is at the conjunction of two high valleys.

Tête de la Maye. Directly over the hamlet is a small rocky dome, the Tête de la Maye (2,516 m/8,254 ft), from which there is a panoramic view of many of the big peaks in the area (there are fixed cables near the top on a few steep, rocky sections; this route should not be taken in wet weather).

Refuge du Châtelleret. To the north is the valley of the Etançons, the stream that flows down from La Meije. A trail alongside its left bank leads gently up to the Refuge du Châtelleret, with a view of a grand cirque, in the center of which is the south face of La Meije, flanked on one side by Le Râteau and on the other by the Pic Gaspard. The south face of La Meije is severe, not less formidable than its north face; it projects above the Glacier des Etançons like a sheer plane of rock, topped with savage teeth.

Upper Valley of the Vénéon. From La Bérarde another trail leads southeast through the upper valley of the Vénéon. Partway up the valley is the Refuge du Plan du Carrelet, beyond which is a junction. From there, the trail to the left climbs steeply eastward to the Refuge du Temple des Ecrins

(2,410 m/7,907 ft), over which towers the Pic Coolidge (3,774 m/12,382 ft) and the fearsomely named Pointe des Avalanches (3,584 m/11,758 ft). The trail to the right (southeast) leads toward the Refuge de la Pilatte, with a superb view of the broad Glacier de la Pilatte. Above this glacier is a group of mountains of which the highest is Les Bans (3,669 m/12,037 ft).

THE EASTERN ECRINS: VALLOUISE

Barre des Ecrins

The Vallouise offers the closest approach to the Barre des Ecrins and the other great mountains and glaciers that form the crown of the Ecrins massif. Until the early nineteenth century, when France annexed the Savoie and with it Mont Blanc, the Barre des Ecrins was the highest mountain in France. Its massive form sits amid a constellation of peaks, including Mont Pelvoux, L'Ailefroide, Pic Coolidge, and Pic des Agneaux, making this area one of the premier centers for alpinism in France. Unlike La Meije, the "Ecrins" has no cable car on it or anywhere near it. Though it can be seen from various distant viewpoints, hikers can get close to it from the upper end of the Vallouise, on the eastern edge of the Ecrins massif. The Barre des Ecrins was first climbed in 1864 by the Englishman Edward Whymper, who one year later made the first ascent of the Matterhorn.

Access to this area is gained from L'Argentière-la-Bessée, almost midway between Briançon and Guillestre. From L'Argentière, a road leads northeast past the village of Vallouise to Pré de Mme.-Carle, which consists mainly of a large parking lot. (Several hamlets along the road, including St.-Antoine, Pelvoux, and Les Claux, offer simple accommodations.)

Pré de Mme.-Carle

The approach to Pré de Mme.-Carle is very impressive, through a long valley between high, rough-hewn cliffs, below the huge rock wall of Mont Pelvoux. Near the end of the road an alpine scene of mountains and glaciers opens up. The severity of the rock walls precludes alpine skiing, and the absence of any ski lift has preserved the wild, unspoiled character of the area. From the parking lot there is a short, almost level walk along the gravel bed of the stream; even from here there are good views. There is soon a junction: the trail to the right (north) climbs to the Glacier Blanc ("white"); the trail to the left (west) to the Glacier Noir ("black"). These two glaciers sweep around the walls of the Barre des Ecrins; the Glacier Noir separates the Ecrins from Mont Pelvoux. A "black glacier" is one strewn with rocks and small stones.

Perilous crevasses such as those on Glacier Blanc occur on glacial slopes. They may be hidden under snow and plunge as deep as 200 ft/60m.

The Glacier Blanc. The trail to the Glacier Blanc climbs to a shelf just below the snout of the glacier—a big, rounded hump of ice, topped with séracs. The route continues to a higher shelf and the Refuge du Glacier Blanc (2,550 m/8,366 ft), amid grand high-alpine scenery: the northeast face of the Barre des Ecrins, with the Glacier Blanc plunging below it, and Mont Pelvoux across the valley.

The Glacier Noir. The Glacier Noir trail continues on a knife-edge ridge, the top of a lateral moraine, directly under the big south wall of the Barre des Ecrins. There is a fine view across the twisting glacier of the north face of Mont Pelvoux and the peaks around it; however, only trained and properly equipped mountaineers can venture onto the glacier farther along this route.

From Ailefroide you can hike partway up a deep, narrow valley along the southern edge of Mont Pelvoux, toward the cirque of L'Ailefroide (3,953 m/ 12,969 ft) with its multiple glaciers. The Refuge du Sélé is near the base of this cirque.

THE SOUTHERN ECRINS: VALGAUDEMAR

The Valgaudémar cuts along the southern edge of the Ecrins massif, providing access for hikers and climbers to the Pic d'Olan (3,564 m/11,693 ft) and

The views from La Bérarde, a popular mountain-climbing and hiking center, are among the French Alps' finest.

Les Bans. The entrance of the Valgaudémar is from N 85, between the towns of Corps and Gap. The lower valley has a gentler aspect, with grassy banks along the river; the upper valley becomes narrow and steep. Accommodations are available at St.-Firmin, St.-Maurice, and La Chapelle.

La Chapelle-en-Valgaudémar

La Chapelle-en-Valgaudémar is a simple, quiet village at the base of the Pic d'Olan. On the southern slope above the village is the hamlet of Les Portes, with a good view of this mountain. Below Les Portes is the Oules du Diable, a swift mountain torrent that almost boils between its steep banks; care should be taken to remain on the path, as the slopes over this torrent are steep and slippery.

East of La Chapelle the road becomes difficult, climbing steeply through the narrow valley to Gioberney. The GR 54 also extends up the valley, so it is possible to walk to the end as well. The Casset waterfall, about 2.5 km/1.5 mi past La Chapelle, is impressive.

The Refuge-Hôtel du Gioberney. This simple hotel is scenically located below a fine cirque. Les Rouies (3,589 m/11,775 ft) is above the western wall, Les Bans above the eastern side. A trail leads up to the Lac du Lauzon, a small lake with a very fine view of these mountains.

Vanoise National Park

THE VANOISE MASSIF IS a region of mountains and glaciers in the French Savoie near the Italian border, adjoining the Gran Paradiso National Park in Italy. The mountains on both the French and Italian sides of the border belong to the same geographic unit, the Graian Alps, but are politically divided into the western or French and the eastern or Italian Alps.

The Parc National de la Vanoise, the first national park in France, was established in 1963. Its more protected central zone covers 53,000 hectares/ 131,000 acres; along with its peripheral zone, the park extends across the entire Vanoise massif. Together with the Gran Paradiso, this area is the largest nature reserve in western Europe. A major reason for the establishment of this park was to protect the ibex in France. The species had already been hunted to extinction throughout almost the entire Alps, except the Gran Paradiso. About forty years after the great Italian national park was created, in part to preserve this species, the French followed suit. The Vanoise is now home to the largest colony of ibex in France, estimated at more than 700, as well as other alpine mammals and birds.

The visual effect of the Vanoise landscape is more consistently high alpine compared with that of the Ecrins, though the highest peak in the Vanoise is minimally lower than the highest mountains in the Ecrins. The central Vanoise is a high plateau above tree line, in the zone of high alpine meadows and moraines. With unrestricted vision across sections of the plateau, there are extensive views of distant clusters of mountains. Much of the Vanoise, part of the Pennine nappe, is made of schist and mica schist, with an area of limestone near the center of the region, around the Col de la Vanoise.

There is no road that traverses the entire park, although several penetrate the region fairly deeply. The approaches to the Vanoise must be made from the perimeter of the massif, chiefly from the south or north.

Southern Vanoise

TERMIGNON

The southern edge of the Vanoise massif rises abruptly and to a great height above the narrow valley of the Maurienne, the bed of the River Arc. This is not a region of big resorts. The simple little town of Termignon is a point of entry to the biggest mountains of the Vanoise and there is cross-country skiing in winter along the valley floor. Though Termignon has several modest hotels, it is more a quiet country town than a resort.

Refuge du Plan du Lac

From Termignon, a road climbs high and steeply to a point called Belle-combe. The road is paved, but stones may have rolled down onto it from the steep slopes above. Beyond a few deserted stone buildings is a large parking lot at the end of the public road. A path leads through a defile past an alpine tarn, the Plan du Lac, to the Refuge du Plan du Lac, a large, handsome French Alpine Club hut. The walk to the hut takes less than an hour. (There is bus service to this hut, and also to the Refuge d'Entre Deux Eaux.) Because you start so high (Bellecombe is at 2,307 m/7,569 ft), you are already above tree line. The effect is vaguely comparable to that of the American West, with great open spaces and long, sweeping views.

The hut is located on a long slope of high meadow, with extensive views. You can look back a great distance to the mountains to the south, on the other side of the Maurienne valley. The finest view is to the east, where a broad system of glaciers, the "Glaciers de la Vanoise," is slung among a series of peaks, extending for approximately 13 km/8.1 mi and constituting the largest glacier mass in the park. The first big mountain to the southwest is the Dent Parrachée (3,697 m/12,129 ft), followed to the north by the Dôme de l'Arpont (3,599 m/11,807 ft), Dôme de Nants (3,570 m/11,712 ft), Dôme de Chasseforêt (3,586 m/11,765 ft), and Mont Pelve (3,261 m/10,698 ft), among others. As the ice pours over the rim of the steep wall that forms this ridge of mountains, it breaks into zones of séracs and big crevasses. Beyond Mont Pelve, as your eye sweeps northward, are the Pointe de la Réchasse (3,212 m/10,538 ft), then the steep, narrow gap of the Col de la Vanoise, and then a cirque, carved out under La Grande Casse (3,855 m/12,648 ft) and La Grande Motte (3,653 m/11,985 ft). These last two peaks are the biggest mountains in the Vanoise National Park. La Grande Casse has two summits; the lower one (3,783 m/12,411 ft) is named Pointe Mathews for the Englishman who made the first ascent of the mountain in 1860, accompanied by Michel Croz, a guide from Chamonix who later died in the first descent of the Matterhorn.

From the Refuge du Plan du Lac, the land falls away steeply northward to the streambed of the Torrent de la Rocheure. At Entre Deux Eaux there are some alpages, or summer farms, and the Refuge d'Entre Deux Eaux. You can continue steeply northwest to the Col de la Vanoise (the trail is part of the GR 55), or you can turn northeast, also along the GR 55, on a more gentle grade through the Vallon de la Leisse. This is a long valley, curving and distinctly U-shaped, carved out below a wall of rock, the cliffs at the base of La Grande Casse and La Grande Motte. It is a very wild, lonely, lovely place. Beyond the Refuge de la Leisse the trail climbs toward the Col de la Leisse. Yet another route from the Rocheure stream heads due east through the Vallon de la Rocheure.

Refuge de l'Arpont

The Refuge de l'Arpont is located at the base of the Glacier de l'Arpont, a hanging glacier. From the western end of Termignon, you first take the road north to the Pont du Chatelard. From there a trail climbs steeply west and northwest to join the GR 5 and reach the hut. This gives a much closer look at the Glacier de l'Arpont and the Dent Parrachée, but as the hut is on the slope below the glacier wall the view is foreshortened and the full sweep of the Glaciers de la Vanoise is not visible.

AUSSOIS

Another approach into the Vanoise from the south can be made from Aussois, slightly larger than Termignon but also unspoiled. Aussois is a small winter resort with several ski lifts. You can drive up to a pair of artificial lakes, the Plan d'Aval and the higher Plan d'Amont, above which, to the northeast, is a cirque topped by La Dent Parrachée. A path connects the two lakes and the GR 5 also loops around them. From the Plan d'Amont, a trail leads northwest to the Refuge du Fond d'Aussois, below the western face of La Dent Parrachée and the Glacier de Labby; a little farther on is the Col d'Aussois (which can, however, require ice axes and crampons). The full expanse of the Glaciers de la Vanoise, however, cannot be seen from this side of the mountains.

COL DE CHAVIERE

Farther west along the Maurienne Valley the industrial town of Modane gives access to the westernmost glaciers of the Vanoise. On the edge of the town above the northern bank of the Arc, you can pick up the GR 5. To the north, this joins the GR 55 and ascends to the Col de Chavière (an ice axe may be advisable here), between the Aiguille de Polset (3,531 m/11,585 ft) and the Pointe de l'Echelle (3,345 m/10,974 ft), with glaciers on both sides.

Northern Vanoise

The northern slope of the Vanoise massif is gentler than the southern, and the valley of the Isère (known as the Tarentaise) is broader than that of the Arc and consequently it is more built-up. Because the terrain is so much more

The scenic walk from Bellecombe to Refuge du Plan du Lac takes less than an hour.

accessible and moderate in grade, there are a number of major French ski resorts on this northern side of the Vanoise. From N 90, the national highway through the Tarentaise, the view is only of low hills; you must turn south on secondary roads to approach the big mountains and glaciers at the center of the Vanoise massif.

There are three major towns along the Isère. Albertville is a large town, the administrative center for the 1992 Winter Olympics. Its new indoor skating rink is the site of the figure skating and speed skating events. The highest nearby mountains, however, are not quite 2,500 m/8,200 ft, and Albertville is rather far from the high country of the Vanoise. Moutiers, more centrally located, is a good gateway for the ski resorts and climbing centers. The old town has a pleasant center but high-rise apartment houses are being built around it. Most outdoor travelers will probably want to get closer to the mountains if accommodations are available upcountry. Bourg-St.-Maurice, an unpretentious small town, is one possibility, but Pralognan is closer to the mountains.

PRALOGNAN-LA-VANOISE

The village of Pralognan-la-Vanoise brings you closest to the heart of the Vanoise, the glaciers and high peaks that you see from the trails above Termignon on the southern side of the massif. To reach Pralognan, take the road from Moutiers southeast and then continue south from Bozel. Pralognan is at the end of the road, attractively sited on a grassy terrace that ends abruptly below a long and impressive wall of mountains with sheer rock faces—the sharply defined edge of the Vanoise massif. Facing the village to the south are the Petit Marchet (2,568 m/8,425 ft) and Grand Marchet (2,654 m/8,707 ft), with the Moriond (2,297 m/7,536 ft) forming an angle to the east.

Pralognan is a modest resort for both skiing and hiking—something of a rarity in the French Alps. Its hotels are not concrete high-rises, but are mainly chalet-style, harmonizing with the village houses. Most of the new apartments are small chalets, only two or three stories tall; the highest new development is a small cluster at the edge of the village, with buildings of about six stories—low, as French ski developments go.

The Mont Bochor cable car serves sightseers in summer and skiers in winter.

Refuge du Col de la Vanoise and Col de la Vanoise

The major hiking route from Pralognan leads to the Col de la Vanoise (2,552 m/8,274 ft), the steeply pitched saddle visible on the southern side of the Vanoise from the trail above Termignon. From Les Fontanettes (east of the village) it climbs up from forest to alpine meadow to glacial moraine, then contours around the Aiguille de la Vanoise (2,796 m/9,173 ft), a huge, scarred slab that narrows at the very top to a point. The trail passes Lac Long, facing La Grande Casse, which is surrounded by glaciers, and continues to the Refuge du Col de la Vanoise, also known as the Refuge Félix Faure. A plaque commemorates the arrival here in August 1897 of Félix Faure, then president of the French Republic, along with the ministers of war and commerce and seven generals and their staff officers, to inspect military maneuvers. The col is just beyond the hut; on the other side, the GR 55 descends southeast, connecting with a trail southward, from which you can reach the Refuge du Plan du Lac.

The marvelous view includes the nearby Grande Casse and the Aiguille de la Vanoise, which from the hut changes its aspect completely, looking more like a slender spire than a big, blank wall. To the south is the Mont Pelve massif; between the Pointe du Dard (3,206 m/10,518 ft) and the Pointe de la Réchasse is the northern edge of the Glaciers de la Vanoise, the biggest glacier area in the park.

Refuge de Péclet-Polset

From the southern tip of Pralognan, the GR 55 leads southwest up the valley of the Doron de la Chavière (*doron* means "stream" in the dialect of Savoie), past the big wall of mountains facing the village. The trail climbs to the Refuge de Péclet-Polset, on the route to the Col de Chavière. Above the hut is the Aiguille de Péclet (3,561 m/11,683 ft), the highest point on a long rock crest rising above the Glacier de Gebroulaz.

CHAMPAGNY-LA-VANOISE

From the junction at Bozel, the road to Champagny continues eastward. Beyond the village of Champagny-la-Vanoise there is a difficult stretch of road, requiring extreme caution, through the Gorges de la Pontille, leading to the upper valley of Champagny-le-Haut with several hamlets. From the end of the road, a trail leads southeast to the Refuge de la Glière, in a superb location facing the Glacier de l'Epéna, the Aiguille de l'Epéna (3,421 m/11,224 ft), the Pointe de la Grande Glière (3,392 m/11,129 ft), and above these the north face of La Grande Casse—very difficult climbs that attract expert alpinists. From this hut you can continue northeastward to the Col du Palet, with a grand view of the magnificent north face of La Grande Casse.

From Landry, between Moutiers and Bourg-St.-Maurice, the north–south valley of the Ponturin also extends deeply into the Vanoise massif. Partway up this valley a pair of linked villages, Peisey-Nancroix, comprise a pleasant small resort, with hiking opportunities and skiing facilities, including extensive cross-country trails and a school for cross-country skiing.

The upper end of the valley lies between the imposing Mont Pourri, the second highest mountain of the Vanoise (3,779 m/12,398 ft), and the Dôme (Sommet on some maps) de Bellecôte (3,417 m/11,210 ft). The Refuge du Rosuel, near the end of the road, offers an impressive view of the Cirque de la Gurraz, streaked with waterfalls, descending from the glaciers of Mont Pourri. From Les Lanches, a trail climbs steeply to the Refuge du Mont Pourri, directly below this peak. From the hut, you can pick up the GR 5 southeast to the Refuge du Palet at the edge of a little lake (the Lac de Grattaleu), between the steeply pitched slopes of the Pointe du Chardonnet (2,870 m/9,416 ft) and the Aiguille Noire (2,885 m/9,465 ft). A short climb leads to the Col du Palet. (This col can also be reached from the Lac de Tignes west of Val d'Isère, and from the valley of Champagny-le-Haut.)

BLACK VANILLA ORCHID
Nigritella nigra

Atop a low, slender stalk, a small head of astonishing color—black, or a deep carmine—is sometimes seen in alpine pastures. This is the black vanilla orchid. In the subspecies *rubra* (rosy vanilla orchid), the flower is a bright, lighter red. The plants' heads consist of dense clusters of tiny flowers.

With an odor of vanilla, this is one of the rare number of alpine flowers with any scent. It reaches heights of 5 to 20 cm/2 to 8 in, and flowers from June to August on alpine meadows between 1,300 and 2,700 m/4,265 and 8,858 ft, mostly on limestone soil.

Facing page: Stones lead the way across a shallow lake on the upper portion of the hike to the Col de la Vanoise.

COL DE L'ISERAN

One of the most spectacular drives in the French Alps is the route over the Col de l'Iseran (2,764 m/9,068 ft), along the eastern edge of the Vanoise National Park. Only the road over the Col de la Bonette (2,802 m/9,193 ft) is higher; however, the mountains surrounding the Col de l'Iseran are much higher and closer as well as more numerous, so that the effect is much grander. The considerable height of the Col de l'Iseran makes this trip dramatic not only because of the scenery at the col but because of the contrasting zones through which the road passes, from the lower, wooded slopes through open meadows and then up to the barren zone of rock and snow.

The road is good, though precipitous. It links the valleys of the Arc (the Maurienne) and the Isère (the Tarentaise); indeed, both rivers have their sources in the mountains clustered around this great pass. The southern approach to the pass is from Lanslebourg-Mont-Cenis; the northern from Bourg-St.-Maurice.

Bonneval-sur-Arc

On the southern approach to the Col de l'Iseran, the road passes through Bonneval-sur-Arc, a small alpine center that has preserved its village character. From Bonneval, climbers depart for a group of glaciers and mountains near the Italian border: the Pointes du Grand Fond (3,460 m/11,352 ft), L'Albaron (3,637 m/11,932 ft), and, on the Italian side, La Grande Ciamarella (3,676 m/12,060 ft). Hikers can ascend these slopes as far as the glacial moraines. Bonneval is also a minor ski center.

The road from Bonneval climbs steadily, with many hairpin turns, up a deep, dark valley; its narrowness and somberness enhance the dramatic view of glaciers and high mountains—the sort of view usually gained only by climbers and the hardiest hikers (in fact, the GR 5 climbs over this col). To the east are the Aiguille Pers (3,386 m/11,108 ft) and the Pointe du Montet (3,428 m/11,247 ft); there is summer skiing below these peaks on the Glacier du Gran Pisaillas, accessible from the Col de l'Iseran by ski lift. A sign at the col tells that it took twenty years to build the road because of the snows that block the pass for two-thirds of the year.

The road descends north from the Col de l'Iseran to Pont St.-Charles, where you can park for the walk to the Col de la Galise. This route passes through the Gorges du Malpasset and then climbs steeply from the Refuge du Prariond; above is the Glacier des Sources de l'Isère on the Italian border. After Pont St.-Charles, the road descends to Val d'Isère.

Val d'Isère

Val d'Isère is a major French ski resort, but not a wholly artificial community. A few older houses among the new hotels and apartment buildings are a testament to its former existence as a mountain village. At the edge of the resort are a cluster of high-rise apartment houses, 10 and 12 stories high. Val d'Isère is the site of most of the men's alpine skiing events in the 1992 Olympics, including the downhill and giant slalom competitions.

Tignes

Just beyond Val d'Isère is the Lac du Chevril reservoir; a side road climbs from the lake to Tignes, a ski resort that shares the same terrain ("l'Espace Killy") and lift system as Val d'Isère. Together, Tignes and Val d'Isère are two of the most important ski resorts in France with some of the best skiing (all above tree line) in the world for expert skiers. Tignes is the site of the freestyle ski events for the 1992 Olympics. Tignes subdivides further into several small resorts: Tignes Le Lac and Le Lavachet on the northern side of the little Lac de Tignes, and Val Claret, 2 km/1.2 mi away, on the south side of the lake; collectively, they are known as Tignes.

Tignes is beautifully situated on a high terrace, facing a small cirque. Skiing resources are excellent, including summer skiing made possible by a cable car from Val Claret that runs up to the Glaciers de la Grande Motte, just below the peak of the third highest mountain in the Vanoise. Tignes is one of France's specially constructed ski communities, built expressly for skiing, with no trace of any previous village. In Tignes Le Lac, six-story apartment houses are built close together, while Val Claret, closer to La Grande Motte, is a cluster of modern, high-rise buildings.

TROIS VALLEES

Some of the finest ski resorts in France are in the Vanoise. On its eastern side, Tignes and Val d'Isère are notable. A greater number of resorts are closer to the center and west of the massif. An important group of these, consisting of four resorts in three neighboring valleys, is called the "Trois Vallées." These resorts—Les Ménuires, Val-Thorens, Méribel, and Courchevel —have ski slopes linked together by lifts, creating one of the largest ski areas in the world. The roads that ascend these valleys all begin at Moutiers, on the northern edge of the Vanoise.

Les Ménuires and Val-Thorens

The long valley of the Doron de Belleville has several ski resorts. (St.-Martin-de-Belleville, a small, more modest ski center, is midway up the valley.) Closer to the end of the valley is Les Ménuires, one of the new "purpose-built" resorts. It has extensive runs and is highly mechanized, with automatically operated lifts for skiing from your front door. Les Ménuires is the site of the 1992 Olympic men's special slalom race. The valley culminates at Val-Thorens in a dramatic location below the Glacier de Péclet, which is topped by the Aiguille de Péclet. At 2,320 m/7,611 ft, Val-Thorens is one of the highest ski resorts in Europe. There is summer as well as winter skiing on the several glaciers that surround the Aiguille de Péclet. This is another artificial community with flashy, high-rise hotels and apartments.

Méribel

The valley of the Doron des Allues extends to Méribel, the site chosen for the women's downhill skiing events and for ice hockey in the 1992 Olympics. This is a tasteful resort (less slick than others); the buildings are not concrete boxes but chalet-style, with wood trim, balconies, and pitched roofs, and they are not packed together. Its site is attractive, though less dramatic than that of nearby Pralognan, where the mountains have a more abrupt, rugged face and are much closer to the village. But Méribel has superb facilities and ski slopes for all levels. You can reach the Sommet de la Saulire (2,738 m/8,983 ft) by either cable car or hiking trail; both the trail and another cable car descend on the other side of the ridge to Courchevel. Hiking trails extend deeper into the big mountains to the south. The trail past the Lac de Tuéda ascends a narrow valley to the Refuge du Saut, below La Grosse Tête (2,728 m/8,950 ft); hikers can continue from there to the Col de Chanrouge (2,531 m/8,304 ft) or the higher Col Rouge (2,731 m/8,960 ft), scenically pitched between Mont Coua (2,871 m/9,419 ft) and the Aiguille des Corneillets (3,055 m/10,023 ft).

Courchevel

The most famous and most chic ski resort in "the Three Valleys" is Courchevel, with excellent skiing for all levels. This is the site of the ski jumping and nordic events in the 1992 Winter Olympics. Courchevel actually consists of three sections, numbered according to their altitude, and linked by a shuttle bus. The smallest and most modest is Courchevel 1550, consisting mostly of two-story chalets. Courchevel 1650 (also called Moriond) is small, but with an urban quality; it is constructed like an American strip, with its six- and seven-story buildings lined up along a main road. Courchevel 1850 is the most elegant of the three. Though modern, it has somewhat lower buildings, mainly three to five stories, displaying more wood trim than concrete, and with a more uniform building style. There is only one real high-rise (about 10 stories). This highest part of Courchevel has a grand view of the mountains. There are many ski lifts in the center of town; Courchevel 1850 is actually built in a semicircle around the major lifts. It is more densely built than Courchevel 1550, but this also means that most buildings are closer to the centrally located lift system.

LA CLUSAZ

Although not within the Vanoise, this ski resort is in the Savoie, near the Col d'Aravis, amid low mountains. Its distinction is that it is a pleasant-looking place of mainly small chalets, spread out over the slopes, with only one cluster of apartment houses of middle height—about six stories. There is good skiing for all levels.

The Col de la Vanoise may be reached by a day hike across meadows and past formations such as the Grande Aiguille de l'Arcelin, located south of the trail.

Mont Blanc and Chamonix

MONT BLANC (4,807 m/15,770 ft) is the highest mountain in the Alps and in western Europe; on the continent of Europe, only Mont Elbrus (5,642 m/ 18,506 ft) in the Caucasus is higher. Mont Blanc is the culminating point of the Mont Blanc massif in eastern France. This massif appears as a vast mountain wall, capped by the snowy dome of Mont Blanc and bristling with other peaks as well, some of which are fingers of bare rock, so narrow and pointed that they are known as "aiguilles," or needles. Many superb glaciers swirl down from this mountainous crown. Unlike the other French alpine areas, no national park has been established on the Mont Blanc massif, but there is a nature reserve on the slope facing Mont Blanc, the Aiguilles Rouges.

On a relief map, the Mont Blanc massif appears as a sort of hinge between the north–south line of the Alps of France and western Italy and the more west–east line of the rest of the Alpine chain. North of the massif, toward Lake Geneva, the mountains fall away to much lower elevations. The massif, part of the Helvetic nappe, is formed of ancient core crystalline rock, with a predominance of granite.

The Mont Blanc massif is a fairly compact unit, unlike most other alpine ranges, which generally have a more linear form. This massif is almost oval in shape, as if a giant fist had punched it up from beneath the earth's crust. The Tour du Mont Blanc, a circular route around the perimeter of the massif, has become one of the classic Alpine walking routes. This tour may take 10 or 12 days, more or less, the route extending through France, Italy, and Switzerland, whose territories converge within the massif. The Tour du Mont Blanc is often abbreviated as TMB on maps and signposts.

The area is best known, though, as one of the premier climbing centers in Europe. Mont Blanc has a singular place in mountaineering history. In 1760 a Swiss naturalist, Professor Horace de Saussure, offered a reward to anyone who could climb the great peak. In the course of de Saussure's own research he had circled the mountain, making the first recorded "tour du Mont Blanc." The mountain was first climbed by Dr. Michel-Gabriel Paccard and Jacques Balmat in 1786, after many others had failed. In 1787, de Saussure himself climbed it with Balmat. Since then, numerous routes have been developed, and the mountain's satellites, the very difficult aiguilles, also have been conquered.

Mont Blanc may be seen from either the north or French side, or from the south or Italian side. The French-Italian frontier does not run precisely over the mountain's top, which lies in France, but loops to the south over a slightly lower summit, Mont Blanc de Courmayeur (4,748 m/15,577 ft). On the French side, the traveler can best see the mountain from Chamonix, and on the Italian side, from points near Courmayeur. The Tour du Mont Blanc enables hikers to view the massif from different angles; motorists can make a similar although often more distant loop. (For the Italian approach, see Courmayeur.)

CHAMONIX

The base for viewing or climbing Mont Blanc from the French side is Chamonix, situated upon the bank of the River Arve, at the virtual foot of Mont Blanc. The great massif presents itself as a long, blunt, abrupt wall, rising starkly above Chamonix. As the town is fairly low and the massif very high, this is a very impressive sight; however, the actual summit, a rounded, snowy hump, does not appear to stand much above its neighboring peaks. (By contrast, such peaks as the Matterhorn or the Weisshorn have strong, well-defined shapes, distinct from the mountains near them. The configuration of the valleys radiating out around Zermatt, with 4,000-m/13,120-ft mountains spread all around in every direction, is also more complex than the simple, straight wall above Chamonix.)

The scene from Chamonix, however, is undeniably grand. Its visual force comes not so much from the peak of Mont Blanc itself as from the entire effect of a huge mass of peaks at such great height, and especially of the vast, handsome glaciers so steeply pitched upon the wall. From Chamonix and nearby viewpoints, the most dramatic of these is the Glacier des Bossons, which descends from Mont Blanc almost to the valley floor, touching near tree line, an extraordinarily low point for an alpine glacier. Broad on top, the glacier narrows to an almost pointed bottom, like a great beaver's tail. Close by to the west is the Glacier du Taconnaz, exactly parallel to the Glacier des Bossons and almost as long. Above the glaciers, the principal peaks that can be seen include the Aiguille du Midi (3,842 m/12,605 ft), Mont Blanc du Tacul (4,248 m/13,937 ft), Mont Maudit (4,465 m/14,649 ft), and the Dôme du Goûter (4,304 m/14,121 ft), as well as Mont Blanc itself.

Chamonix has permitted unrestrained growth and become a large, densely built town, with several high-rise hotels. The small, traffic-free zone in the center of Chamonix is perhaps the most attractive part of town, with public gardens and statues of the first conquerors of Mont Blanc. Nearby is an interesting alpine museum. Chamonix is also on a major international traffic route: the Mont Blanc tunnel to Italy. Congestion, excessive construction, and

Pages 66 and 67: Apex of the Alps, Mont Blanc rises from a massif of soaring peaks. The Tour de Mont Blanc, a seven-to-twelve-day hike that may be started anywhere en route, is most popular in August.

motor traffic have destroyed any resemblance to an alpine village. As you walk the trails above the valley of the Arve, facing the great spectacle of the Mont Blanc massif, the only thing that spoils the effect is the occasional sight of Chamonix sprawling on the valley floor below.

The best viewing point for Mont Blanc and its closest peaks and glaciers is either upon the slope of Mont Blanc itself or upon the slope that faces it across the Chamonix valley.

Chamonix and the neighboring villages offer opportunities for all the major winter and alpine sports. This is, of course, one of the great climbing centers of Europe. There are guides' associations at several points in the valley, and two in Chamonix, of which one (La Compagnie des Guides de Chamonix–Mont Blanc) is the oldest in the Alps. Paragliding is also very popular here, and two schools offer instruction. At Chamonix there is year-round skating, and also tennis, swimming, and golf, with very modern sports facilities.

Chamonix is accessible by rail from Paris and also from Switzerland, via Vallorcine and Martigny. It can be reached by bus from Annecy and Grenoble. Chamonix is at one end of the Mont Blanc tunnel, through which you may drive or take a bus to Aosta in Italy. The Tour du Mont Blanc automobile route circles the massif, from Chamonix west to Albertville, then south to Moutiers, east over the Col du Petit St.-Bernard to Courmayeur, then to Aosta, north over the Col du Grand St.-Bernard, north again to Martigny, then west over the Col de la Forclaz and the Col des Montets to Chamonix.

Aiguille du Midi

A two-section cable car mounts to the top of the Aiguille du Midi. The intermediate station, at Plan de l'Aiguille, is just below a serried line of sharp peaks known as the Aiguilles de Chamonix. From this station, the Grand Balcon Nord trail leads over the shoulder of the ridge to Montenvers, overlooking the Mer de Glace. From Plan de l'Aiguille, the cable car swings over the Glacier des Pèlerins, then climbs up the rocky shaft of the Aiguille du Midi to its north peak (Piton Nord) at 3,802 m/12,474 ft. The viewing terrace of this upper station overlooks the great glaciers, with views toward the summit of Mont Blanc, the Aiguille Verte, the Grandes Jorasses, and the Dent du Géant. A footbridge crosses to the mountain's central peak (Piton Central) at 3,842 m/12,605 ft, where there is an elevator to the top. The view from there embraces not only Mont Blanc and all the aiguilles but extends to Mont Dolent and, in the distance, the Grand Combin, the Matterhorn, and Monte Rosa. Another viewing platform overlooks the famous Vallée Blanche, a valley of snow upon the glacier; experts may ski this dangerous route with guides.

Vallée Blanche Cable Car. Another extraordinary excursion may be taken from the Aiguille du Midi: an aerial traverse over the crest of the Mont Blanc massif to the Italian side. From the Aiguille du Midi a cable car passes over the Vallée Blanche and the great Glacier du Géant, east of Mont Blanc and Mont Maudit, and stops at the Pointe Helbronner on the Italian border, next to the Col du Géant. The view shows the Dent du Géant and Grandes Jorasses from a different perspective, as well as the southern wall of the Mont Blanc massif. (Bring your passport if you plan to cross the border.) From the Pointe Helbronner you can descend on the Col du Géant cable car in three stages to La Palud, near Courmayeur. Except for the fact that you are suspended over the glacier instead of being upon it, this trip provides an unforgettable view of the high alpine world normally available only to mountaineers.

Montenvers and the Mer de Glace

The Mer de Glace (sea of ice) is a very long and impressive glacier, easily accessible from Chamonix. From its origin in the Glacier du Géant it is 14 km/ 8.7 mi in length, forming a gigantic S. It is the second largest glacier in the Alps after the Swiss Grosser Aletsch glacier.

From Chamonix, a cog railway climbs to Montenvers, above the west bank of the Mer de Glace. There is a spectacular view of the broad, supple curve of this river of ice, which is ripped into numberless crevasses. A cable car takes visitors down to a cave artificially hollowed out inside the glacier. Above the glacier's banks are many of the most famous pointes and aiguilles—big, vertical spires that look as sharp as needles. Among them are some of the most severe climbs in the Alps. Above the glacier's west bank are the Grépon and Charmoz, famous not for their height but for their extreme difficulty; above the east bank are the celebrated Drus, a couple of immensely challenging, vertical peaks shaped like harpoons, and also the Aiguille Verte (4,122 m/13,523 ft).

Above the Mer de Glace are the tributary glaciers that feed it, and higher still is a rocky crest of peaks, including the fang of the Aiguille (or Dent) du Géant (4,013 m/13,166 ft), the Grandes Jorasses—a group of spires that includes the Pointes Walker (4,208 m/13,806 ft), Whymper (4,184 m/ 13,727 ft), and Young (3,996 m/13,110 ft), named for the celebrated British alpinists who climbed them, and the Pointe Croz (4,110 m/13,484 ft), which honors the great French guide. The Italian-French border extends along the summits of these peaks.

Glacier des Bossons

While the Mer de Glace is a valley glacier, the Bossons is an icefall with an acutely steep pitch, its surface torn into séracs. From Les Bossons in the Chamonix valley, a chair lift climbs to the glacier's base. Besides the glacier, the view includes the Aiguilles de Chamonix. An ice cave has been dug inside the glacier and may be visited.

Mont Blanc Tramway

Starting from Le Fayet or St.-Gervais, west of Chamonix, this trolley (or light railway) climbs first to the Col de Voza and then to the Nid d'Aigle, or "eagle's nest," a point below the Aiguille de Bionnassay (4,052 m/13,294 ft) and its glacier, directly west of Mont Blanc. A footpath from the tram station leads to the edge of the moraine for a superb view of this great glacier and its séracs.

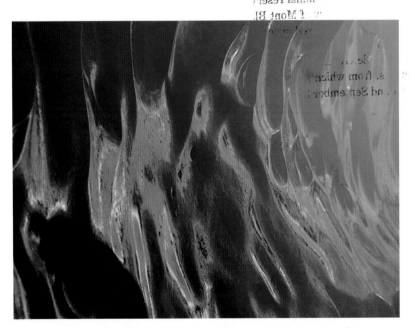

Visitors to Glacier des Bossons below Mont Blanc may visit a man-made ice cave dug into the glacier. Accessible by chairlift, Les Bossons also offers spectacular views of Aguilles de Chamonix and surrounding peaks. Facing page: Dwarfed by nature, well-equipped glacier climbers take on one of the Alps' most formidable challenges. Inexperienced climbers should never attempt this sport unless roped and accompanied by licensed guides.

Bellevue Cable Car

The Bellevue cable car from Les Houches, midway between St.-Gervais and Chamonix, rises to a point between the Col de Voza and the Nid d'Aigle. Both this lift and the tram to the Col de Voza are often used by hikers on the Tour du Mont Blanc.

Le Prarion Cable Car

This lift also commences from Les Houches, and provides a panoramic view of the Mont Blanc massif from the northwest. A footpath leads to the top of Le Prarion (1,969 m/6,460 ft) for an even more extended view.

Parc du Balcon de Merlet

This is an open-air animal reserve on a flank of the Aiguillette de Brévent, with a very fine view of Mont Blanc. It is not a zoo: the animals are free to roam within an enclosed space of 23 hectares/57 acres; visitors may wander among the animals. Besides European Alpine animals, there are other high-altitude creatures such as llamas and yaks. The park is north of Les Houches, from which it is accessible by a small road, and is open between May 1 and September 30.

AIGUILLES ROUGES

Facing Mont Blanc from across the Arve valley are the Aiguilles Rouges, a range of lower mountains that offers many superb viewpoints. A trail known as the Grand Balcon Sud extends along their slope, from the Col des Montets past Le Brévent to Les Houches. This is a section of the Tour du Mont Blanc, perhaps the most stunning part of the route because of the panorama it presents: the entire north slope of the Mont Blanc group, with all its beautiful glaciers. Several cable cars intersect the route, making it possible to ascend or descend to the valley from intermediate points along the way.

Le Brévent

One of the classic views of Mont Blanc is obtained from Le Brévent (2,525 m/8,284 ft), the mountain facing Mont Blanc almost directly across the valley of the Arve. From Chamonix, a two-section cable car ascends to its summit. You may also hike up this mountain; a popular compromise is to ride up to the intermediate station at Planpraz and then hike to the summit. This gives a comprehensive view of the entire group, with Mont Blanc and the other great peaks and glaciers spread before you in a grand tableau. This is the best place from which to view the Bossons and Taconnaz glaciers as they sweep down toward the valley floor.

La Flégère—L'Index

From Les Praz de Chamonix, a village directly northeast of Chamonix, a two-section lift rises first to La Flégère and then to L'Index on the slope of the Aiguilles Rouges. This viewpoint faces the Aiguille Verte and the Drus, and looks down upon the Mer de Glace; there is also a good view of the whole north face of the massif. A trail from La Flégère climbs to Lac Blanc, a small lake with a grand view. The Lacs des Chéserys are a group of small lakes nearby to the east, accessible by the network of trails upon this slope.

Réserve Naturelle des Aiguilles Rouges

The Aiguilles Rouges Nature Preserve is upon the eastern edge of the Aiguilles Rouges massif. Hikers on the Grand Balcon Sud between the Col des Montets and La Flégère walk through part of this terrain. There is a small exposition building and a short botanical walk at the entrance, near the Col des Montets, which is north of Argentière in the Arve valley.

Argentière

This is a pretty town on the Arve, full of flowers in summer—a refreshing contrast to urbanized Chamonix. It also enjoys fine views of the massif, extending to Mont Blanc. Argentière is at the foot of the 11-km-/6.8-mi-long Argentière glacier, second in this region only to the Mer de Glace. A nearby two-stage lift system ascends to Lognan and then the Aiguille des Grands Montets (3,295 m/10,810 ft), near the icy Col des Grands Montets—not to be confused with the much lower Col des Montets mentioned above. The upper lift station, Grands Montets, is encircled by glaciers and looks out upon the Glacier d'Argentière. The scene includes the Aiguille Verte directly above, a group of sheer-sided rock and ice peaks called Les Droites (4,000 m/13,123 ft at the highest point), and Mont Dolent (3,823 m/12,543 ft) across the glacier. From the lower station at Lognan, a footpath leads to the edge of the big glacier's left bank.

The Swiss Alps

T hough the highest mountain in the Alps is in France, the greatest number of peaks 4,000 m/13,000 ft or higher are in Switzerland; all in all, this country embodies the glory of the Alps.

Switzerland's small size—and its extraordinarily good system of public transportation as well as roads—make even its high alpine valleys easily accessible. The Swiss Post Office (PTT) runs the country's long-distance and rural bus system, and the yellow and red PTT buses stop at most villages.

Across the southwest of Switzerland stretch the Valaisian Alps, a magnificent chain of high peaks and splendid glaciers, the grandest scenic expanse in the Alps. On the other side of the Rhone Valley, the Bernese Alps display peaks almost as high and harbor the largest glacier in Europe; these two chains are close enough to be seen from the other at certain points. In southeastern Switzerland, the Rhaetian Alps are also renowned for their glaciers and fine mountains. The Glarus Alps, a smaller group in central Switzerland, are scarcely less Alpine than the mountains of the larger chains, and the Lepontine Alps, in the Swiss

The banks of the Bachalpsee on the hike to First in the Bernese Oberland, with their grand views of the Wetterhorn, make fine picnic spots.

Ticino, are a generally lower but complex and rugged group, offering some of the charm of Italian culture. The traveler in these various mountain chains can also enjoy an interesting contrast of regional cultures: Swiss French, German, Italian, and Romansch.

A good share of spectacular scenery is accessible to travelers by means of the excellent and abundant Swiss cable cars and cog railways; some of the roads over the alpine passes, including the Furka-Grimsel-Susten route and the Klausen Pass road, bring motorists into the high mountains. As in other Alpine countries, though, some of the finest alpine landscapes can be seen only by hikers.

The Swiss Alpine Club (SAC) huts are primarily climbing huts, based as close as possible to the starts of technical climbing routes. Hikers, however, are welcome and often stay at huts. Another option for hikers are the *Berghotels* (*auberges de montagne*), simple mountain inns that are privately owned. These inns offer the same kind of dormitory accommodations as the huts, but private rooms are also available. Only a few are equipped with warm water or showers. These modest establishments, some of which are very old, are a true national institution, appreciated and greatly beloved by the Swiss. Like Alpine Club huts, mountain inns are generally found in very scenic locations and most can be reached only by foot.

Addresses. For information on Switzerland, contact the Swiss National Tourist Office.

In the U.S., the addresses are: for the East Coast, 608 Fifth Avenue, New York, NY 10020; (212) 757-5944. For central and midwestern states, 150 N. Michigan Avenue, Chicago, IL 60601; (312) 630-5840. In the West: 260 Stockton Street, San Francisco, CA 94108-5387; (415) 362-2260.

In Canada, the tourist office address is: P.O. Box 215, Commerce Court West, Toronto, ONT M5L 1E8; (416) 868-0584.

In Great Britain, the address is: Swiss Centre, New Coventry Street, London W1V 8EE; (44) 1-734 1921.

For information on joining the Swiss Alpine Club, write to: Schweizer Alpen Club (SAC) or Club Alpin Suisse (CAS), Helvetiaplatz 4, 3005 Bern, Switzerland; (41) 31-43 36 11. Applicants for membership require sponsors.

The Valaisian Alps

THE PENNINE ALPS CONSTITUTE the highest mountain wall in western Europe, though the single peak of Mont Blanc in France is higher. These mountains mark the front line of the monumental collision of the Eurasian plate and the Italian prong of the African plate, which began millions of years ago and is still continuing. They now form the barrier separating western Switzerland from Italy. On average, this spectacular range contains both the highest Alpine peaks (among them the Matterhorn) and the largest areas of glaciers in the entire Alpine complex.

Geographers call these mountains the Pennine Alps, a term that includes both their Swiss and Italian sides. The Swiss slope of these mountains, falling within the canton of the Valais, or Wallis, is the Valaisian Alps. Unlike most Swiss cantons, this one contains two linguistic units: the western valleys are French-speaking, the eastern ones German-speaking, and the line of demarcation runs quite cleanly through the center of the canton.

These mountains were formed by the movement and folding of the complex Pennine nappes, which consist of a core of crystalline rock, mainly granite, gneiss, marble, and marine sediments. This core was altered by metamorphism, which converted the sediments to mica schist. The mountains formed by the important St. Bernard and Monte Rosa nappes consist largely of granite surrounded by mica schist and serpentine. They include the Allalinhorn and Grand Combin. However, due to the complex manner in which different Pennine nappes intersect, adjacent mountains can have very different geology. Thus, the Matterhorn, which is almost a next-door neighbor of the Monte Rosa, is made of crystalline gneisses, metamorphosed granite, and gabbro (coarse-grained igneous rock) because it derives from the Dent Blanche nappe (itself a segment of the Austro-alpine zone) that also formed the Ober Gabelhorn, Zinalrothorn, Weisshorn, Dent Blanche, and Dent d'Hérens.

The Valais has the driest climate and the greatest number of sunny days of any region in Switzerland, even in winter; the region thus attracts many skiers from fogbound northern Europe.

The watercourses issuing from these mountains and glaciers flow northward to the Rhone, creating a series of lateral valleys. To explore the region, visitors travel from the Rhone Valley southward up these valleys that rise high into the mountains. Some valleys are linked by high passes that hikers can sometimes cross, but travelers proceeding by road or rail must return in each case to the Rhone Valley, or some branch point near it, in order to set off up another valley.

THE COUNTRY OF THE THREE DRANCES

The three westernmost valleys of the Valaisian Alps, the Vals Ferret, d'Entremont, and de Bagnes, are each drained by a stream called the Drance, with the name of its valley attached—thus this area is called "Le Pays des Trois Drances."

The starting point for a visit to any of these three valleys is Martigny, an agreeable little town at the western end of the Rhone Valley. Though decidedly Swiss, Martigny has a French air, especially in its central square, with neat rows of trees surrounded by cafés and little restaurants. A ruined medieval fortress crowns a hill overlooking the town, a token that this was once an important crossroad—the junction of the great Rhone Valley and the route to the St. Bernard Pass and Italy. Martigny is the home of an excellent museum, the Fondation Pierre Gianadda, which mounts important art exhibitions and also displays a permanent collection of Gallo-Roman objects and antique automobiles.

Val Ferret

This westernmost valley of Canton Valais is sparsely inhabited, unspoiled, and unfrequented. From Sembrancher, a crossroads at the head of the valley, the road continues south through Orsières. Champex, on a small shelf above Orsières, is a pretty village on a small lake. Beyond Orsières there is very little motor traffic. The upper end of the valley is narrow and green, bordered on the west by steep, rocky ridges from which numerous waterfalls plunge into the Drance de Ferret. The eastern slope is lower, gentler, and wooded. Beyond La Fouly and Ferret, the land rises to a high grassy terrace, dotted with a few alpine farms (*alpages* or *pâturages*), below the cirque that closes the valley off to the south.

Though the valley is picturesque, the grandest scenery is accessible only to the hiker. The trail from Ferret southwest to the Grand Col Ferret, the pass to Italy, yields a superb panorama of Mont Dolent and the Glacier de Pré de Bar. This section of trail is part of the Tour du Mont Blanc, the walking route that circles the Mont Blanc massif. The Val Ferret is actually a trough between the Mont Blanc massif and the Pennine or Valaisian Alps.

Champex and Orsières offer the widest range of accommodations in the Val Ferret. At the upper end of the valley, where hardly anyone ever comes, there are few facilities for tourists. Hikers on the Tour du Mont Blanc

Near the vertical walls and snowy peaks of Mt. Collon, a pristine glacial ice formation soars into the late afternoon sky.

descending from the Grand Col Ferret stop at Ferret or La Fouly, where there are a few simple hotels. If you like to feel that you are at the end of the world (a pleasant, green world here), then a night at Ferret might charm you. From Martigny you can travel by narrow-gauge railway to Orsières, at the junction of the vals Ferret and d'Entremont. A PTT bus connects Orsières and Ferret, where the paved road ends.

Val d'Entremont and the Great St. Bernard Pass

This valley is the northern gate to the Col du Grand St.-Bernard—the historic Great St. Bernard Pass, which since prehistoric times has been the major pass route over the western Alps into Italy. The term *Pennine* derives from "Penn," the name the Gauls gave to their mountains, or perhaps to one of their gods. After the Romans discovered the St. Bernard Pass they named it Mont Jovis, or Mount Jupiter, but an earlier name for the pass survived as well—Mons Penninus; a temple to Jupiter Poeninus was located in Roman times near the pass. Conquered by Caesar Augustus, the pass was used by the Romans as their main access route to the north. Charlemagne crossed it upon returning from his coronation in Milan in 774, and Napoleon led his army here—40,000 men and 5,000 horses—across the Alps in 1800 en route to the battle of Marengo. The pass only acquired its present name during the late Middle Ages, several hundred years after St. Bernard founded a hospice here in the eleventh century. Perhaps the pass is best known for the dogs who were once dispatched from the Augustinian hospice in winter to find and rescue travelers marooned by snowstorms. Today, the chapel of the hospice, the kennels, and a small museum containing Gaulish and Roman artifacts found at the pass are open to the public.

Because of its heavy automobile traffic, the Val d'Entremont is less attractive to the traveler seeking alpine air and silence. Though the rocky tower of Mont Vélan (3,734 m/12,250 ft) rises behind the hospice, the scenery at the pass is not the finest in the range. The pass itself, at 2,469 m/8,100 ft, is stony and bleak, and often streaked with snow even in summer.

From Martigny you may drive to the pass, or take the narrow-gauge railway to Orsières and then a PTT bus to the pass. Motorists may drive through a tunnel or over the surface road, which is open from approximately mid-June to November. On the Italian side, the road descends to the Val d'Aosta.

Val de Bagnes

The Val de Bagnes, which leads nowhere, is much less frequented than the Val d'Entremont, its busy neighbor to the west, and its villages remain quiet and unspoiled. Yet this valley is the gateway to the Grand Combin, the first great peak on the western side of the Valaisian Alps. The Val de Bagnes has been a federally protected nature preserve since 1906.

From Martigny, follow the Drance upstream to Le Châble. Verbier, a chic ski resort, occupies a broad terrace above Le Châble. Verbier is composed entirely of new hotels and apartment houses—an almost French-style artificial community that bears no apparent relation to the character and architecture of the rest of the Val de Bagnes. There are a few small, simple villages on the narrow valley floor below: Champsec, Lourtier, and Fionnay. The road beyond Fionnay becomes steeper, ending at the Barrage (dam) de Mauvoisin, part of the Grande Dixence hydroelectric system—an extensive power project drawing water from tunnels and reservoirs throughout the Valaisian Alps. Most of the works, including power lines, are underground.

The long reservoir above the dam, the Lac de Mauvoisin, extends far into the mountains, below the shadow of the Grand Combin (4,141 m/13,586 ft). This massive and complex mountain, with huge, snowy flanks and a curving, rocky summit ridge, belongs to the group known as the "four-thousanders," the mountains over 4,000 meters high.

The Grand Combin is the greatest but not the only feature of the Val de Bagnes. The southern end of the valley fronts a fan-shaped series of ridges leading to the central spine separating Switzerland and Italy; from these mountains a series of glaciers, including the big Glacier d'Otemma, feeds the Drance de Bagnes. To the southeast, the Val de Bagnes is separated from the Val d'Hérémence by a loop of mountains that includes Mont Blanc de Cheilon.

From Verbier there are cable cars to a plateau from which there is a good but distant view of the Grand Combin, but for the best views you should get closer to the mountain. As there are no ski lifts in the upper end of the Val de Bagnes, you must hike in order to see the grand scenery above the end of the valley. Simple accommodations are available in Fionnay and Mauvoisin.

Mauvoisin. Most hikers begin their walks at the dam wall, where the paved road ends. Some courageous (or foolhardy) motorists shorten their hike by driving to the end of the lake, a distance of about 5 km/3 mi along the western shore on a pitted, one-lane gravel road. Initially, the road proceeds through a series of narrow tunnels. There are virtually no shoulders or turnouts, and you must drive to the end of the road to turn around. Traffic proceeds in one direction at even-numbered hours, in the other direction at odd ones.

Three hiking routes in this area provide superb and different views of the gigantic Grand Combin, with its sweeping glaciers and the constellation of peaks that surround it. Trails along both the western and eastern shores of the Lac de Mauvoisin lead to the Cabane de Chanrion, an SAC hut with a

A field of cotton grass on the upper Mauvoisin hike in early September conveys the sense of openness long associated with Alpine meadows in flower. Above timberline, there are more than seven hundred species of flowering plants; some, like the edelweiss, are protected by law and may not be picked.

splendid view of the Grand Combin and the mountainous folds that block the valley to the south. The trail to the high meadows of La Tsessette provides a closer view of the glacier cirque below the east side of the Grand Combin. The grandest view of the Grand Combin is seen from the Cabane de Panossière. This SAC hut is positioned directly above the Glacier de Corbassière, a broad river of ice more than 6 km/3.7 mi long and 2 km/1.2 mi wide, which descends northward from the mountain. The hut can be reached from either Fionnay or Mauvoisin, or by a loop trip combining both sections of the route. The trail up from Mauvoisin is steeper and more difficult but provides additional magnificent views from the Col des Otanes, the notch above the hut. Inexperienced hikers should take the trail from Fionnay, and return the same way.

Besides hiking or climbing, summertime visitors can fish in the Lac de Mauvoisin; winter visitors can have a choice of ski mountaineering or cross-country skiing along the valley bottom. At Verbier, however, there is an immense network of ski lifts and a great variety of ski runs.

To reach the Val de Bagnes by train, one must take the narrow-gauge railway from Martigny to Le Châble, which is the transfer point for the bus to Verbier or the Val de Bagnes. The latter bus continues to Mauvoisin.

MONT BLANC, THE VANOISE, THE GRAN PARADISO, AND THE WESTERN VALASIAN ALPS

Autobahn   ● Points of Interest

Main Roads   ▲ Peaks

Connecting Roads   ⚒ Passes   🛖 Huts

0   15 Mi

0   15 Km

VAL D'HERENS AND VAL D'HEREMENCE

The Val d'Hérens penetrates close to the great central crest of the Valaisian Alps, providing access to some of the region's greatest scenic splendors, with big, snow-covered mountains and some of the most impressive glaciers in the Valais. Despite this, it has remained mostly untouched by the large-scale development that has accompanied the establishment of modern ski resorts. Its unspoiled villages give the traveler a rare glimpse of what a place such as Zermatt was like when it was a simple mountain village.

The starting point for a trip into these valleys is Sion, an interesting old town in the Rhone Valley and the capital of Canton Valais. Two steep, conical hills, almost improbably close to each other, rise abruptly above the old quarter and reflect in a curious way the history of the town. In the Middle Ages, the bishops of Sion became not only its spiritual but also its temporal lords when they were granted the title of Counts of the Valais. The northern of the two hills is topped by the ruins of a thirteenth-century episcopal palace, the Château de Tourbillon; the southern hill culminates in the Château de Valère, a medieval fortress containing within its walls the church of Notre-Dame. The church contains a charming organ with painted panels, said to be the oldest playable organ in the world (there are organ recitals in the summer), and some fine frescoes and choir stalls. Adjacent to the church is a museum containing medieval armor, religious objects, and furniture. In the town below, the archaeological museum has a small but good Roman collection.

The road ascending southward from Sion forks at Vex, the junction for the Val d'Hérens and the Val d'Hérémence. But the geographical junction for these two valleys is at Euseigne, a little farther south on the road into the Val d'Hérens. At this point their two streams join: the Dixence, which drains the Val d'Hérémence, and the Borgne, which drains the Val d'Hérens. At Euseigne the road passes some curious pointed towers, les Pyramides d'Euseigne. These are the result of a natural phenomenon in which soft rock and moraine debris were eroded into columns that retain their height because of boulders perched above them.

Val d'Hérémence

The chief feature of the Val d'Hérémence is the Lac des Dix, 5.5 km/3.4 mi long, created by the Grande Dixence dam. This dam, at 285 m/935 ft the highest in the world, is the center of the vast alpine hydroelectric system, the Grande Dixence. The Lac des Dix stores water derived from the melting snow and ice in spring and summer. During these seasons, water is pumped into this lake from throughout the Valaisian Alps through a series of complicated tunnels. During the winter the water is released to fall to the Rhone Valley, where it generates hydroelectric power. This is a remarkable feat of engineering, with minimal environmental impact. One can reach Le Chargeur, at the foot of the dam, by car or bus; a little cable car ferries visitors to the top of the dam wall. From there, you can walk the length of the west shore of the lake, and obtain fine views of Mont Blanc de Cheilon. (Strong, experienced hikers can continue to the Cabane des Dix, or cross the Col de Riedmatten to the Val d'Arolla.)

Val d'Hérens

From Vex, the road enters the Val d'Hérens, reaching Evolène and, a few kilometers later, Les Haudères. Besides its access to very fine alpine scenery, this valley is remarkable because many women here still wear the traditional dress of the region. Both villages are good bases from which to explore.

Evolène. Evolène is slightly larger, with a wider choice of accommodations and a sprinkling of new concrete "chalets," mostly on the road leading out of the village. Across the valley to the west is the Pic d'Artsinol (2,998 m/ 9,836 ft), a favorite excursion spot. At Lana, a nearby hamlet across the Borgne, a chair lift operates during the summer for a limited time in the morning and afternoon, giving hikers a partial boost up the trail leading to this small mountain, from which there is a panoramic view.

Les Haudères and the Val de Ferpècle. Les Haudères is the point where the Val d'Hérens branches into the Val de Ferpècle and the Val d'Arolla. It is a charming, unspoiled village, composed mostly of old Valaisian houses and their little gardens. The view here is more varied than at Evolène. The Val de Ferpècle, shorter than the Val d'Arolla, rises southeast; it is the approach route to the highest mountain in this region, the Dent Blanche (4,357 m/ 14,295 ft). The view from the slopes above Les Haudères is dominated by the tilted peak of this great "white tooth," as it is named. There are multiple opportunities at Ferpècle for hikers, who can climb up to Bricola and even a little farther, to Les Manzettes, for views of the Dent Blanche and the impressive glaciers of Ferpècle and Mont Miné.

On the slopes above Les Haudères are three hamlets, La Forclaz, La Sage, and Villa, from which several trails lead up to points along the eastern wall of the Val d'Hérens. One trail climbs to the Col de Torrent, the pass to the Val de Moiry to the east.

Val d'Arolla. From Les Haudères, the main road climbs south and slightly west into the long, narrow Val d'Arolla, which extends deep into the high Alps to the south. The southern end of this valley is half encircled by some of the biggest Valaisian Alps outside those above Zermatt and Saas-

Fee. This region also presents a splendid array of glaciers. From the road approaching Arolla, Mont Collon (3,637 m/11,932 ft) fills the view to the south, a great, snow-capped trapezoidal block standing squarely at the valley's end. Mont Collon appears like an island encircled by glaciers—the Haut Glacier d'Arolla to the east and the Glacier de Mont Collon to the west, which join at the mountain's base to flow into the Bas Glacier d'Arolla. Slightly to the west, the Pigne d'Arolla (3,976 m/13,044 ft) sits between the Glacier de Piece to the east and the Glacier de Tsijiore Nouve to the west. Nonhikers can obtain a splendid view of this mountain from the terrace of the Grand Hotel and Kurhaus, about 80 m/262 ft above Arolla. Still farther west is the impressive Mont Blanc de Cheilon (3,870 m/12,697 ft), at the head of the Glacier de Cheilon and presiding over the Val d'Hérémence; you must proceed on foot, however, to see it.

The namesake of Arolla is the Arolla pine, one of the chief alpine conifers, which flourishes here. Arolla was never a village, but rather the highest of the summer farms—now the highest settlement—in the Val d'Hérens. The advent of mountaineering and skiing turned it into a "station de montagne": a small center for mountain sports. There are several hotels, some chalets with apartments for rent, a little grocery store, and a couple of sport shops. Several ski lifts operate during the winter.

For hikers, Arolla offers many possibilities. The trail that climbs above the east slope of the Bas Glacier d'Arolla yields close views of Mont Collon and its

Located near the foot of the Arolla glacier, the tiny mountain village of Arolla commands a spectacular view of Mt. Collon's formidable peak. Facing page: Near the Pigne d'Arolla, a peak named for the region's famous pine tree, a windswept ice face looks south across the clouds toward Italy.

glaciers. To see Mont Blanc de Cheilon, follow the trail west to the Pas de Chèvres, which overlooks the big Glacier de Cheilon and provides impressive views of the mountain at its head. From the nearby Col de Riedmatten, hikers may cross to the Val d'Hérémence without having to step out onto the ice of the glacier. The trail from Arolla northwestward to Pra Gra, an *alpage*, gives splendid, comprehensive views of Mont Collon and the Pigne d'Arolla; continuing in this direction, experienced hikers can reach the Cabane des Aiguilles Rouges ("red needles"), an SAC hut at the foot of the red, jagged peaks separating the Val d'Arolla from the Val d'Hérémence.

Besides the superb opportunities for hiking throughout this region, it is also a noted center for climbing. There is a guides' office in Arolla, through which you can obtain the services of a licensed mountain guide, and the Club des Randonnées in Les Haudères also organizes excursions onto the glaciers. Arolla operates two chair lifts during the winter. A couple of ski lifts serve Les Haudères and Evolène, and there is cross-country skiing along the valley floor.

From Sion you can travel by bus or car to the Val d'Hérens. At Les Haudères, bus travelers change for Arolla, Ferpècle, La Forclaz, La Sage, and Villa. To reach the Lac des Dix, you can drive or take the bus through Vex to Le Chargeur.

VAL D'ANNIVIERS

Although close to some of the highest mountains in Europe, the Val d'Anniviers and its collateral valleys do not penetrate very deeply into the Valaisian range, and long glaciers block the valley approaches to these mountains. Thus, much of the finest scenery can be viewed only by technical climbers. Nevertheless, these valleys provide some pleasant excursions. The starting point is the town of Sierre in the Rhone Valley. At Vissoie, the road branches for the Val de Moiry to the west, and the Val de Zinal to the east.

Bella Tola

The pretty village of St.-Luc sits on a terrace above the eastern slope of the Val d'Anniviers and serves as the starting point for trips to a small peak, the Bella Tola (3,025 m/9,924 ft), that can be ascended by hikers. This climb was such a favorite for Victorian visitors that tiny St.-Luc had an English church to serve them. The Bella Tola is the highest point on the ridge separating this valley from the Turtmanntal, its neighbor to the east. Rising above everything within sight, it provides a completely panoramic view, extending not only to the Valaisian Alps but also northward to the mountains of the Bernese

Oberland across the Rhone Valley. A chair lift from St.-Luc to Tignousa gives hikers a boost. South of the Bella Tola is the Meidpass, which hikers can cross to reach the Turtmanntal; the ridge serves as a sharp linguistic dividing line—the eastern limit of the French-speaking Valais: all place names on the other side of the pass are Swiss-German.

Val de Moiry

The Val de Moiry is rather short and culminates in the dammed-up Lac de Moiry, part of the Grande Dixence system. Its stream, La Gougra, joins La Navisence just below the flower-bedecked village of Grimentz.

Val de Zinal

The lower Val de Zinal is rather narrow, with wooded slopes. Its well-known resort, Zinal, is positioned several kilometers before the end of the valley, and there is no great view to be had from the village; the only mountain visible is a peak called Besso (3,668 m/12,034 ft), which blocks the view of the magnificent Zinalrothorn from much of the valley. From Zinal a path continues up a very gentle grade along the Navisence stream for several kilometers southward before the view opens out. The trail then continues along the crest of the moraine of the Zinal glacier on a knife-edge ridge, where the route requires some expertise. The steep route southeast of Zinal to the SAC Cabane d'Ar Pitetta provides good views of the western wall of the Weisshorn, Schalihorn, and Zinalrothorn group.

Though hiking opportunities are not very extensive here, there is very good climbing, and Zinal is a popular ski resort, with one cable car and several chair lifts. There is a small network of cross-country ski trails along the valley floor, a skating rink, and an attractive indoor swimming pool.

All the villages of the Val d'Anniviers can be reached by car or by postal bus from Sierre.

THE VISPERTAL

The Vispertal is the gateway to the glory of the Swiss Alps, a magnificent range of thickly clustered 4,000-m/13,000-ft peaks that are the roof of western Europe. So extensive are the glaciers that this was once called the Swiss Greenland. These valleys are very deep, with a great differential between their base and the summits of the peaks that surround them.

Like its neighbors to the west, the upper Vispertal splits into two branches. Both are watered by streams called the Visp—the Mattervispa and the

Saaser Vispa. As with all the Valaisian valleys, the Vispertal is approached from the Rhone Valley to the north. The closest town is Visp (in French, Viège); Brig, a short distance to the east, is the transportation center of the upper Rhone Valley.

Zermatt and the Mattertal

At the southern end of the Mattertal, the western branch of the Vispertal, is Zermatt, a celebrated European center for climbing, hiking, and skiing. Above Zermatt stands the Matterhorn, one of the most famous mountains in the world. Yet this magnificent peak, with its unique form, is far from being the sole attraction in Zermatt: more 4,000-m/13,000-ft peaks loop around the Mattertal than around any other valley in the Alps.

The glaciers that carved out these mountains are spread in a broad fan around Zermatt in every direction except north. Five valleys are easily accessible from Zermatt, with glorious scenery in every direction. The southern end of the Mattertal is roughly T-shaped, with Zermatt near the crossing of the T. From this junction, the Zmutt valley and glacier extend to the west, and the great Gorner glacier to the east. Hemming these valleys to the south is an almost linear wall of tremendous mountains.

THE AROLLA PINE
Pinus cembra

This pine, which reaches a height of 20–25 m/65–82 ft, is among the most characteristic of alpine trees. Unlike the spruce, fir, and larch, its appearance is thick and bulky rather than light or pyramidal; the branches of the Arolla pine grow out from the trunk and then curve abruptly upward, like raised arms. From a distance, its long needles look bushy on the boughs, like bottle-brushes. These needles grow in tufts of five, bound together at the base.

The cone is shaped like an artichoke—roundish and tapering slightly toward the tip. The Arolla pine prefers an acid soil and may be found at the upper limit of the forest.

The majestic Matterhorn is incomparably beautiful. Nearby Zermatt offers day tours and, for the braver and more prosperous, climbing expeditions.

Zermatt is thus superbly located for viewing grand alpine scenery. It is the base for many hiking trails—more than are accessible from any other village in the Alps—and some of the routes here rank among the finest walks in Switzerland. It is also one of the premier mountaineering centers of Europe, offering numerous climbs ranging from easy to extremely difficult. Because of Zermatt's several cable cars and its cog railway, much of this scenery can be enjoyed by travelers who neither climb nor hike. Zermatt is also a major year-round skiing resort, with good summer skiing on the big glacier plateau behind the Klein Matterhorn and Breithorn.

The Matterhorn, Zermatt's signature mountain, is visible from every street. The other great mountains, however, cannot be seen until you climb the slopes above Zermatt, by cable car or on foot. Although Zermatt has grown to be a large place, almost a town, there are still a few traditional old Valaisian houses and granaries, as well as gardens between many chalets and hotels. It retains the feeling of a village more than some other large resorts such as Chamonix or St. Moritz. The main street is thronged with tourists during July and August, many of whom are day-trippers, who come specially for the excursion to the Gornergrat. In the mountains, people cluster at the cable-car stations and their viewing terraces, but hikers leave the crowds behind.

The great valleys accessible from Zermatt are the Täsch, Trift, Zmutt, Gorner, and Findel. In many other Valaisian valleys, the highest peaks are found only to the south. But some of the biggest mountains in the Alps crown the walls of the Mattertal somewhat north of Zermatt. Above the western side of the valley are a group of important mountains including the Weisshorn (4,505 m/14,780 ft), the Zinalrothorn (4,221 m/13,848 ft), and the Ober Gabelhorn (4,063 m/13,330 ft), along with a host of other peaks just under 4,000 m/13,120 ft, set amid a series of high glaciers, 1,000 to 1,500 m/3,280 to 4,920 ft above the valley floor.

The Weisshorn. The Weisshorn, with its long, glittering flanks of ice, has sometimes been considered the most beautiful mountain in the Alps. It stands at the northern end of this range, above the village of Randa. There is no cable-car access to the Weisshorn, so the mountain must be enjoyed from viewing points across the valley. The hiking trail from Sunnegga (above Zermatt) to a point called the Ober Sattla (above Täsch) provides good views of the Weisshorn; it can also be seen from the Gornergrat.

Täsch. The Mischabel group separates the Mattertal from the Saastal to the east. The biggest of these peaks—the Dom (at 4,545 m/14,91 ft, the highest mountain entirely within Swiss borders), Täschhorn, Alphubel, Rimpfischhorn, and Allalinhorn—can be viewed from the slopes above Täschalp, high above the village of Täsch, which is about 5 km/3 mi north of Zermatt. The Ober Sattla is a high shoulder east of Täsch from which there are very fine views of these mountains. It can be reached by a trail from the top of Zermatt's Sunnegga funicular, or from the village of Täsch. A taxi may be taken between Täsch and Täschalp. The Mischabel group can also be viewed from the trails above the Trift region across the Zermatt valley.

Trift. The narrow, steep valley of the Triftbach, a brook that courses directly into Zermatt from the west, is topped by a coronet of great mountains, most notably the Ober Gabelhorn, Wellenkuppe, and Zinalrothorn, and the Gabelhorn, Trift, and Rothorn glaciers. There is no cable car to Trift, but the magnificent scenery provides ample compensation for the initial steep trudge up the gorge. From the *Berghotel* at Trift, there are trails in several directions.

The hike from Trift southwest and then westward over Höhbalm is surely the finest walk not only in Switzerland but in all the Alps. It presents a continually unfolding panorama; during the course of the day you see sixteen 4,000-meter peaks: the Ober Gabelhorn, Zinalrothorn, Dom, Täschhorn, Alphubel, Allalinhorn, Rimpfischhorn, Strahlhorn, Monte Rosa, Liskamm, Castor, Pollux, Breithorn, Matterhorn, the Dent d'Hérens, and the tip of the Weisshorn, as well as numerous other mountains just below the 4,000-meter mark. Moreover, the middle section of the walk passes directly opposite the great north wall of the Matterhorn—a sight that alone would make any hike thrilling.

One of the lesser peaks above Trift, the Mettelhorn (3,406 m/11,174 ft), often climbed by hikers, provides a panoramic view of the entire range as well as more distant views of the Bernese Oberland to the north. By climbing up partway from Trift to the Triftchumme, the high meadows between Trift and the Mettelhorn, you can gain a breathtaking view of the Ober Gabelhorn, Wellenkuppe, Zinalrothorn, and the mountains near them, as well as stunning, close views of the glaciers around them. (Hikers should inquire about snow conditions before attempting the Mettelhorn peak.)

The terrace outside the upper Sunnegga funicular station (above Zermatt) and the cable cars continuing up to Blauherd and the Unterrothorn also provide excellent viewing points for the mountains above Trift, as does the Gornergrat cog railway.

Zmutt. The Zmutt glacier, southwest of Zermatt, carved out the broad valley separating the Dent d'Hérens (4,171 m/13,684 ft) and the Matterhorn (4,478 m/14,691 ft) from the southern edge of the Gabelhorn massif. Hiking trails along the northern edge of the Zmutt valley provide magnificent views of the north wall of the Matterhorn, one of the three great "faces" of Alpine climbing, and of the vast arc of glaciers and ridges that enclose the western end of the valley. These trails include the high route from Zermatt to the hamlet of Zmutt, the Höhbalm route mentioned above, and the trail to the Schönbiel hut. In a spectacular location, this hut faces the beautiful Dent d'Hérens, shaped like a helmet of ice, as well as the Matterhorn's Zmutt (northwest) ridge. The Dent Blanche rises behind the hut, and to the west is a wall of hanging glaciers.

The Matterhorn. The Matterhorn itself, just southwest of Zermatt and visible from every part of the village, is a pyramid with four faces and four ridges, a classic example of what geologists call a "horn," a sharp, jagged peak carved out by glaciers. This mountain is distinctive in every respect. Although part of a long line of peaks, almost a linear wall of tremendous mountains stretching west to east along the Swiss-Italian border, the Matterhorn stands alone in proud isolation. Seen from the Zermatt side, this huge tower of rock rises from an immense base with a long, crouching posterior, so that it resembles a sphinx, with its head slightly inclined. It is perhaps the most beautiful mountain in the world, an image of power and grace.

The Italian border runs up the mountain's southwest ridge, over the summit, and down the southeast ridge; the "normal" climbing route is the northeast ridge, the Hörnligrat. A cable car takes climbers and tourists to the little Schwarzsee at the base of this ridge. Hikers can continue up the trail to the Hörnli hut, the starting point for the climb. While this approach offers a close

view of the mountain (more precisely, of the east face and the northeast ridge), it is foreshortened, and you can obtain a better view of the Matterhorn's full and magnificent shape from other points across the valley.

Gornergrat. The immense Gorner glacier, over 12 km/7.5 mi long, flows into the Mattertal from the east, terminating just below the Matterhorn massif. High above the northern side of the glacier is a ridge, known as the Gornergrat, that can be reached by the Gornergrat cog railway from Zermatt, or by foot. The terrace above the Gornergrat Kulm Hotel (3,135 m/ 10,285 ft) is the finest single viewpoint in the Alps. To the southeast is the vast, complex mass of the Monte Rosa, the highest of whose eight peaks (the Dufourspitz) reaches 4,634 m/15,203 ft—the highest point in Switzerland. The mountain sits enthroned between two massive glaciers, the Gorner and the almost equally broad Grenz glacier. Beyond the Monte Rosa stretches a tremendous wall of snowcapped mountains and hanging glaciers. To the west is the Liskamm, with two snowy summits high above vertical black walls; this is followed by the twin snow cones, Castor and Pollux, the Breithorn, with its long, ferocious black wall, and then the Matterhorn. The Gornergrat closely and directly faces this line of six 4,000-meter peaks, with hanging glaciers pouring down their flanks and separating their ridges. On a clear day, this

The twin peaks of mounts Castor and Pollux in Italy can be seen from the Gornergrat, one of the Alps' best mountain viewpoints accessible by lift or train. Facing page: The Gornergrat's vistas also include the Monte Rosa massif. The Monte Rosa hut sits on a rock protrusion in the middle of the Gorner glacier.

mass of snowy peaks and glaciers blaze against the blue sky, creating an incomparable effect. A total of eighteen 4,000-meter mountains can be seen from the Gornergrat, the greatest number of these giant peaks that can be seen from any viewpoint in the Alps.

Hikers who start early in the morning and take the especially scenic Gagenhaupt route variant between Riffelberg and Rotenboden on the way up to the Gornergrat may see chamois or ibex on an outcrop of rock just west of the Riffelhorn, a small rock peak that you pass while climbing to the Gornergrat.

Klein Matterhorn. The Klein Matterhorn cable car, the highest in Europe, brings visitors up to the summit of this 3,884-m/12,743-ft peak called the Little Matterhorn, just to the east of its great neighbor. Though it provides a close view of the Matterhorn and the Breithorn, and views of many other peaks, the overall scene is not as fine as the one from the Gornergrat. Skiers in summer and winter, and climbers bound for the Breithorn or the "twins," Castor and Pollux, make use of this lift as well.

Findel. Another huge sheet of ice, parallel to the Gorner glacier and just to the north, is the Findel glacier. Above the northern rim of the Findel glacier is a little lake, the Stellisee; just a few minutes' walk farther, the terrace of the *Berghotel* at Flühalp is a favorite viewing spot for hikers. From these points there are excellent views across the valley to the Matterhorn, and eastward toward the Rimpfischhorn, Adlerhorn, and Strahlhorn. The Flühalp hotel also serves as the base for climbers heading for the latter three mountains. From the trail beyond Flühalp there are excellent views down onto the Findel glacier, its broad surface ruptured into a labyrinth of crevasses.

From Zermatt, an underground funicular train serves as a quick shuttle to Sunnegga, from which you can continue by cable car to Blauherd; this provides a boost almost to the level of the Flühalp hotel. From Blauherd, you can continue by another cable car to the summit of the Unterrothorn (3,103 m/10,180 ft). This "little" peak is separated by a narrow, U-shaped valley from its bigger sister, the Oberrothorn (3,415 m/11,204 ft). Like the Mettelhorn, the ascent of the Oberrothorn requires no technical skills and its summit provides a superb panoramic view, making it a favorite excursion for hikers and climbers in training.

Zermatt is reached by the BVZ railway, which starts in Brig on a narrow-gauge track in front of the main station. The train stops in Visp before climbing up the Mattertal. You can also drive up the Mattertal as far as Täsch, where there are several large parking lots. Although the road continues to Zermatt, it is open only to residents' automobiles; traffic is banned entirely from the village, which permits only electric vehicles. From Täsch there is shuttle rail service to Zermatt.

IBEX
Capra ibex

These relatives of the goat are the largest animals that frequent the high alpine slopes, and because of their size and their long, magnificent horns, they appear to be kings of the mountains. In many places, these handsome creatures were hunted to extinction, but the species was saved because of a pioneering preservation effort in Italy's Gran Paradiso National Park. They have since been successfully reintroduced into many parts of the Alps and are now generally protected.

The coat of the male ibex is brown, with a lighter underside. It is almost beige in spring, during the moult, then darkens to medium brown in summer and chestnut in winter; females remain lighter in color. Males have a small beard. The animal's most notable feature is its long horns, marked by a series of ring-like notches.

This animal's habitat is rocky areas from tree line to about 3,000 m/ 9,842 ft, and sometimes as high as 3,500 m/11,482 ft. During winter ibex may descend to lower slopes for food, but they climb to higher altitudes again as the snow melts and new plants grow. Ibex's feet are wonderfully adapted for rocky slopes and cliffs; a viewer may watch how their hoofs, separated into two distinct toes, grip the edges of rock.

Ibex are very fond of salt, and may be seen licking certain rocks or, in national parks, places where salt has been left out for them by park wardens. The sexes live separately; females and the young live together in groups, and old males are solitary. Ibex may tolerate a rather close presence or approach by a quiet visitor.

The Saastal

This valley lies under the flank of the Mischabel range, one of the most important mountain groups in Switzerland, which separates the Saastal from the Mattertal to the west. To the east, the Saastal is bounded by another big wall, rising to 4,023 m/13,199 ft at the Weissmies. The valley is punctuated by several villages with the prefix *Saas-*, including Saas-Balen, Saas-Grund, and Saas-Almagell. Saas-Grund lies at the foot of the Weissmies group of mountains and is the starting point for many hikes and climbs; other excursions begin at Saas-Almagell, the southernmost village in the valley.

Saas-Fee. At the upper end of the valley, Saas-Fee has one of the most spectacular locations in the Alps. Originally a group of summer farms, or *alps*, rather than a year-round settlement, it is now the most famous, often referred to simply as "Saas." Saas-Fee is located on a terrace several hundred meters above the valley floor, where the looming wall of the Mischabel range wraps halfway around its site. The village sits within the curve of this steep, massive glacial cirque, an enormous rampart of rock, ice, and snow — one of the biggest in Switzerland. Above rise some of the highest mountains in the Alps. Whereas from Zermatt one must climb or take a cable car to see the mountains above the village, the entire crown of the Mischabel stands plainly visible from every part of Saas-Fee.

Besides its beautiful location, Saas still has some of the charm of an Alpine village. It is much less overbuilt and less crowded than Zermatt, with many more traditional Valaisian houses. In contrast to the main street of Zermatt, now a continuous line of shops and hotels, cabbages and strawberries are still cultivated in the vegetable gardens on the main street of Saas. This is a major center for hiking, climbing, and year-round skiing; the Felskinn cable car and the Metro funicular are used for the summer ski slopes. Saas is also the starting (or end) point for the Haute Route, a difficult, week-long ski-mountaineering event over the glaciers to Chamonix, done in the spring. The village has a modern indoor swimming pool and sports complex, and many tennis courts facing the mountains.

On the west side of Saas, the Hannig cable car rises to an excellent viewing point; hikers who continue up to the area known as Mellig have superb views across the bowl of the cirque to the whole curved wall of the Mischabel range.

To reach Saas-Fee by public transportation, take the train from Brig or Visp to Stalden and change there for the bus to Saas-Fee. Visitors arriving by car must park at the entrance to the village, where there is a parking garage and several lots. No automobile traffic is allowed in Saas-Fee. Saas-Grund and Saas-Almagell are a few minutes away by car or bus.

Längfluh. The glacial cirque that towers above Saas is a true icefall, presenting a front of hanging glaciers, torn by the steepness of the wall into deep crevasses and towering, jagged pillars of ice called séracs. To view such a wild, tumbled glacier is an experience usually reserved for mountaineers, but at Saas-Fee the sight is available to everyone via the Längfluh cable car, which lofts over the ice and deposits the visitor on a narrow finger of rock amid the séracs. The slopes around the middle station, Spielboden, are honeycombed with marmot burrows; this area is a favorite with children, who like to sit in front of marmot holes, exhibiting unusual patience as they hold out carrots and wait for a marmot to appear.

The Felskinn cable car climbs over the eastern part of the glacier, from which (during a normal season) you can walk without a guide over the glacier to the SAC Britanniahütte on a well-marked and almost level route that is monitored daily for signs of crevasses. (Hikers should, of course, wear boots and dark glasses, and use protective cream for the skin and lips.) This is one of the very few glacier routes in the Alps where it is safe for inexperienced persons to walk without a guide. From Felskinn, you can also take the "Metro," an underground funicular that emerges on the Mittel Allalin ridge at 3,500 m/11,483 ft, an island in a sea of glaciers; there is a revolving restaurant at the top. The Metro is used to shorten ascents of the Allalinhorn and Alphubel, and for summer skiing.

The Plattjen cable car rises to the shoulder below the Mittaghorn, from which hikers can follow a longer route than the one from Felskinn to the Britannia hut. This trail offers views east and south across the Saastal.

Britanniahütte.   The view from this SAC hut is remarkable, presenting a sea of high glaciers amid which rise the Rimpfischhorn (4,199 m/13,776 ft) and the Strahlhorn (4,190 m/13,747 ft), two mountains that cannot be seen from Saas, as well as a close view of the Allalinhorn (4,027 m/13,212 ft).

Grächen and Gspon.   These two popular hiking routes are traverses on high trails (*Höhenweg*) above the Saastal, with varying scenes of the mountains on each side. Hikers staying in Saas take the bus down the valley. They can either get off at Stalden and take the cable car to Gspon for the Gspon–Saas-Grund hike, or continue by bus to Grächen and take the cable car up to the Hannigalp, starting point for the Grächen–Saas-Fee hike. The Grächen trail takes you into wilder country; the grim Balfrin (3,796 m/12,454 ft) dominates the central part of this high mountain walk. The shorter, easier Gspon trail offers more extensive, though distant, views of some of the mountains above Saas-Fee, such as the Allalinhorn and Alphubel.

Saas-Almagell.   From this southernmost village in the Saastal, there are three walking routes into Italy. The Furggtal leads southeastward to the Antrona pass. This beautiful U-shaped trough, almost a textbook example of a valley scooped out by a glacier, is now wild and uninhabited; the only trace

ALPINE CHOUGH
Pyrrhocorax graculus

This black bird is the aerial daredevil of the Alps, performing daring flips, abrupt turns, and suddenly plummeting through the air to land neatly a few feet from a picnic spot. No alpine bird is more commonly seen by hikers and climbers, especially when food is unpacked from a rucksack, whereupon two or three often seem to materialize from nowhere. They compete passionately for any sandwich crumb, even catching a morsel in midair while fending off a rival.

Their black dress is set off by their red feet and yellow beaks. Averaging about 38 cm/15 in in length, they are about half the size of a crow.

The chough's habitat is from tree line to about 3,000 m/9,842 ft. Though they do not migrate, they may descend in winter to search for food in fields and even villages at the bottom of valleys. They make their nests in holes and cracks in rock walls.

of human presence is a concrete sluice in the Furggbach, showing evidence of the Grande Dixence hydroelectric system, and a few sections of medieval paving left from the days when this was a major route for the import of salt from Italy. A second valley, the Almagellertal, rises eastward below the Weissmies massif to the Zwischbergen Pass and a majestic view of the Mischabel range. There is a *Berghotel* at Almagelleralp, and a new SAC hut just below the pass. The third route is more frequented and less scenic but also requires less exertion: hikers can climb above the Mattmark dam and lake up to the Monte Moro pass, which offers a view of the Monte Rosa. A cable car descends from this pass to Macugnaga on the Italian side of the Monte Rosa.

Saas-Grund. This village is the point of departure for the normal route up the Weissmies (4,023 m/13,199 ft), as well as for the Lagginhorn (3,971 m/ 13,028 ft) and Fletschhorn (3,904 m/12,808 ft). The Kreuzboden-Hohsaas lift rises to a point close to the Weissmies hut. From the middle station, Kreuzboden, a trail curves around the shoulder of the Weissmies massif, with excellent views of the Mischabel range.

The trail from the Felskinn lift to Brittaniahutte is short and fairly level.

The Bernese Alps

THE HUGE ALPINE MASS of the Bernese Alps rivals the Valaisian Alps as the most impressive European Alpine range. These mountains are the highest land within the Swiss canton of Bern and overlook the city of Bern, Switzerland's capital, hence their popular name—the Bernese Oberland. On a fine day, from the terrace behind the Berner Münster, Bern's splendid medieval cathedral, you can see the distant line of snowy peaks, which appear to float against the blue sky. Some authorities limit the term "Bernese Oberland" to the central portion of this range, however this book follows the broader, more common definition and includes the entire range spanning Canton Bern.

Amid the constellation of glaciers upon the crown of this range is the Grosser Aletsch glacier, the biggest glacier in the Alps. Though the Bernese peaks are not as high on average as those of the Valaisian Alps, they constitute some of the most formidable challenges that mountaineers have ever faced. This is one of the premier skiing regions in Europe, as well as a favorite among hikers, strollers, and cable-car riders. The weather in the "Oberland," as the Swiss call it, is more unsettled than that of the Valais, with greater annual rainfall. The combination of additional moisture and generally lower altitudes of villages and pastures results in a landscape that is alpine yet luxuriously verdant. The well-known image found on Swiss calendars— dazzling green meadows spangled with profuse, brilliant wildflowers against a backdrop of snowy mountains—is the image of Bernese Oberland.

On a relief map, the Bernese Alps appear as a great band stretching horizontally across the lower third of Switzerland. They are mainly accessible from the north, through a series of valleys that penetrate the range.

The geology of the Bernese Oberland derives from the Helvetic nappe; large masses of the nappe's underlying core rocks—granite, schists, and gneisses—have been exposed by glacial activity. The folding, movement, and overthrusting of rock layers have produced extremely complex rock formations. For example, the summits of some major peaks near Grindelwald— the Wetterhorn, Mönch, and Jungfrau—are core crystalline rock that was overthrust on top of the sedimentary limestone layers that originally were deposited above the core rock; in contrast, the nearby Eiger mountain is for the most part limestone. Similar differences occur throughout the Bernese mountains.

A long-distance hiking route traverses the mountains of the entire canton of Bern, using the passes that connect one valley with the next. Before roads and railways, these passes were the shortest and fastest, albeit steepest, way to get from village to village. Today their only pedestrian traffic consists of people who love walking in the mountains, or an occasional shepherd. The pass route can be walked in about ten days (depending on the weather), but you can also take a day's walk on any single portion of the route.

THE WESTERN BERNESE ALPS

Gstaad and the Saanenland

Fashionable Gstaad is remarkably different from other stylish resorts such as St. Moritz. With restrictions on growth, Gstaad has preserved its character as a village set amid farms and pastures; fields and woodland can easily be seen from the center of Gstaad. New houses and hotels must be made predominantly of wood, to retain the traditional look of Swiss chalets. Most shops and even banks are built in chalet style. The result is that, despite the celebrated film stars and writers who come to ski, and the fine boutiques and elite hotels, Gstaad retains the small scale of a mountain village.

Gstaad is located in the heart of an area called the Saanenland, among mountains that have truly alpine peaks and glaciers, although they have not yet attained the full height and ruggedness found in the center of the Bernese Alps. The resort is set in a broad basin, and the landscape in its immediate vicinity has a soft, pastoral quality—the mountains visible from the village are of low to moderate height, below 2,500 m/8,200 ft. Gstaad sits at the crosspoint of four valleys. Because of the regional topography, excursions can be made in several directions, yet everything is nearby and hikers and skiers have easy access to the entire area.

From Gstaad, the Eggli cable car climbs to high pastures, with good views of the Rübli (2,285 m/7,497 ft), Gummfluh (2,458 m/8,062 ft), and Oldenhorn (3,122 m/10,240 ft); you can walk down to Gstaad. From nearby Rougemont, the Videmanette cable car rises to a terrace below the Rübli, offering a lovely view of the Bernese Alps, including the Eiger, Mönch, and Jungfrau.

The region around Gstaad is known not only for alpine skiing but also for its excellent cross-country ski-trail network, and in the spring there is organized ski touring. Gstaad is accessible by road, rail, and bus.

Glacier des Diablerets. The grandest feature in the vicinity of Gstaad and its neighboring villages lies to the south: the Glacier des Diablerets, a broad expanse of ice and snow at an altitude of 3,000 m/9,842 ft, beneath the jagged teeth of Les Diablerets (3,210 m/10,531 ft) and the rocky point of the Oldenhorn (3,122 m/10,243 ft). This is a year-round skiing center. The Reusch cable-car system serving this area begins near Gsteig, just south of Gstaad. It mounts to the edge of the glacier, with a fine view of snowy peaks, including the distant Grand Combin.

The Oeschinensee has a striking backdrop of vertical limestone walls topped by snow and ice; it is a short hike or cable-car ride from Kandersteg. Facing page: In summer, lush green meadows and a picturesque lake are highlights of the trail from First to Faulhorn in the Bernese Oberland.

Lauenental. One of the most attractive excursions for hikers in this area is up the Lauenen Valley toward the Wildhorn (3,248 m/10,656 ft). The Lauenensee, a small lake, sits in the center of a flowery meadow with a backdrop of mountains and a fine waterfall. From Gstaad, you can reach the village of Lauenen by bus or car, and then hike up to the SAC Geltenhütte, from which there is a view of the glacial cirque above.

The Wasserngrat. The Wasserngrat is a long, narrow ridge, what hikers and mountaineers call a "knife-edge ridge," though here the term is an exaggeration because there is room to walk on top of it. These striking landforms are the result of the great glacial movements of the past: as the glaciers advanced, they deposited some of the debris they carried along their sides. These became lateral moraines, which are often knife-edge ridges. The Wasserngrat is like a big bulwark with a beveled top, forming the eastern wall of the Lauenen Valley. From Gstaad you can take a cable car to the northern end of this ridge and then hike along it; the trail connects to the Trüttlisberg Pass, from which you can walk down to Lenk in the Simmental, the neighboring valley. The Trüttlisberg route is a section of the great pass route across the Bernese Oberland.

Lenk and the Simmental

Lenk is the chief village of the upper Simmental, the longest valley in the Bernese Oberland. Broad and gentle, with comparatively fertile soil and a relatively mild climate, this valley is the home of the well-known brown-and-white Simmental cows, which are exported all over the world. Some of the most beautiful old wooden houses in Switzerland, their façades carved and painted with whimsical folk-art motifs, are found in both the lower and upper Simmental.

Lenk is a quiet alpine village with a small ski center and access to hiking trails. There is also a spa with mineral baths here. It is situated on the banks of the river Simme, between low mountains, and the view from the village is not exceptional; however, a trail south from Lenk leads to the foot of the Wildstrubel (3,244 m/10,643 ft), a broad peak surrounded by glaciers—so extensive, indeed, is the Wildstrubel that it dominates both the upper Simmental and the next valley, the upper Engstligental. Several torrents rushing down from these alpine heights feed the Simmenfalle, a big waterfall. To the east, the Hahnenmoos Pass leads to Adelboden; Lenk is one of the connecting points on the Bernese Oberland pass route, midway between Gstaad and Adelboden. It is also the northern approach for the Rawil Pass over the mountains to Sion and the Rhone Valley.

Among the usual winter sports offered at Lenk there is also a school that teaches ski ballet, a combination of elegant turns, small leaps, and pirouettes, the skier's equivalent of figure skating.

Lenk can be reached by car from Zweisimmen, or by rail.

Adelboden

Adelboden is like an outer gate to the great mountains in the center of the Bernese Alps. It is set in a deep fold between two mountainous ridges; the highest point on the ridge to the east is the peak of the Lohner (3,049 m/10,001 ft); the opposing ridge, to the west, culminates at the Albristhorn (2,761 m/9,056 ft). But the grandest scenery is to the south; there, Adelboden faces a cirque that includes the snowy Wildstrubel, with the Enstligen Falls at its base.

A small family resort, Adelboden offers skiing without crowds and several possibilities for hikers. Unter dem Birg, south of the village, is reached by bus or car; from there you can hike or take the cable car to the terrace of Engstligenalp for a closer view of the Wildstrubel, its glacial cirque and waterfalls; several trails can take you even higher. One leads southeast to the Gemmipass and Leukerbad (an alternative to the routes from Kandersteg to the same destinations). From Adelboden, a trail eastward climbs to the steep

Bunderchrinde Pass, with extensive views, then descends to Kandersteg, another section of the Bernese Oberland pass route.

Adelboden can be reached by road only from the north, via Frutigen, a town just south of Lake Thun. From the Frutigen rail station there is bus service to Adelboden.

Kandersteg

A charming small resort situated on the green banks of the Kander stream, Kandersteg is at the foot of steep and massive mountains—some of the most rugged in the Bernese Oberland. The contrast between the village's pleasant, grassy, almost level terrace and the stark, rugged walls that rise abruptly above it is an unexpected and delightful sight. English visitors were first attracted to Kandersteg during the Victorian era, and there are still several spacious, picturesque Victorian hotels; the lovely Reformed church was once used for English services. Despite its attractive location, Kandersteg is not overbuilt. Hotels and chalets are scattered along the banks of the stream and across the meadows, with plenty of space between most of them.

Kandersteg is frequented by skiers in winter, and by hikers and climbers in summer. Paragliding is also very popular here. The town is approached by road from the north and by rail via Spiez and Frutigen. The Lötschberg rail tunnel between Kandersteg and Goppenstein is the only link to the south (cars are transported through the tunnel).

The Oeschinensee and Hohtürli. A very popular outing is the short trip up to a stunning turquoise lake, the Oeschinensee, set below broad, towering walls of sheer rock laced with waterfalls and topped with glaciers. This beautiful spot is easily reached by footpath or cable car. You can stroll around the lake or continue up to the beautiful meadows and little alps at Unter and Ober Bergli, which sell fresh milk. The scenery here is dominated by one of the most impressive mountain groups in the Alps: the Blümlisalp cluster, a series of big peaks from which a spectacular set of steep, hanging glaciers tumble toward the lush green meadows directly below. (The Blümlisalphorn is another example of a mountain that is geologically very different from those nearby: it is limestone, whereas the nearby Bietschhorn, at the end of the Lötschental, is largely granite.)

Above the Ober Bergli summer farm, the trail becomes extremely steep, exposed, and eroded, as it climbs to the magnificent Hohtürli Pass and the SAC Blümlisalphütte. Just above the hut stands the Wilde Frau (3,260 m/ 10,695 ft) and behind it a line of six higher mountains, including the Blümlisalphorn (3,664 m/12,021 ft). Five glaciers pour down the slopes, torn into crevasses and séracs by the steepness of the wall. (The trail on the other side of the Hohtürli Pass descends to the Kiental and is part of the Oberland pass

MARMOT
Marmota marmota

Marmots are perhaps the most commonly seen alpine animals. These bushy-tailed, plump little rodents, related to woodchucks, are often seen scampering over mountain slopes or sitting upright outside their burrows to scan the area.

Marmots are usually found above tree line, in meadows or grassy areas or on sunny, rocky slopes between 1,500 and 2,700 m/4,921 and 8,858 ft; however, in favorable habitats, they may be found as low as 1,000 m/3,280 ft and as high as 3,000 m/9,842 ft. The entrance holes of their burrows are scattered everywhere on the alpine slopes. In early summer, visitors may see young marmots tumbling about and chasing each other over the slopes.

In some parts they are accustomed to human presence and will emerge from their burrows or may be lured out by an offer of food. One such spot is the slope near the Spielboden cable-car station at Saas-Fee; the area is honeycombed with burrows and it is easy to see and often to feed marmots. Their paws have long claws and an almost finger-like structure, so that when they sit up and nibble food they seem to be holding it with little hands. Visitors are requested not to give them sweets and cakes.

Marmots are entirely vegetarian, subsisting upon grass and other plants. Their main predators are golden eagles; foxes also prey on them. They were once considered game and were actively hunted by alpine people. Their alarm call is a high-pitched whistle that at first may be taken for a bird call.

At the end of summer, marmots accumulate grass, which they cut, dry, and stuff inside their burrows. They sleep on beds of this hay during their winter hibernation and live on their reserves of fat. Depending on the weather, the last marmots are usually seen in September and October. A dozen or so spend the winter in each burrow, with the entries stopped up with earth. In April or May, after they awaken, they clear away the grass on which they have slept.

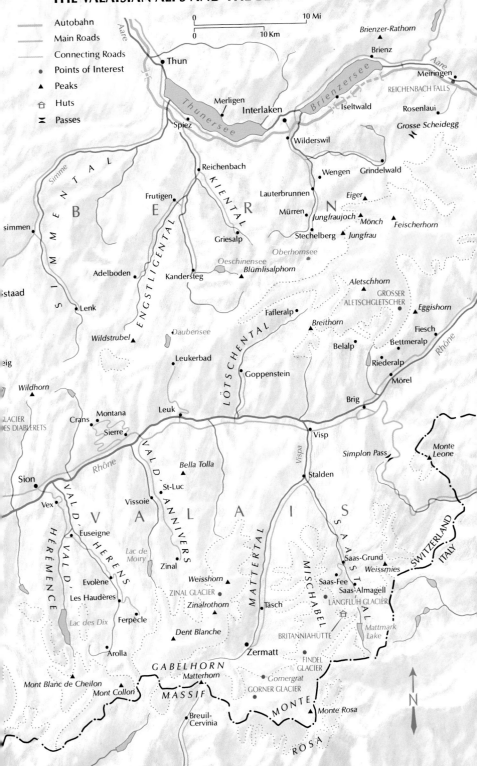

THE VALAISIAN ALPS AND THE BERNESE OBERLAND

Autobahn
Main Roads
Connecting Roads
• Points of Interest
▲ Peaks
⌂ Huts
⋈ Passes

0   10 Mi
0   10 Km

Thun
Aare
Brienzer-Rathorn
Brienz
Meiringen
Aare
Merligen
Thunersee
Brienzersee
Iseltwald
REICHENBACH FALLS
Interlaken
Spiez
Rosenlaui
Grosse Scheidegg
Wilderswil
Reichenbach
Wengen
Grindelwald
Frutigen
KIENTAL
Lauterbrunnen
Eiger
Mürren
Jungfraujoch
Mönch
Feischerhorn
Simme
Stechelberg
Jungfrau
Griesalp
B   E   R   N
simmen
Oberhornsee
Oeschinensee
ENGSTLIGENTAL
Adelboden
Kandersteg
Blümlisalphorn
Aletschhorn
staad
Lenk
Fafleralp
GROSSER
ALETSCHGLETSCHER
Eggishorn
Daubensee
Breithorn
Fiesch
Wildstrubel
LÖTSCHENTAL
Belalp
Bettmeralp
Rhône
Leukerbad
Riederalp
eig
Goppenstein
Mörel
Wildhorn
Brig
GLACIER
DES DIABLERETS
Crans
Montana
Leuk
Visp
Monte
Leone
Sierre
Bella Tolla
Simplon Pass
Sion
Rhône
St-Luc
Stalden
Vispa
Vex
Vissoie
VAL D'ANNIVIERS
V   A   L   A   I   S
VAL D'HÉRÉMENCE
Euseigne
Lac de
Moiry
SWITZERLAND
ITALY
VAL D'HÉRENS
Zinal
MATTERTAL
Saas-Grund
Weissmies
Evolène
Weisshorn
Saas-Fee
Les Haudères
ZINAL GLACIER
Saas-Almagell
MISCHABEL
LÄNGFLUH GLACIER
Ferpècle
Zinalrothorn
Täsch
Lac des Dix
Dent Blanche
BRITANNIAHÜTTE
SAASTAL
Arolla
Mattmark
Lake
Zermatt
FINDEL
GLACIER
GABELHORN
Mont Blanc de Cheilon
Matterhorn
Gornergrat
Mont Collon
MASSIF
GORNER GLACIER
MONTE
Breuil-
Cervinia
Monte Rosa
ROSA

N

route.) Beyond the little farms, the route over Hohtürli and down to the Kiental is the most difficult and demanding pass route in the Swiss Alps, and should be attempted only in good weather conditions by experienced, fit, and well-equipped hikers. Even if you walk only partway, however, the view is superb. Pastoral beauty is juxtaposed sharply with the high-alpine landscape; glaciers and grassy slopes are so close together that with one glance the eye can see the dazzling contrast of green meadows and brilliant white glaciers hanging above them—a contrast of both colors and planes.

Gemmipass

Before the Lötschberg rail tunnel was built in 1910 connecting Kandersteg with Goppenstein, travelers who wanted to go from the Bernese Oberland to the Rhone Valley had to make a great loop around one edge or the other of the Bernese Alps. But there was a shortcut, although a steep one: the Gemmipass, linking Kandersteg and Leukerbad (above the Rhone Valley), was by far the fastest way to the Valais. Few other passes would serve, because much of the terrain along the spine of the Bernese Oberland is blocked by glaciers. The scenery along this route is very different from that of the country above the Oeschinensee and the route to Hohtürli.

Hikers from Kandersteg can take a bus south to the Stockbahn, and then a cable car up the slope. The Gemmipass trail follows the bank of the Schwarzbach, passing near the small Arvensee. At Schwarzenbach the valley contracts, and there is a *Berghotel;* beyond this is a larger lake of dark and gloomy aspect, the Daubensee. For much of the route, the landscape is rough, barren, and stony; the plateau extends between exposed rock slopes powdered with scree. The scene looks arctic, perhaps, rather than Swiss. Near the Gemmipass there are views of the Wildstrubel and its glaciers, but no green meadows at its base. From the pass, the route descends in a series of zigzags down an extremely steep rock wall to Leukerbad (hikers may choose to use a cable car here). Earlier travelers sometimes descended the pass on horseback, but this was prohibited after an accident in 1861 when a countess fell from her saddle here and was killed.

Gasterental. Wild and beautiful, this is the upper valley of the Kander stream. From Kandersteg station you can take a minibus (places should be reserved) or hike up through the steep, narrow gorge of the Klus, through which the Kander falls to the lower valley. The road, just wide enough for a van, is cut dramatically through vertical rock walls. Beyond Selden, where there are a few *Berghotels,* the path extends along the stream to a big rock wall streaked with waterfalls, above which lies the broad Kanderfirn, or glacier. Above the glacier stand the Tschingelhorn (3,577 m/11,733 ft) and Mutthorn (3,043 m/9,981 ft), two mountains that are also seen from the upper Lauterbrunnental on the other side of the glacier.

The Kiental

The Kiental is a quiet valley with some surprises. From even the lowest part of the valley floor, you can see the great snowy wall of the Blümlisalp group shimmering in the distance. Yet while it leads to some of the great Oberland passes, the Kiental contains nothing resembling a resort, though there are a few hotels and inns (*Gasthöfe*) sprinkled about among its unassuming hamlets. After meandering along through gentle farmland along the almost level valley floor, the road suddenly appears to bolt almost upright through an astonishingly steep gorge; the roadbed is a corkscrew of hairpin turns blasted out of thick walls of rock, and is often only an inch or so wider than the PTT bus that plies this route several times a day. (This part of the road is private; cars are allowed up, but must pay a toll.)

Just above the gorge are some simple *Berghotels*—Pochtenalp, Griesalp, and Golderli—at the edge of a high, grassy plateau. Above these rich green meadows rises the great Blümlisalp wall, topped with snow. The Griesalp area is often the midpoint for hikers on the Bernese Oberland pass route between the Sefinenfurke and Hohtürli. There are no cable cars up here, no means of getting anywhere but your own legs, and nothing to do but climb and hike, or lie in a very peaceful meadow.

The Kiental is reached from Reichenbach, which is on the rail line between Spiez and Kandersteg. From Reichenbach there is bus service to Griesalp, above the gorge at the upper end of the Kiental. From here, experienced hikers set off for Hohtürli, the pass to Kandersteg, or for the Sefinenfurke, the pass to the Lauterbrunnental. For hikers going over the highest passes of the Bernese Oberland route, the Kiental serves as an "escape point" should conditions be poor or the weather turn bad.

THE CENTRAL BERNESE OBERLAND

Bernese Lakes: The Thunersee and Brienzersee

The highest mountains of the Bernese Alps overlook the Thunersee and Brienzersee, the two major Bernese lakes. On a fine summer day, this contrast of lake and mountain is both delightful and surprising. Lake Thun, especially, presents a subalpine, almost Mediterranean, appearance: the blue-green waters are streaked with white sails and the brilliant colors of windsurfing craft; swimmers glide through the water and sunbathers bask along the shore.

This reveals an unexpected aspect of the Alps: that people come not only to ski, hike, and climb, but also to swim, sail, and fish in clean, pure water. In these alpine lakes you can enjoy a full range of freshwater sports: swimming, sailing, windsurfing, water-skiing, kayaking, and fishing. There is a sailing school at Lake Thun, the oldest among several in Switzerland. At the Strandbad at Thun, the largest beach on these twin lakes (where the beach consists of a huge, neatly cropped lawn), the scene has the color and gaiety of a bathing resort at a more southern latitude but also presents a startling view. Over the blue waters appears a great white mass, gleaming in the distance: the sovereign peaks of the Bernese Oberland—the Eiger, Mönch, and Jungfrau.

On the western edge of the Thunersee is the picturesque old town of Thun, with its turreted castle and curious, two-level arcades. The drive along the north shore of the lake is scenic; beyond Merligen the road follows a corniche above a little cliff, another feature that briefly calls to mind the Mediterranean coast.

Hemmed in more closely by steep mountain slopes and cliffs, the Brienzersee has a wilder aspect than that of the Thunersee. Above its southern shore are the Giessbach Falls, an impressive set of multiple waterfalls. The falls are approached from Iseltwald, a village that may be reached by road or by steamer from Brienz or Interlaken. Brienz, on the lake's north shore, is an attractive small town famous for its woodcarvers. Above Brienz is the Brienzer-Rothorn (2,349 m/7,706 ft), which provides a view of the Bernese Alps. Switzerland's only steam-powered cog railway mounts nearly to the summit. Near Brienz, at Ballenberg, is the Freilichtmuseum Ballenberg, an open-air museum containing examples of traditional Swiss farmhouses from many parts of the country, with rural craft displays.

Interlaken

The Thunersee and the Brienzersee were once one lake, which was divided in two by the accumulation of alluvial deposits. Interlaken, the gateway to the heart of the Bernese Oberland, occupies the neck of land between the two lakes. The River Aare flows through the town, connecting the lakes.

Interlaken is a prosperous, cheerful, and fairly large town devoted to tourism. The Hoheweg, the tree-shaded central drive connecting the east and west sections of the town, is bordered by lawns, public gardens, and some of Switzerland's finest hotels—extravagant Victorian constructions, preserved and kept meticulously up-to-date—as well as the Kursaal (Casino). The view of the Jungfrau from this jaunty promenade is impressive. Interlaken is

Staubbach Falls is one of many hanging waterfalls in the striking Lauterbrunnen Valley, which is dominated by rocky, cliff-like mountains.

divided into two sections, Ost (east) and West, and has separate rail stations as well as steamer docks.

Interlaken is a base for day trips to Grindelwald, Wengen, Mürren, and other points high in the mountains. Rail and road communications are excellent. You can make Interlaken your base and go up on day trips to ski in the winter, and tour or hike in the summer, but visitors who wish to be close to the mountains should make one of the alpine villages their base. It is one thing to see the Jungfrau in the distance, another to have it rising starkly above you. Interlaken's little downtown has an almost urban quality, while the mountain resorts have retained more of a village atmosphere.

The Lauterbrunnental

This valley is a dramatic sight, a deep, clean-cut trench scooped out between towering, sheer cliffs. It is, in fact, a classic example of a glaciated U-shaped valley. Scores of waterfalls plummet over the vast expanse of bare rock. But the most exceptional feature here stands high above the valley's eastern wall—the famous alpine trio, the Eiger, Mönch, and Jungfrau, three grand conformations of ice, rock, and snow. They are followed in close order by the rest of this long line of peaks: the Rottalhorn, Gletscherhorn, Ebnefluh, Mittaghorn, Grosshorn, and Breithorn.

At the head of this valley is the village of Lauterbrunnen, the main transit point for the higher resorts of Mürren and Wengen, as well as for Stechelberg at the upper end of the valley. (No traffic is allowed in Mürren and Wengen; visitors may leave their cars in the parking lot at Lauterbrunnen.) Among the innumerable cascades that lace the cliffs of the Lauterbrunnental, the two grandest are the 300-m/984-ft Staubbach Falls, and the even more extraordinary Trümmelbach Falls. From viewing points hollowed out inside the cliff at Trümmelbach, visitors may watch the cataracts created by the snowmelt of the Alpine giants overhead. Compressed into a narrow fissure and plunging from a great height, the water emerges with propulsive force.

Wengen. Wengen (1,275 m/4,183 ft) sits on a terrace above the eastern wall of the Lauterbrunnental. This attractive resort offers a superb view of the Jungfrau towering above; it is also a good vantage point for looking into the great trench of the Lauterbrunnental. The finest walk here is the trail between Wengen and Kleine Scheidegg, which leads past the Jungfrau and the Mönch with their magnificent glaciers, waterfalls, and cliffs. You can shorten the walk by picking up the cog railway at Wengernalp, the intermediate stop on the cog railway between Wengen and Kleine Scheidegg. Wen-

The Lauterbrunnen Valley between Stechelberg and the Oberhornsee is unspoiled and accessible only by foot; relatively few hikers pass through it.

gen is also one terminus for the Männlichen cable car (the other is in Grindelwald); from its top station or from Kleine Scheidegg you can climb the little peak of the Lauberhorn (2,472 m/8,110 ft) for a good view of the region. Wengen is reached by cog railway from Lauterbrunnen or Kleine Scheidegg; the trains originate in Interlaken.

Mürren. While Wengen is located almost opposite Lauterbrunnen, Mürren is set deeper into the valley, on its western side. Its location—on a narrow balcony high above sheer cliffs—is breathtaking. At 1,645 m/5,397 ft, Mürren is the highest resort village in the Bernese Oberland. From here the view is spectacular: across the narrow valley, the Eiger, Mönch, and Jungfrau are spread like a banner before you. From Wengen the view is only of the Jungfrau—the closest view of the mountain from any village—whereas the area near Mürren provides the finest view of the great Oberland trio as an ensemble.

From Mürren there is excellent hiking in both directions along the balcony above the Lauterbrunnental. Trails to the north, toward Suls and the Lobhornhütte (a remote hut with no guardian), yield spectacular views of the Eiger directly across the valley, as well as of the Mönch and Jungfrau. On trails to the south, at such points as Wasenegg and Boganggen, hikers enter a wild, grassy landscape presenting an exceptional view of the entire mountainous wall extending beyond the Jungfrau. A trail continues past Boganggen to the Sefinenfurke Pass (a section of the Oberland pass route), descending to Griesalp and the Kiental; this is a route for experienced, fit hikers.

There are two ways to reach Mürren from the Lauterbrunnen valley: you can take the funicular from Lauterbrunnen to Grütschalp and then the little train along the cliff to Mürren; or you can reach Mürren by cable car from Längwald, near Stechelberg. This cable-car line continues above Mürren to the Schilthorn.

Schilthorn. One of the most popular excursion points in the Lauterbrunnental is the Schilthorn (2,960 m/9,711 ft), a mountain west of Mürren. Atop the Schilthorn is a revolving, circular restaurant, the Piz Gloria; besides the sight of the famous nearby mountains, it offers the best view of the Blümlisalp group available to nonhikers. The restaurant rotates slowly, and by spending 55 minutes at your table you can watch the whole great panorama revolve around you. You can hike on a steep trail between Mürren and the Schilthorn or take a cable car part or all of the way.

Stechelberg and Oberhornsee. At the upper end of the Lauterbrunnental is the last village in the valley, tiny Stechelberg, set among fields and pastures. It can be reached by car or bus from Lauterbrunnen (there are intermediate bus stops for the Trümmelbach Falls and the Mürren–Schilthorn cable car). Beyond Stechelberg, hikers may continue up the valley to the high slopes above, where meadows abloom with wildflowers lie at the foot of a semicircle of mountains and glaciers. This is undeveloped, unspoiled country. There are only a few hikers and cowherds; the upper part of the valley is a nature preserve, and chamois and ibex can often be seen. A beautiful turquoise lake, the Oberhornsee, is a favorite destination for hikers. A route continues beyond the Oberhornsee to the Schmadrihütte (no guardian or restaurant) in a stunning location below a group of big glaciers, the Tschingelfirn, Breithorngletscher, and Schmadrigletscher. Above the hut is a huge wall hung with ferocious glaciers and gigantic séracs. Here you are close to the mountains that hem in the upper end of the valley—the Breithorn, Tschingelhorn, and Mutthorn.

There are two *Berghotels* along the trail above Stechelberg—the Tschingelhorn and Obersteinberg—used by hikers exploring the area.

The Lütschental

This valley is narrow and heavily wooded, and it is only as you emerge into the open at Grindelwald that its scenic splendor is revealed. Above the south bank of the Schwarze Lütschine stands a wall of incomparably vast proportions, stretching 15 km/9 mi and rising to heights of between 3,000 m/9,840 ft and almost 4,000 m/13,000 ft. The wall is deeply notched in two places by the Unterer and Oberer Grindelwald glaciers; the frontal peaks surmounting each section are, from east to west, the Wetterhorn (3,701 m/12,142 ft), Mättenberg (3,104 m/10,184 ft), and Eiger (3,970 m/13,025 ft). Despite their many differences, these immense rock faces create an effect comparable to that of the Yosemite Valley.

This stupendous rock wall is, however, only the outer edge of the alpine world within: a constellation of mountains and glaciers that form the crown of the Bernese Alps. Beyond the Eiger the outer line of peaks continues with the Mönch (4,099 m/13,448 ft) and Jungfrau (4,158 m/13,642 ft). Because these three famous mountains rise abruptly from the valley floor, they are easy to view and even, using mechanical transportation, to visit. And there are several vantage points from which nonmountaineers can view parts of the inner sanctuary of glaciers and icy peaks hidden behind the outer wall.

The Eiger. The Ogre, the Monk, and the Virgin, like three characters from a fairy tale, dominate the region. The Mönch (which separates the Ogre and the Virgin) wears the white cowl of a Carmelite monk, and the Jungfrau, robed in sparkling white, is fresh and beautiful. But it is the gray Eiger (the word means "ogre" in local dialect)—or more specifically, its North Wall—that has seized the imagination of both the mountaineering world and the general public. There is a special Eiger mystique. This mountain is to

The north face of the Eiger is truly awesome; it is the ultimate goal of the true Alpine climber.

Grindelwald what the Matterhorn is to Zermatt, with one important difference: the climbers who flock to test their skill and will on the Matterhorn are mostly average mountaineers, whereas those whom the Eiger hurls down from its grim wall are often top-grade climbers. The North Wall, or North Face, of the Eiger has taken the lives of more expert climbers than any other route in the Alps. The biggest face climb in the Alps, exposed to harsh weather and savage conditions, climbers have wryly called it "the final exam"—the ultimate test of their ability and nerve (and some would say, of luck). Among the many north walls in the Alps, it alone is referred to simply as The North Wall.

Grindelwald

At the base of the massive stone rampart of the Wetterhorn–Mättenberg–Eiger, with the Eiger's north and east walls towering overhead, Grindelwald enjoys one of the most spectacular locations in the entire Alpine chain. Hotels both elegant and moderate cluster along the main street. Above this, the ground begins to rise, climbing steeply northward to a ridge that faces the great Oberland wall. Near the top of this ridge is a natural terrace called

First, which can be reached from Grindelwald by a series of connected chair lifts or, more laboriously, by foot. (A cable-car replacement is scheduled to open in 1991–92.)

First. This place is a sort of open-air balcony with superb panoramic views of some of the ice-wrapped peaks that loft above the interior mass of glaciers. From First, there are trails in several directions along this high terrace. A favorite, easy walk leads to the little blue Bachalpsee, with dazzling views of the Schreckhorn (4,078 m/13,375 ft), Finsteraarhorn (4,274 m/ 14,019 ft), and the two Fiescherhorner peaks (4,049 m/13,281 ft). From this lake, hikers may descend through flowery meadows to the restaurant at Mittelläger on the slopes of Bussalp, and return by bus to Grindelwald. From the Bachalpsee they may also continue to Schynige Platte, passing just below the Faulhorn, a low mountain with a rounded top upon which there is a *Berghotel* and a fine view. The walk to Schynige Platte is a full day's excursion through magnificent wild country; across the deep Lütschental is an unfolding view of the Eiger, Mönch, Jungfrau, and the continuing line of peaks extending southwest toward the Blümlisalp group. At Schynige Platte there is an alpine garden. A quaint, open-air cog railway descends to Wilderswil, a village on the outskirts of Interlaken, which is on the main railway. You can return from Wilderswil by train to Grindelwald, Lauterbrunnen, or Interlaken.

Other hiking routes may also be taken from First. You can hike northward over the mountains to Axalp and the town of Brienz, returning by lake steamer to Interlaken. And the trail from First eastward to Grosse Scheidegg is part of the Bernese Oberland pass route, between Grindelwald and Meiringen.

Jungfraujoch. The most famous rail excursion in the entire region is the trip to the Jungfraujoch, the snowy notch connecting the Jungfrau and Mönch. This extraordinary feat of nineteenth-century engineering climbs to the highest railway station in Europe. The "Jungfrau Express" originates in Interlaken, though you can pick up the train in Grindelwald, Lauterbrunnen, or Wengen. Wherever you board, however, you must change trains at Kleine Scheidegg, a high, narrow saddle closing off the Lütschental to the southwest. The view here is of the Eiger North Wall looming straight above, flanked by the Mönch and the Jungfrau. (North Wall climbers start their ascent near Kleine Scheidegg.) There are several hotels near the cog railway station, and the area between the tracks and the hotels is usually swarming with tourists. But you can walk over the meadows away from the crowds for a closer look at the awesome North Face, with its usual afternoon theatricals of snow and ice avalanches and boulders thundering down the wall.

Beyond Kleine Scheidegg, the train climbs through a tunnel inside the Eiger and the Mönch, emerging at the Jungfraujoch station at 3,475 m/ 11,401 ft, after rising 1,393 m/4,570 ft from Kleine Scheidegg in about 50 minutes. Tourists can rise a little higher by elevator to the Sphinx, a tiny perch above the glaciers, between the nearby Mönch and Jungfrau.

To the southeast you look down to the Grosser Aletsch glacier, the biggest glacier in Europe—a long flow of ice under a blanket of dazzling snow; to the west, you look across great depth and distance beyond the Grindelwald valley and the Thunersee to the very borders of Switzerland.

From Grindelwald, numerous other excursions are possible, both for the hiker and the cable-car mountaineer. The lift to Pfingstegg takes you to the edge of the gorge above the Unterer Grindelwald glacier. Hikers may continue to the little restaurant at Stieregg, with impressive views: along this trail you see the huge, magnificent east face of the Eiger, the glacier below—both moraine and crevassed ice—and the Fiescherhorn.

Besides being a center for skiing and hiking, Grindelwald is one of Switzerland's major climbing centers, with a large guides' organization offering climbs, tours, and classes. Two-day group tours start from the Jungfraujoch and descend the Aletsch glacier, with a night's stop at the SAC Konkordiahütte. As everywhere else in the Alps, the guide will provide the rope, but otherwise you must be properly clothed and equipped with a harness.

Rosenlaui.   East of Grindelwald is Grosse Scheidegg, a neck of land slightly lower but also longer than Kleine (or little) Scheidegg. (The road between Grindelwald and Grosse Scheidegg is a private one, not open to automobiles, but served by a bus line.) On the other side of the notch is the Reichenbachtal, whose scenery is commanded by the tremendous expanse of the Wetterhorn: a vast cliff striped with the silver plumes of innumerable waterfalls. In the center of this valley, reached by road or footpath, is Rosenlaui, site of an old and well-known climbing school and a *Berghotel.* Here you can visit the Gletscherschlucht, a gorge cut by the torrent from the Rosenlaui glacier. The deceptively pretty, pale blue ice of this steep, hanging glacier shimmers above, enclosed between the Wellhorn on one side and, on the other, the rocky pinnacles known collectively as the Engelhörner, where highly technical climbing is practiced. This is a segment of the Bernese Oberland pass route between Grindelwald and Meiringen.

The Reichenbach Falls.   Past Rosenlaui there is a pleasant meadow at Gschwantenmad; the road then plunges steeply to the floor of the Haslital (many hikers take the bus between Rosenlaui and Meiringen). The impressive Reichenbach Falls are on the west side of the road, and may be visited. At these falls, Sherlock Holmes wrestled the villainous Dr. Moriarty to their supposedly mutual deaths—until a public outcry forced Sir Arthur Conan Doyle to resurrect his hero. The volume of water is so great that from Meiringen, across the Aare, you can see the upper falls (looking, from a distance, like a solid glass column) and even hear their roar.

THE EASTERN BERNESE OBERLAND

Meiringen

Meiringen is located at an Alpine crossroads (routes lead from here to Interlaken, Lucerne, and the Grimsel and Susten passes), and it is a stop on the east-to-west Oberland hiking route. Though well-equipped with hotels, it is a quiet residential town, its back streets lined with houses and gardens—an agreeable contrast to the fashionable resort villages in the central Oberland. As a rail and transportation junction, it has a commercial life of its own outside of tourism, yet it is a center for hiking and mountaineering. In winter, Meiringen is an informal, low-key ski resort. From here, you can visit the very narrow gorge of the Aare (Aareschlucht), impressively cut between sheer, almost sculpted rock walls. Though Meiringen, on the flat terrace of the Aare, is at the relatively low altitude of 600 m/1,968 ft, steep walls hem in the valley. To the south rises the huge Oberland massif, while north of Meiringen is the Hasliberg. On the eastern side of this mountain is a balcony situated above a rocky wall that drops abruptly to the Gental, the valley below. From Meiringen, a series of lifts ascends to Planplatten, above this balcony. A popular excursion for hikers in summer is to ride up to Planplatten and then walk high above the floor of the Gental toward one of the lakes on the upper terraces of this ridge—the Melchsee, Tannensee, or Engstlensee.

Engstlenalp. The Engstlensee, though the lowest, is the most scenic of the lakes above the Gental. Beside the lake is Engstlenalp, consisting of a few summer farms and an old *Berghotel.* The clear, blue-green lake and the little alp lie on the upper slope of a U-shaped valley cut between two rocky walls. Rearing above the lake to the north is the rocky prow of the Graustock (2,661 m/8,730 ft); the Wendenstöcke (3,042 m/9,980 ft), the long ridge opposite Engstlenalp, is frosted with glaciers. Above the upper end of the valley, to the east, is the round, snowy head of the Titlis; to the west there is an impressive view of the Wetterhorn, the edge of the great Oberland wall.

Hikers can continue eastward over the Jochpass to Engelberg (thus crossing out of Canton Bern, although the mountains are still considered part of the Bernese range). This is yet another stage along the Oberland pass route. You can ride down from the Jochpass to Engelberg by chair lift and cable car.

Pages 122 and 123: Seen from Kleine Scheidegg, the Mönch and Jungfrau mountains form part of the famous Lauterbrunnen Wall, which, also including the Gletscherhorn, Breithorn, and Eiger, presents a stunning array of strikingly individual silhouettes. While buses, cable cars, funiculars, and cog railways take visitors to the resorts of Wengen, Mürren, and Stechelberg and to viewpoints high above, hikers who set off on foot experience the most spectacular panoramas of all.

Engelberg

Engelberg is a small, lively, attractive family resort and a center for climbing, hiking, and skiing—one of the oldest ski resorts in Switzerland. It is also of cultural interest, being the site of a twelfth-century Benedictine monastery, rebuilt in the eighteenth century, which may be visited.

Engelberg's location is scenic and interesting; it is cut off by mountains on three sides, creating an impression of remoteness. Engelberg is at the foot of the Titlis (3,238 m/10,623 ft). A series of cable cars rises almost to the snowy mound of its summit, giving fine views of the eastern Bernese Alps. There are also cable cars from Engelberg to Ristis, below the SAC Brunnihütte and the Rigidalstock (2,593 m/8,507 ft), and to Fürenalp, below the Wissberg (2,627 m/8,618 ft), with trails from both cable-car stations. Hikers may extend the Oberland pass route beyond Engelberg by continuing eastward past the towers of the Gross Spannort (3,198 m/10,492 ft) to the Surenenpass, and then descending to Altdorf.

Though hikers can walk to Engelberg from the west, southwest, or east, those traveling by road or rail can only approach it from the north, through Stans. To reach Engelberg from Meiringen, you must drive in a big loop through the Brunigpass and Stans. A pleasant way to travel to Engelberg is to take the steamer from Lucerne to Stansstad and then the train, which becomes a cog railway beyond Stans.

The Susten–Furka–Grimsel Passes

At the eastern edge of the Oberland massif are a series of great alpine passes that connect the Bernese Oberland with other parts of Switzerland. The Susten, Furka, and Grimsel passes can be visited by a circular driving tour that starts just south of Meiringen. The traverse of these three passes gives nonhikers a glimpse of the high Alps.

Sustenpass. Innertkirchen, the first town south of Meiringen, is the gateway to the Gadmental, the valley that leads to the Sustenpass. The road climbs steeply, and there is an abrupt change from the woods and pastures of the Gadmental to stark, high alpine scenery. Just below the pass, on the western side, is a little lake, the Steinsee, at the base of a magnificent backdrop: below the massive Sustenhorn (3,504 m/11,496 ft) is the big Steingletscher, a broad glacier with multiple tongues, descending in a series of steps to the lake. From the pass (2,224 m/7,297 ft) there is a view of a cluster of rock towers, whimsically named the Funffingerstock or "five-finger stick" (2,994 m/9,823 ft). The road descends to the Meiental, a narrow, deep valley cut between rugged, rocky slopes, to Wassen, where you can turn south for Andermatt.

Furkapass. The Furkapass (2,431 m/7,976 ft) is west of Andermatt, a small, attractive old town strategically located near the junction of several major passes: the St. Gotthard and Oberalp, as well as the Furka. From Andermatt, the approach to the Furkapass climbs through a U-shaped valley with bare green slopes. The Galenstock (3,583 m/11,801 ft), a triangular rock ridge with a glacier below, dominates the Furkapass. Beyond here, heading west, you can stop near the Belvedere (2,300 m/7,546 ft), an old Victorian hotel, for a grand view of the big Rhone glacier and the source of the Rhone River. The glacier originates in a horseshoe-shaped cirque formed by jagged gray teeth of rock; as it plunges downhill, the ice breaks up into big, pale blue séracs. The effect of the whole is of a mass of ice, streaked with gray from the rock the glacier has ground up; the glacier is perched above a rounded, furrowed rock wall. The stream emerging from the glacier's snout, cascading at first over the rocks, is the source of the Rhone: it pours down to a flat, narrow terrace on the valley floor below, the bed of the young river. (At the Belvedere, you can step into a grotto hollowed out inside the blue ice.)

The road descends to Gletsch and the Goms valley—a pastoral region whose little villages still consist of traditional wooden chalets, with ornamental folk-art motifs carved onto many house gables and windowframes. A special feature of the Goms is its excellent cross-country skiing, with tracks extending along the valley for more than 30 km/19 mi. The groomed track between Oberwald and Niederwald is 21 km/13 mi long, and is lighted until 10 P.M. for the most avid skiers. Skiers can also use the Furka–Oberalp railway to start or finish the track at any stop along the line.

Grimselpass. From Gletsch you turn northwest for the Grimselpass (2,165 m/7,103 ft), the most direct route connecting the upper Rhone Valley and the Bernese Oberland. On the ascent from Gletsch there is a good view to the northeast of the Rhone glacier. This pass is noted for its cluster of lakes: the Totensee (Lake of the Dead: so-named because of a battle at these heights in 1799 between the Austrians and the French) and two artificial lakes, the Grimselsee and the Räterichsbodensee, sunk below rugged slopes of scored rock. The big Unteraargletscher drops to the edge of the scenic Grimselsee, and behind the lake rise the stark shapes of some of the high Bernese Alps, including the Finsteraarhorn. The Grimsel Hospice stands on a little promontory above this lake. The road descends from the pass through the valley of the upper Aare to Meiringen, thus completing the circle of these three passes.

Pages 126 and 127: Caressed by clouds, the Finsteraarhorn is one of the magnificent sights on the splendid high-country walk from First to Bussalp.

THE SOUTHERN SLOPE OF
THE BERNESE OBERLAND

Although the valleys that penetrate the Bernese Alps from the south belong politically to Canton Valais, they are sited on the massif of the Bernese Alps. Sion in the Rhone Valley is the western access point for rail, bus, or automobile access to these valleys and their resorts.

Crans, Montana, and Leukerbad

Crans and adjoining Montana are known collectively as "Crans"; this resort complex is actually on the southern side of the Wildhorn and Wildstrubel, the mountains that you see near Gsteig, Lauenen, and Lenk, which provide the slopes for many of the Crans ski runs. At Crans there are several lakes, an 18-hole golf course, and walking trails, but it is best known as a chic ski resort in the contemporary French style, with many five- and six-story modern, concrete buildings and several high-rise structures.

Leukerbad is a curious combination: both a resort for skiers and hikers, and one of the most up-to-date thermal spas in Switzerland. In Europe, spas retain their traditional function based on natural mineral or thermal waters, which people drink or bathe in. Leukerbad has an exceptionally well-equipped medical center with physical therapy for people recovering from accidents or surgery such as hip or knee replacement. A combination of baths, massage, and exercise is also used to relieve chronic problems of the joints, muscles, and bones. Yet far from having a clinical appearance, Leukerbad is bright and attractive, with gracious hotels and an assortment of handsome swimming pools. On a winter's day in Leukerbad you can ski in the morning and swim in the afternoon in one of the thermal outdoor pools, with a view of the snowclad mountains. There is hiking and skiing (alpine and cross-country) in several directions. The cliffs of the Gemmipass (the walking route to Kandersteg) tower above the town, but a cable car eases the ascent. Above the Gemmipass are trails to Adelboden and Kandersteg.

Lötschental

The Lötschental is a beautiful, unspoiled valley at the foot of the broad Fafler glacier. Because of the mountain barrier to the north, it has traditionally been approached from the Rhone Valley. As the valley rises beyond Goppenstein it

Towering and protective walls of stone line the serene Aareschlucht Gorge near Meiringen. Hikers in the area may also try the trail that works its way down the side of the Reichenbach Falls, where tons of water roar in thundering cascades.

narrows, and big mountains and glaciers can be seen high above on either side. At the upper end of the valley is the Fafler glacier, cradled between rocky peaks and ridges. One of the most striking local features is the Bietschhorn (3,934 m/12,907 ft); to hikers and climbers above Zermatt and Saas-Fee, this mountain appears across the Rhone Valley, in the distance, as a huge, snow-streaked rock pyramid. Here in the Lötschental, its rugged form towers above all other peaks. Among the hiking routes here, the high trail (*Höhenweg*) from Fafleralp to Ferden is a favorite, offering splendid views of the Fafler glacier, the Bietschhorn, and other mountains.

The Lötschental is known for the grotesque wooden masks that are still made and sold here, echoes of an ancient pagan culture. The masks have the faces of trolls and giants, with long black hair and crooked teeth.

From the Rhone Valley you can drive or travel by rail to Goppenstein, the entry point to the Lötschental. It is also the southern end of the Lötschberg rail tunnel to Kandersteg (with automobile transport through the tunnel), the only route connecting the Rhone Valley with the central part of the Bernese Oberland. There is bus service up the Lötschental to Fafleralp.

Grosser Aletschgletscher

Some of Switzerland's major glaciers originate in the Bernese Alps and flow southward toward the upper Rhone Valley. The Grosser Aletschgletscher— the Great Aletsch glacier—extending 23 km/14.4 mi, is the longest glacier in the entire Alps. It originates on the Jungfrau massif and flows southwest in a serpentine curve, terminating on a shelf high above the upper Rhone Valley. From the Jungfraujoch station (accessible from Lauterbrunnen, Wengen, and Grindelwald), nonalpinists can view it at its birthplace, where the glacier is covered with deep snow. But there are other excellent viewpoints as well farther down the glacier from which you can enjoy equally close and in some ways more interesting views. The great reach of this giant glacier is also more clearly seen from a midway viewpoint. Toward its lower end the ice is more exposed, revealing the long, curving lines of the medial moraines that mark the glacier like the bands on a serpent. This vast natural phenomenon may be viewed from a cluster of points above the upper Rhone Valley: Belalp, Riederalp, Bettmeralp, and the Eggishorn.

Belalp. Belalp is poised just above the tongue of the glacier, providing a grand frontal view of the ice in all its breadth. This minuscule community, consisting of a simple hotel, a couple of houses, and a little church, is closed to nonresident automobile traffic. With a guide, you can cross the glacier to Riederalp, on the left bank of the glacier. Other interesting excursions from

Belalp include the route to the Sparrhorn, a nontechnical climb up a small mountain with good views of both the Grosser Aletsch and the Oberaletsch glaciers. To reach Belalp, take the bus or drive from Naters, just north of Brig, to Blatten; from there a cable car ascends to Belalp (2,130 m/6,988 ft at Hotel Belalp).

Riederalp and Bettmeralp. Riederalp (1,925 m/6,316 ft) and Bettmeralp (1,957 m/6,420 ft) are small resorts situated a little farther up the glacier on its left bank. From both places you can descend to the glacier, cross it with a guide, and climb up to Belalp. You can also follow a trail along this bank of the glacier (it is actually a lateral moraine), with excellent, close views of the ice. One route leads to the Märjelensee, a small lake sometimes filled with large blocks of floating ice. (The lake was created because the glacier blocks the stream emerging from the Märjelen valley.) Another route leads to the summit of a small mountain, the Bettmerhorn, overlooking the glacier. Near Riederalp, on these alpine slopes above Europe's biggest glacier, there is an odd sight: a four-story Victorian structure with a mansard roof. Erected as a summer home by Sir Ernest Cassel, an English banker, and now the property of the Swiss League for the Protection of Nature, it was the first Swiss ecological center for the study of the environment. Among the excursions you may take from this side are a walk along the Oberriederi bisse, one of the old Valaisian irrigation canals. Riederalp is reached by cable car from Mörel, northeast of Brig in the upper Rhone Valley, and Bettmeralp is reached by cable car from Grengiols, a little farther east of Mörel.

Eggishorn. From Fiesch, northeast of Brig in the Rhone Valley, a cable car climbs almost to the top of a small mountain, the Eggishorn (2,927 m/9,601 ft). From the upper station, a stone path leads in 20 minutes to the summit of this little peak, which in another landscape would count as a big mountain. It is a tremendous viewpoint. The Eggishorn is superbly positioned above the great curve of the Aletsch glacier as it winds past the mountains on the southern edge of the Oberland. One of the mountains visible from here is the Aletschhorn (4,195 m/13,763 ft), the second highest peak in the Bernese Alps. Across the Rhone Valley to the southwest are the Mischabel massif, the Matterhorn, and the Weisshorn, among others. But the main attraction is the ice. From the Eggishorn, the glacier appears in all its sinuosity, striped by the fine, almost elegant parallel black lines of the medial moraines. And from here, you can look up to the great Oberland peaks and see the tremendous sweep of this river of ice, immensely wide at its head, pouring down from the Jungfrau and the Mönch. The ice below is scored and gashed by a thousand crevasses. Toward its tip, near Belalp, the curves of the moraine and the tongue slide into a final graceful curl.

The Lepontine Alps

THE CENTRAL PORTION OF the Lepontine Alps is in Canton Ticino, the Italian-speaking part of Switzerland. Sometimes called the Ticinese Alps, the region's attractiveness is enhanced by the simple but charming mountain villages. Though this is rugged, mountainous terrain, the peaks are lower than the mountains to the north and west. There are no long stretches with insuperable obstacles, as in the Valaisian Alps, and the mountains are cut through not only by the Simplon and St. Gotthard passes, two of the most important of all alpine passes, but by several lesser passes as well.

The Lepontine Alps comprise very different rock formations: some derive from a complex set of Pennine nappes and consist of crystalline rock, while others consist of sedimentary rocks. Most of the mountains north of Locarno are crystalline gneiss and other metamorphosed rocks. South of Locarno, granite prevails, although bands of sedimentary rocks such as sandstone, limestone, and dolomite can be found. The Hinterrhein region, in contrast, is part of a group of sedimentary and mica schist mountains.

Simplon Pass (Passo del Sempione)

After struggling across the Great St. Bernard in 1800, Napoleon decided that an alpine pass road was necessary—somewhere else. As the Simplon (2,005 m/6,578 ft) is lower than the Great St. Bernard, Napoleon ordered that a road be cut here. The route extends between Brig, in the Rhone Valley, and Domodossola in Italy.

There are scenic views on both sides of the pass. To the north are the Bernese Alps; the Aletschhorn and Finsteraarhorn especially stand out. Just south of the pass is the Fletschhorn, one of the big mountains of the Saas Valley. The view from the pass itself is dominated by the Kaltwassergletscher. Above this broad glacier rises Monte Leone (3,553 m/11,657 ft), the highest mountain in the Lepontine Alps. To see it, however, you must walk up toward the glacier. The Swiss-Italian border runs over the summit of Monte Leone; its two glaciers, the Kaltwassergletscher and the Alpjengletscher, both face the Swiss side. There is a hospice, run by the monks of the Great St. Bernard. South of the pass, the road descends through the Gondoschlucht, a very deep,

Typical Ticinese farmhouses in the Val Verzasca were constructed entirely of dry stone slabs. Many were abandoned during hard times in the late nineteenth century, when inhabitants left for America. A valley footpath leads to the unspoiled village of Sonogno, with charming stone houses and streets, flowers blooming on balconies, and rock walls that encompass much of the village.

narrow gorge. Motorists may drive over the Simplon Pass, or take the rail tunnel (the longest in the world).

Nufenen Pass

The Nufenen Pass (2,478 m/8,130 ft), between Ulrichen in the Upper Rhone Valley and Airolo in the Val Leventina, swings across the northwestern section of the Lepontine Alps. Opened in 1969, this is the newest pass road in Switzerland. It is also the highest pass road entirely within Swiss borders; only the Umbrail Pass (2,501 m/8,205 ft), which crosses the Italian border at the most southeastern point of Switzerland, is higher. The Nufenen Pass gives travelers between the Rhone Valley and the central valley of the Ticino an alternative to the Furkapass.

There is an outstanding panoramic view from the Nufenen Pass. To the southwest, the Griessee lies below the broad Griesgletscher. The blue water edging the white glacier creates a bright and startling contrast. A group of jagged peaks, of which the highest is the Blinnenhorn (3,374 m/11,070 ft), rise around the glacier like canine teeth around a broad tongue. Within this group of mountains and glaciers is the source of the Ticino River, which gives its name to the canton. Farther off, across the Rhone Valley, you can see the Aletschhorn, Finsteraarhorn, Oberaarhorn, and Lauteraarhorn.

Directly south of the Griessee is the Italian border; a trail from the Nufenen Pass leads past the lake on the eastern side (thus avoiding the glacier, which is west of the lake) to the Griespass. From the Griespass there is a very steep descent into the Italian Valle di Morasco. Near the hamlet of Riale this route joins the bed of the Toce River; the river falls in a series of impressive cascades into the Val Formazza, which descends to Domodossola. (The upper end of the Formazza protrudes into Swiss territory, and the northern villages have historically been German-speaking.) The upper basin of the Toce contains several large artificial lakes, the largest and most scenic of which is Lago del Sabbione. This lake is set deeply below the curving mountain wall that here forms the Swiss border. The lake is almost surrounded by steep slopes; at its head is the steeply pitched Ghiacciaio (glacier) del Sabbione, enfolded between the Blinnenhorn, the Hohsandhorn or Punta del Sabbione (3,182 m/10,443 ft), and the Ofenhorn or Punta d'Arbola (3,235 m/10,614 ft). (These mountains are directly on the Swiss-Italian border and so have dual names.) There is bus service across the pass from Ulrichen to Airolo.

Val Bedretto. East of the Nufenen Pass is the Val Bedretto, a bleak, lonely valley, scantily populated, set between deep walls topped with a barrier of rough crags. Unlike most of the valleys of this region, which run north to south, the Val Bedretto runs west-east athwart the grain of the land.

South of the Bedretto is a high, mountainous plateau, strewn with lakes. This is one of the most beautiful parts of the Ticinese Alps, perhaps the heart of this region. To reach this alpine plateau, you must hike over the steep southern wall of the Val Bedretto; otherwise you can approach the plateau from the Val Maggia or the Val Verzasca, which penetrate these mountains from the south.

St. Gotthard Pass

This pass is the most direct connection between central Ticino and central Switzerland. It is now traversed by rail and also by the world's longest road tunnel, but there is also the old road over the pass. Until tunnels and bridges were built, travelers using this route to the north had to negotiate the nearby Schöllenen gorge, where the turbulent Reuss River flows between deep, sheer walls of rock. In 1799 the Russian field marshal Suvorov forced a passage through this defile against French opposition during the war that followed the French Revolution. Motorists can walk down to the old road for a look at the Teufelsbrücke, or Devil's Bridge, where pitched battles were fought; an inscription in the rock nearby commemorates Suvorov's feat.

Val Maggia

The Val Maggia and Val Verzasca must both be approached from Locarno, a beautiful Ticinese city on the northern shore of the Lago Maggiore. From there, both valleys strike northward into the Lepontine Alps, through some of the finest scenery in the chain.

The Val Maggia is the westernmost Ticinese valley. (Only the lower part of the valley is known by this name; each of the upper branches has its own name.) The Val Maggia is wide at first, with a very gentle gradient; the bed of the Maggia is stony and broad, though the river is narrow except in spring. Farther upstream, the valley narrows; big slabbing cliffs appear along its sides. Cevio is an unusual and pretty village, built around a central lawn rather than a traditional paved square, thus resembling a New England "green." But there the resemblance ends, for the houses in Cevio are made of stone, some dating from the Renaissance. The seventeenth-century house of the *Landvogte* (provincial governors) displays many of their armorial shields painted on its façade. From Cevio, a road leads west to Bosco-Gurin,

Pages 136 and 137: A scenic hiking trail follows the Verzasca River, crossing a number of footbridges and an arched medieval bridge at Lavertezzo. The area's picturesque construction utilized the plentiful local stone.

at 1,506 m/4,941 ft the highest village in Canton Ticino, where the inhabitants still speak the Swiss-German Walliser dialect. Bosco-Gurin has a small ski center with a lift. At Bignasco, a little farther upstream from Cevio, the Val Maggia branches northwest to the Val Bavona and northeast to the Val Lavizzara.

Val Bavona and the Robiei Area. Val Bavona is especially enchanting, with typical Ticinese villages and excellent hiking in the mountains above the end of the valley. Along the valley floor are a number of tiny, exceedingly charming, and utterly unspoiled hamlets, inhabited only in summer. Some have only four to eight houses, and most have no shop, not even a café, though a few villages have a simple restaurant. (In this region, some "restaurants" are really small inns with rooms, as at San Carlo, and there are simple hotels down the valley at Cevio and Bignasco.) The houses are in the style of the upper Ticinese villages, of dry stone, laid horizontally, and roofed with the same material, with perhaps a simple wooden balcony along one wall. Often there are flowers growing near the front door, their bright colors standing out delightfully against the gray stone. There is a striking contrast between the verdant meadows and woods on the narrow valley floor and the deep valley walls of slabbed, sheer rock—a startling opposition of savage cliffs and charming hamlets.

San Carlo, the last village in the Val Bavona, has a large cable car of rather marvelous construction: there are towers on one side only, so the whole system is cantilevered. It looks out of place in this remote, unfrequented, and undeveloped valley, which has not a single village that can be called a resort. It owes its existence to the great Robiei dam and hydroelectric project in the mountains above San Carlo. The scene is dramatic: after hoisting you past gigantic walls of sheer rock, the cable car swings over the topmost cliff (an ascent of almost 1,000 m/3,280 ft over a distance of 4 km/2.5 mi) and deposits you onto a green meadow among several artificial lakes—it is like riding up into another world. On top is the high plateau that extends northward to the Val Bedretto. Near the cable-car station is an unexpected sight: a six-story, octagonal, modern hotel, but nothing else; there is no shop, no other house, only wild, open country—and a group of trail signs. Even from the cable-car station the scenery is dominated by the big, rounded, sloping Basodino glacier, beneath the biggest peak in the area, the Basodino (3,272 m/10,735 ft).

The country above Robiei is splendid hiking terrain, but only a small number of hikers come to this remote place. Though the mountains are not very high compared to the biggest Valaisian and Bernese Alps, they are rough and jagged, with rocky crests. The landscape is impressively rugged and distinctive. Instead of the more even landforms seen in other areas, where slopes are often smooth even though steep and valleys may be gently rounded, the topography here is tortuous, full of twisted valleys and snaky ridges and hollows resembling massive potholes, some of them filled with water. There are also numerous little lakes in this region. The area looks very wild, not just because of its rugged terrain, but also because it is uninhabited: there is an isolated alp or two but not a single village upon this plateau.

From Robiei, you can walk to the Paso di Cristallina. The trail climbs to a viewpoint over Lake Sfundau, whose turquoise surface may be dotted with floating chunks of ice; there is also a fine view toward the Basodino glacier. The route continues past the west face of the Cristallina and up to the pass. From there, a trail continues to the SAC Capanna Cristallina, from which you can walk down to the Val Bedretto, or else over the Paso del Narèt to the pretty Lago del Narèt (and then down to the Val Lavizzara).

From Robiei you can also walk up to the base of the Basodino glacier, or around several of the other lakes on this alpine plateau.

Val Lavizzara. The Val Lavizzara is narrow, with steep, wooded slopes instead of the powerful cliffs of the Val Bavona. The settlements in this valley are a little larger than those in the Val Bavona—they are villages rather than hamlets and have year-round inhabitants—but there are many traditional Ticinese houses. The road ends at the village of Fusio, below the artificial Lago del Sambuco. From Fusio you can walk over the Paso Campolungo to the Val Leventina to the northeast. A more popular trail extends along the Sambuco lake and then leads to Lago del Narèt. On this side of the alpine plateau the land is less contorted, and there is no view of a glacier, as on the side near Robiei. An alternative trail to the Lago del Narèt extends from Piano di Peccia in the Val Peccia, a northwestern arm of the Val Lavizzara.

You can drive from Locarno up the various branches of the Val Maggia. There is bus service from Locarno up the Val Maggia to Bignasco and to several points in the valleys branching off the main valley: to Cimalmotto and Bosco-Gurin; to San Carlo (for Robiei) in the Val Bavona; to Piano di Peccia in the Val Peccia; and to Fusio in the Val Lavizzara.

Val Verzasca

East of the Val Maggia, the Val Verzasca is a beautiful valley, though much shorter and less complex than the upper Val Maggia. Along much of the Verzasca riverbed there are mountain slopes rather than cliffs, giving a comparatively softer look, though still a rugged and mountainous one. At the end of the valley, however, steep, exposed rock walls appear.

Here, as in the Val Maggia, are lovely old Ticinese houses whose walls and roofs are made of dry stone, gray and sometimes golden, with a rich, nubbly texture. Some of the houses are abandoned. (Many poor Ticinese farmers

ALPINE PANSY
Viola calcarata

HAREBELL
Campanula rotundiflora

Alpine pansy.

Harebell.

One of the most common alpine flowers, the Alpine pansy blooms in profusion in high meadows. It grows on an erect stem, reaching 10 or 12 cm/4 or 5 in in height, with oval, toothed leaves growing around the base of the stem. Flowering between June and August, the Alpine pansy grows at altitudes from 1,500 m/4,921 ft to more than 3,000 m/9,842 ft on a variety of soils, with some preference for limestone.

Along with the Alpine pansy, the charming harebell contributes much of the purple color that spangles the alpine meadows. Its hue is distinctly blue-violet and its shape clearly bell-like, with the flower nearly perpendicular to the stem so that it always looks as if it is blowing in the wind. It flowers in July and August in pastures or rocky patches and even in wooded areas on any type of soil, from 1,400 to 3,100 m/4,593 to 10,170 ft.

left their homes at the end of the nineteenth century, a large number emigrating to California and creating an "Italian-Swiss colony," where they established wineries.)

Besides the valley road there is a footpath over the fields and through the woods, connecting each village with the next. At Lavertezzo a handsome medieval arched bridge is still in use. Brione has a church with medieval frescoes and other old buildings. At the end of the valley, in a very scenic location, is Sonogno, below the rocky walls of Madom Gröss (2,741 m/8,993 ft) and Pizzo Cramosino (2,718 m/8,917 ft). Sonogno is very charming—the nearest thing to a tourist center in the entire area, but on such a small and modest scale that it does not diminish the unspoiled character of the valley. Sonogno has a hotel, a simple restaurant, a tiny shop, an *artigianato* selling local crafts, and a small museum of local culture. The houses are stucco or dry stone, with small wooden balconies hung with flowers in summer.

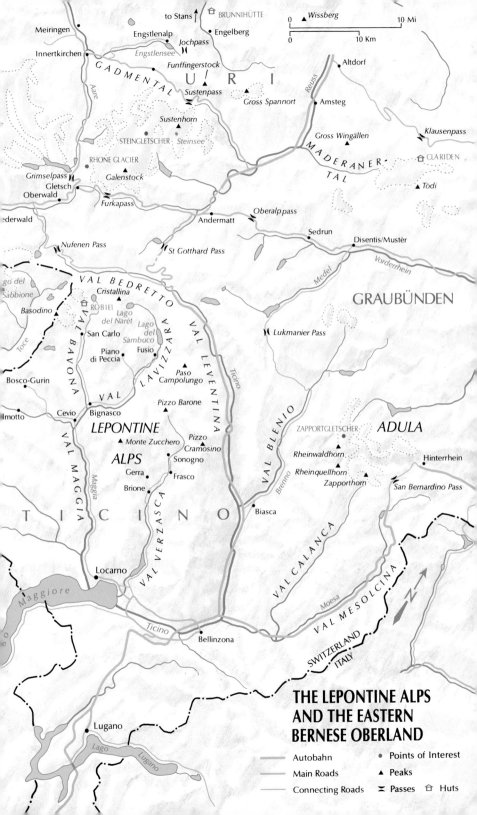

THE LEPONTINE ALPS
AND THE EASTERN
BERNESE OBERLAND

Autobahn • Points of Interest

Main Roads ▲ Peaks

Connecting Roads ⌇ Passes ⌂ Huts

From Sonogno, there are trails in several directions through the clefts in the mountains. You can walk up the Val Redòrta to the Paso (also called Forcla) di Redòrta; the pass goes between Monte Zucchero (2,736 m/8,976 ft) and Corona di Redòrta (2,804 m/9,199 ft), and descends on the other side to the Val di Prato, a branch of the Val Lavizzara. Along the way is the hamlet of Püscen Nègro, whose old stone houses are now almost entirely abandoned. As you climb up through sloping meadows, near a steep rock wall, there are sweeping views down the valley. Another trail follows the Verzasca farther upstream through the Val Vegorness to its source. At the end of the valley is a broad cirque, drained by many streams. The trail climbs past the Rifugio Alpe Barone to the little lake of Barone, just below the Pizzo Barone (2,864 m/9,396 ft). A route over the Paso Barone leads to the Val Leventina.

There are attractive hikes from other points farther down the valley as well. From Frasco, a few miles downstream from Sonogno, a trail climbs to Lago d'Efra, a little lake with a fine view. And from Brione a trail ascends the Val d'Osura, between steep rock walls, to the base of the south side of Monte Zucchero.

There are small hotels in Frasco and Gerra as well as in Sonogno. You can drive or take a bus from Locarno up the Val Verzasca to Sonogno.

Val Leventina

The Val Leventina is the central artery of the Ticino, a big gap running northwest-southeast through the Lepontine Alps. For centuries this was a crucial trade route, much fought over, since it leads south to Lugano, Como, and central Italy. At its northern end is the historic and strategically located St. Gotthard Pass.

On the eastern side of the Val Leventina is an old trail linking the villages on its upper slope; because this path is high above the valley it is called the Strada Alta (*Höhenweg* in German) Leventina. This is a pleasant walk through fields, woods, and simple mountain villages of unmistakably Italian appearance; each little group of stone and plaster houses is clustered around a tall campanile. The view across the valley is of the western Ticinese Alps, but the immediate landscape is not high alpine. The only drawback is that you are occasionally aware of the superhighway on the valley floor below.

You can hike the entire Strada Alta Leventina, which will take up to three days, or walk any small section of it for a day or less, because at many points there are connections down to the valley. The route extends between Airolo, at the southern edge of the St. Gotthard Pass, and Biasca, about two-thirds of the way down the Val Leventina toward Bellinzona. Several villages have simple hotels.

Lukmanier Pass

The Lukmanier or Lucomagno Pass (1,914 m/6,470 ft), which cuts through the eastern group of the Lepontine Alps, connects Disentis in the valley of the Vorderrhein with Biasca in the southern Val Leventina. It is the lowest pass across any part of the Swiss Alps; thus this region has both the highest pass within the Swiss Alps (the Nufenen) and the lowest. The Lukmanier was an important route during the time of the Holy Roman Empire, when the dangerous St. Gotthard was barely passable; today, however, it receives far less traffic than the St. Gotthard.

Disentis is a quiet town in the valley of the Vorderrhein, or Outer Rhine (the major source of the Rhine River, which originates near Oberalp and the Furka Pass). Disentis is also known as Mustér, because of its monastery, one of the oldest Benedictine foundations in Switzerland (the present abbey was built in the seventeenth century). The Medelserschlucht, south of Disentis along the Lukmanier road, is a gorge through which the stream of the Medel plunges to join the Tavetsch River at Disentis, becoming the young Vorderrhein.

The Lukmanier Pass is both a geographical and cultural watershed. From these mountains, the Brenno (Blenio) River flows south into the Ticino, while the Medel flows north into the Rhine. The pass is also the dividing line between Canton Graubünden, where Romansch is spoken, and the Italian-speaking Ticino. Architectural styles and materials differ as well on either side of the pass, with wooden chalets to the north and Ticinese stone houses to the south.

The scenery near the pass is wild and alpine, although the terrain of this eastern part of the Lepontine Alps is less tortuous than that of the high plateau west of the Val Leventina. On the south side of the pass in the Val Blenio are views eastward of the Adula massif, dominated by the Rheinwaldhorn, the highest mountain in Canton Ticino.

Near the southern end of the Val Blenio, a narrow valley opens to the east, climbing to a point below the Rheinwaldhorn: this is the Val Malvaglia, one of the most unspoiled valleys of the Ticino, with several very pretty hamlets hugging its narrow slopes.

Val Calanca

The remote, rarely visited Val Calanca is east of the Val Blenio. It branches off from the Val Mesolcina almost at the entrance to that valley, near Roveredo. Though the Val Calanca is Italian-speaking and close to Bellinzona, it belongs politically to Canton Graubünden.

Weathered formations atop Cristallina Pass in the Lepontine Mountains sometimes resemble petrified wood. Facing page: The jewel-like Lago del Coagno nestles high in the mountains near Cristallina.

The valley walls here are steep and narrow—cliffs, in places. Along the valley, beside the turbulent River Calancasca, is a string of picturesque villages; several others occupy terraces above the valley floor. The old footpaths to some of these villages are virtual stone staircases. The conditions that make the Val Calanca so picturesque meant a harsh, meager life for the villagers, and the valley is now almost depopulated. The rugged walls of the Zapporthorn dominate the upper end of the valley.

Adula Group

The Rheinwald area is the site of the Adula group, which include the Rheinwaldhorn (3,402 m/11,161 ft), the Rheinquellhorn (3,200 m/10,499 ft), the Zapporthorn (3,152 m/10,341 ft), and the large Zapportgletscher. In this area, the Hinterrhein, or Inner Rhine, originates, one of the two sources of the young Rhine River.

To view these mountains, hikers take the trail from the village of Hinterrhein, which is north of the San Bernardino Pass. The trail leads southeast to the Zapporthütte, facing the Adula group.

The Glarus Alps

THE GLARUS (*Glarner* in German) Alps are a small but impressive range in central Switzerland. The profile of these mountains is generally higher than that of the Lepontine Alps to the south, and there is a greater difference in elevation between peaks and valley floors, resembling the Bernese Alps instead. The alpine meadows in most of the Glarus Alps are lush and green, in this respect also resembling the Bernese Oberland. These mountains are part of the Helvetic nappe and consist chiefly of core crystalline rock—granite, schist, and gneiss—along with limestone and sandstone.

Besides their scenic attraction, the Glarus Alps have a special historic interest. In these mountains a Russian field marshal, Aleksandr Vasilyevich Suvorov, carried out one of the most astonishing feats ever accomplished in either the Alps or the history of warfare. In 1798, the French revolutionary army occupied Switzerland; the Austrians and Russians sent armies to drive them out. Suvorov was on his way to Zurich to link up with Austrians and other Russians there when, in 1799, his army was encircled by the French. He enabled his 18,000 foot soldiers and 5,000 Cossack horsemen to escape by leading them across three alpine passes in ten days. The Russian army, having already fought its way north from Italy over the St. Gotthard Pass, was by this time exhausted; the troops were hungry, ragged, nearly barefoot. Their 70-year-old general, however, retained astonishing energy. After escaping first over the Chinzig Chulm, a pass from the Schächental to the Muotathal, he found the French blocking his way. Forced to find another exit, he chose the Pragel Pass to the Klöntal (the valley is now flooded by an artificial lake, the Klöntalersee). The army descended to the town of Glarus, then to Schwanden, and up the Sernftal to Elm. But once again the French army threatened to encircle the Russians, whereupon Suvorov led his men over the most difficult of the passes, the Panixer, which was deep in snow and in any case had no marked route. Sixteen thousand men made it to safety. This was, roughly speaking, an eighteenth-century Dunkirk, but without the help of friendly rescuers. These amazing feats are deeply stamped into the memory of the people of this region, and the name of Suvorov is often found here, designating a house, a path, or a bridge.

The Maderanertal

The lovely Maderanertal rises from the valley of the Reuss River eastward into the Glarus massif. It is approached from Amsteg, a village midway between Andermatt and Altdorf. It is a fairly narrow valley enclosed by some

3,000-m/9,840-ft mountains. Despite its handsome scenery, it is quiet and unspoiled; there is not a single resort in the Maderanertal. Beyond the village of Bristen near the valley's entrance, there are only a few scattered farms. Yet this was a popular holiday center in the nineteenth century, when guests came out on a carriage road to a hotel up the valley. The hotel is closed now, but its presence here is a historical curiosity, an artifact of a bygone era. It offered a ladies' salon, a reading room and library with German and English newspapers, a bowling alley, and Church of England services, all in the midst of the mountains. The hotel had its own barbershop and butcher, and there was a special house for English guests. Yet now hardly anyone comes to the Maderanertal.

The north side of the valley is dominated by the Gross Windgällen (3,188 m/10,459 ft) and the Gross Ruchen (3,139 m/10,299 ft), and the south side by the Oberalpstock (3,328 m/10,919 ft). Along the steep walls on both sides are many long waterfalls. The feature that most attracts the eye, however, is the big, sloping glacier at the end of the valley, the Hüfifirn, below the Gross Düssi (3,257 m/10,686 ft; known colloquially as the Düssistock). A trail up the center of the valley climbs fairly directly to the SAC Hüfihütte on a rock ledge that penetrates the center of the glacier. From the hut there is a fine view of the half-circle of mountains that encloses the glacier.

A system of trails up the valley's northern slope leads to the Stäfel meadows and the Windgällenhütte, offering a superb view that encompasses the upper end of the valley with the glacier, the Düssistock, and the mountains above the south slope of the valley, as well as the Windgällen. On the south side of the valley, a trail from Balmenschachen climbs to Brunni Alp and then to the Brunni glacier. Another trail, starting at Bristen, ascends 1,400 m/ 4,600 ft to the Chrüzli Pass (2,347 m/7,700 ft), and descends to Sedrun in the Vorderrhein Valley.

Klausen Pass

The center of the Glarus Alps is bisected by a pair of great valleys linked at the center by the Klausen Pass. This route extends past the huge massif of the Tödi (3,614 m/11,857 ft), the highest mountain of the Glarus Alps.

At the western edge of the Klausen Pass route is Altdorf, a small, attractive town attached by tradition to the legend of William Tell; here allegedly he shot the apple from his son's head. In the town center is a monument to Tell; here also the *Tell Spiele,* based on Schiller's play about William Tell, is performed in summer in a special theater, with local people playing the roles.

The road east of Altdorf climbs gently at first through a narrow valley, and then more steeply as it rises to the Schächental, the main valley. Above

SPINY or THORNY THISTLE
Cirsium spinosissimum

A characteristic sight along the banks of alpine streams as well as in meadows or among rocks, this large thistle reaches 50 cm/20 in in height. It resembles a dancing, whirling figure, with its leaves flung out or raised like arms, and a yellow head on top. And though its spiny, prickly leaves look forbidding, they do not sting.

The dark green leaves are very deeply notched. In the center of the head, guarded by a protective cluster of shorter yellow leaves (actually bracts), are tightly packed golden flowers. Groups of these thistles are found from 1,500 to 3,000 m/4,921 to 9,842 ft, on any kind of soil. The flowers appear from July to August.

the wooded slopes is a line of mountains with a sharp, pointed profile. Unterschächen, on the south side of the valley, is positioned at the base of the impressive Brunnital; the Hinter Schächen stream curls down this steep, narrow valley cut between two walls scooped out of the rock. Above the Brunnital is a big, rugged mass—the rocky walls of the Gross Windgällen and Gross Ruchen, mountains seen from the Maderanertal to the south. Several trails ascend the slopes of this scenic valley.

The Schächental remains quite narrow, and as the road climbs high along its north slope the views are tremendous. Ahead is a wall of cliffs,

Facing page: The misty land near the top of the Sustenpass is home to the Arolla pine, stunted fir trees, and a variety of alpine shrubs.

culminating in a group of big mountains with pointed crests: the Clariden (3,268 m/10,722 ft), the Chammliberg (3,214 m/10,545 ft), and the Schärhorn (3,295 m/10,810 ft). The glacier below the Schärhorn, the Griessfirn, is the source for the superb Stäuben waterfall. Steep green walls shear down from the pass to the valley floor.

As you descend eastward from the Klausen Pass, the walls at the base of the Tödi mountain swing into view: a huge rampart of rock topped by a glacier and further steps of rock, ice, and snow, mounting to the summit. The pass wall, on the eastern side, is even steeper than on the western side. If you approach the Klausen Pass from the east, you are positioned to see the steep cirque into which the road is cut in switchbacks, with a waterfall streaking down nearby.

You can walk over the Klausen Pass by footpaths along the floor of the two valleys on either side of the pass, the Schächental and the Urnerboden. Some variant routes traverse higher on the slopes.

Urnerboden and Linthal

On the eastern side of the Klausen Pass the valley is also very deep, though somewhat broader: a big, U-shaped trench cut between long cliffs. Along the floor of this higher valley, the Urnerboden, are clusters of alps among rich green meadows. Beyond is another drop to a lower valley, the Linthal, with a small town of the same name. North of Linthal there are numerous villages and the small city of Glarus.

Just east of the Klausen Pass, where the road angles sharply to the south and then turns sharply north again, a trail climbs to Gemsfairen, from which there are good views of the Clariden. Farther east of the Klausen Pass, from the town of Linthal, you can drive (or take a taxi) along a small road southward up the Linth Valley to Reitimatt or Tierfed. A trail from Tierfed heads south along the Sandbach to Ueli, from which there are impressive views of the Tödi. The trail continues to the Fridolinshütte, below the Tödi and the Bifertenstock (3,421 m/11,224 ft); this is a steep, long, and rugged route.

Braunwald. Braunwald, the chief resort of Canton Glarus, is a small, quiet place, the only resort in eastern Switzerland that bars automobiles. It is located on a shelf overlooking the west side of the Linthal, 600 m/1,969 ft above the valley floor. From this perch, it enjoys an excellent view across the Glarus Alps, especially of the Tödi. Braunwald is reached by funicular from the village of Linthal.

Above Braunwald is a band of cliffs; from the top of the Gumen chair lift, you can take the trail that climbs above the cliffs to Bützi. On top is a huge area of white limestone, said to be the largest karst plateau in Switzerland, eroded into furrows and hollows. A blazed route leads to Erigsmatt (in fog you could easily lose your way here); retrace your steps on return.

Klöntalersee

The highest mountain at the eastern edge of the Glarus Alps is the Glärnisch (2,914 m/9,560 ft), topped by glaciers. Below is the lovely Klöntalersee, a long, artificial lake beneath the north side of the Glärnisch. In 1799, Suvorov's army marched through this valley, seeking to evade the French. The Klöntalersee is reached easily by road from Glarus. At Vorauen on the western edge of the lake there is a small beach and boating dock. From here a trail climbs to the SAC Glarnischhütte, northwest of the mountain.

Sernftal and Elm

The Sernftal is a tributary valley east of the Linthal and south of Glarus. At the end of the Sernftal, in a deep pocket of steep green slopes, is the tiny village of Elm, one of the choicest spots in the region. Elm is an extremely pretty, quiet, wholly unspoiled place with handsome old wooden houses that are decked with flowers in summer. The mountains around it include the Piz Sardona or Surenstock (3,056 m/10,026 ft), Piz Segnas (3,099 m/10,167 ft), and the Vorab (3,028 m/9,934 ft). (Some of these mountains form the border between the Swiss-German and Romansch areas, and thus have names in both languages.) Elm is a year-round resort, a center for alpine and cross-country skiing as well as for hiking and climbing.

Despite its present neat, charming appearance, Elm has a tragic and significant history. In 1881, part of the Tschingelhorn, one of the mountains overlooking Elm, fell upon the village, causing extreme devastation—more than 100 people were killed. A plaque on the village church lists the scores of dead by name and family relationship; whole families were wiped out. The villagers brought this disaster upon themselves, however, through a combination of ignorance and greed. They had been mining slate from the mountain, and although ominous noises had been heard for some time, they had continued to mine, until finally the mountain gave way. The Swiss federal government then passed the first laws in Europe prohibiting unrestrained exploitation of the environment. Elm is also associated with the astonishing feat of Suvorov's army; the house in which Suvorov was quartered is protected as a historic site.

Clockwise from top left: The innocent-looking Alpine forget-me-not will grow on any soil type. Alpine toadflax shows a slight preference for lime-free soil. The European cyclamen, which has an intensely sweet fragrance, grows in lime-rich areas. Moss campion grows in a thick mat that helps the plant preserve moisture; it is found on lime-rich soil. The rarely found but graceful St. Bruno's lily prefers a lime-free soil.

A hike on a farm road to Gemsfairen on the northeast side of the Klausen Pass takes visitors to a high pasture with marvelous views of the deep U-shaped valley.

The footpath from Schwanden to Elm, through the floor of the valley along the Sernft River, is known as the Suworowweg—the Suvorov trail. It can be skied in winter. Several higher trails climb the slopes around Elm. A trail to the southeast climbs steeply to the SAC Martinsmadhütte, just below the Vorab glacier. But Elm is best known as the nexus of several pass routes. The Foo Pass leads northeast to Weisstannen, skirting the Piz Sardona-Piz Segnas massif to the north. The Richetlipass heads south and then west, with views of the snowy Hausstock (3,158 m/10,361 ft), over the mountains to Linthal. And the historic Panixer Pass, where Suvorov and his army made their supreme effort, runs south between the Hausstock and the Vorab to Pigniu (Panix) above the Vorderrhein Valley.

The Engadine and the Rhaetian Alps

THE RHAETIAN ALPS EXTEND diagonally across southeastern Switzerland into the southwestern edge of Austria. This mountain range lies almost entirely within the largest, though least populous, of the Swiss cantons— Graubünden (*Grisons* in French, *Grischuns* in Romansch). The region is the central remnant of the ancient state of Rhaetia, once a northern province of the Roman Empire. Though it also extends into Austria and Italy, ancient Rhaetia lies largely in Switzerland today, making up a substantial part of Canton Graubünden.

With one exception, these mountains bear out the general rule that the central and eastern Alps are not as high as the western Alps. The exception, the highest cluster of mountains in this area, is the Bernina group in the Upper Engadine. The Piz Bernina (4,049 m/13,284 ft) is the only mountain above 4,000 m/13,120 ft east of the St. Gotthard Pass in the entire alpine chain. The Upper Engadine is known especially for its magnificent glaciers and beautiful lakes, while the Lower Engadine offers a striking contrast between meadows and rocky, jagged peaks.

The Rhaetian Alps mark the boundary between the exposed core rocks of the western Alps and the lightly metamorphosed "cover" rocks that characterize the crystalline ranges farther east. The Bernina group of mountains of the Upper Engadine are crystalline, composed largely of gneiss and mica schist, but the rock farther down the En Valley is sedimentary. The Lower Engadine Valley, however, constitutes a "window" in which core granite and gneisses similar to those of the Pennine nappes have been exposed by erosion of the cover rock formations.

The main river draining the southeast portion of Graubünden is the En, and the surrounding country is called the Engadine. The En flows northeastward into Austria, where it is called by its German name, the Inn. The Engadine is a Romance-language pocket within an area that is primarily German-speaking. Here, but especially in the Lower Engadine, people still speak Romansch, a language descended from Latin and said to be older than Italian.

The Bernina Group—Upper Engadine

After the Valais and the Bernese Oberland, the Bernina group of mountains (including the Bregaglia) forms the third great alpine region of Switzerland. This is so important a center for alpinism that the training classes and examinations for Swiss mountain-guide candidates are rotated among the Valaisian Alps, the Bernese Oberland, and the Bernina mountains. Though the highest of these are lower than the chief Valaisian and Bernese peaks, they offer challenging climbs on snow, ice, and rock; some of the most difficult rock climbs in Europe are found in the nearby Val Bregaglia. Several alpine resorts, including the internationally known St. Moritz, cluster around the peaks of the Bernina group. Besides its great mountains, the Engadine is known also for exceptionally good weather. In Switzerland, only the Valais has a sunnier, drier climate.

The mountains of the Bernina group are strung in a line along the Swiss-Italian border. Many of the names include the word *Piz*, which means "peak" in Romansch. Flowing around them are some of the most beautiful glaciers in the Alps—the delight of alpinists—but they may also be seen by hikers and cable-car mountaineers.

THE UPPER EN VALLEY

From Maloja, where the main valley of the Upper Engadine begins, to St. Moritz farther northeast, the Upper En Valley is filled almost entirely by a long series of beautiful lakes, each of which flows into the next. This chain of lakes (*lej* in Romansch, *see* in German) looks especially lovely from the mountain slopes above. The Upper En Valley is a center for water sports, particularly sailing and windsurfing. Watching the festive scene, you would scarcely think that these lakes are at almost 1,800 m/5,900 ft. All of the villages along the lakes, including St. Moritz, are famous as well as for winter sports and share many skiing facilities and programs. One of the great Swiss cross-country ski races, the Engadine Ski Marathon, extends along the length of the valley floor and over the frozen lakes.

Maloja

The Maloja Pass is at the western tip of the Lej da Sils (Silser See). Maloja is at a crossroads, both ancient and modern. It is a central point on the road linking the major Engadine resorts with Italy, and it is also an approach to the old Roman route over the still unpaved Septimer Pass. Although Maloja is a small, unpretentious place, very good accommodations are available.

Val Forno. From the Lej da Sils, several valleys cut deeply southward toward the high peaks along the Italian border. Maloja is the starting point for hikes up one of these, the Val Forno. Partway up this valley is the Lac da Cavloc, whose dark blue waters reflect the snowy Piz Forno (3,214 m/

Piz Corvatsch rises in a land of broad green valleys and sparkling white glaciers; a dry climate and frequent blue skies make the area delightful for climbers, hikers, and photographers.

10,545 ft). Beyond the lake, the trail climbs above tree line and the scenery becomes harsh and alpine. The route continues through the wild, lonely upper valley to the foot of the Vadrec (glacier) del Forno.

Val Bregaglia. Below Maloja, to the southwest, is the Val Bregaglia, or Bergell in German. The special charm of this valley is the contrast between the southern appearance of the valley floor—Italianate villages and Mediterranean vegetation—and the glaciers that overhang it. From the Maloja Pass (1,815 m/5,955 ft) there is an almost precipitous drop to the Val Bregaglia, with an accompanying abrupt change in vegetation due to the lower altitude, and the valley's orientation toward the southwest. There are many fine stands of chestnut trees in the Val Bregaglia (the largest chestnut forest in Switzerland is here) as well as vineyards, fig trees, and pomegranates. Among the picturesque villages, Soglio is outstanding. It is perched on a balcony overlooking the valley, a cluster of old houses with beautiful stone roofs,

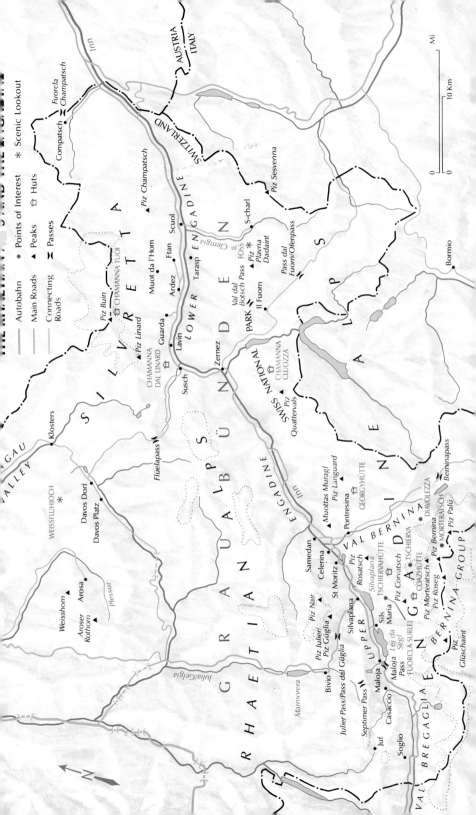

among which are a few Renaissance palaces (one has been converted into a hotel). From the terrace of Soglio there is a view across the valley to the Bondasca glacier and the sharp, pointed granite peaks around it, which include the Sciora Dadent (3,275 m/10,745 ft), Piz Cengalo (3,370 m/11,056 ft), and Piz Badile (3,308 m/10,853 ft). The excellent granite and challenging verticality of these mountains attract expert rock climbers; the sheer-walled Piz Badile in particular has been a magnet for distinguished international climbers. Hikers can take the high trail, or *Höhenweg*, between Casaccio (at the bottom of the Maloja Pass) and Soglio, and return to Maloja by bus.

Val Fex

This most frequented of the valleys south of Lake Sils is reached from Sils Maria, a very small but select resort village between the lakes of Sils and Silvaplana, on the eastern shore. (Sils Baselgia, adjoining Sils Maria, is less expensive.) The Val Fex is on a shelf above the lake; you can hike up through a small gorge to reach it, or take a horse-drawn carriage up from Sils Maria. The valley is broad and grassy, with several alps among the meadows; the effect is gentler and more pastoral than in the wilder Val Forno. The trail leads past the last summer farm to a glacier, the Vadrec da Fex. A cable car from Sils Maria to Furtschellas enables you to ramble along trails high on the eastern slope above the Val Fex, or on a trail above the eastern bank of the lakes of Sils and Silvaplana.

Silvaplana and Piz Corvatsch

Silvaplana lies between the lakes of Silvaplana and Champfer on the western side of the Upper En Valley. It is slightly larger than Sils and Maloja, though still a village in comparison with St. Moritz. A bridge crosses to Surlej on the eastern shore, the base for the Corvatsch cable car. This lift rises to 3,295 m/10,810 ft, near the summit of the Piz Corvatsch (3,451 m/11,322 ft), the highest peak of the mountainous ridge separating the Upper En Valley from the Val Roseg. From the Corvatsch there are splendid views of the Bernina group and the great Tschierva and Roseg glaciers. The Corvatsch is one of the main ski areas for all the resorts along the lakes, including St. Moritz; there is also summer skiing on the Corvatsch glacier. Some hikers use the Corvatsch cable car as a boost for crossing from the En to the Roseg Valley. From the intermediate station, a trail climbs to Fuorcla Surlej (where there are also grand views) and then descends into the Val Roseg, joining a trail heading southwest for the Coaz hut or northeast for Hotel Roseggletscher and Pontresina.

The proximity of Silvaplana to the Corvatsch cable car makes it a good base for skiing, and it shares with the other lakeside resorts the network of cross-country ski trails along the valley. It is also a center for sailing and windsurfing. Silvaplana is on the bus route between St. Moritz and Maloja.

St. Moritz

The best-known place in the Upper Engadine Valley is also one of the most famous and opulent of all alpine resorts—St. Moritz. It has grown into a small town, divided into several sections that wrap halfway around its lake. St. Moritz-Bad, now a modern spa, lies on the south bank of the lake, and St. Moritz-Dorf, the most built-up section, is above the north bank. In this part of St. Moritz are most of its celebrated luxury hotels and fashionable shops.

The Engadine Valley here is broad and the mountains visible from the town are of medium height; St. Moritz is not the place to go to see exciting scenery directly from a town, but cable cars can soon lift you to points from which there are excellent views of the great glaciers and mountains nearby. The Corvatsch cable car is 6 km/3.7 mi from St. Moritz, with connection by bus. Directly above the town is Piz Nair (3,057 m/10,030 ft), whose slopes are enjoyed by both skiers and hikers. A cable car climbs nearly to its summit, from which there are good views. Besides the standard winter sports of skiing (alpine and cross-country), skating, and curling (a game played on ice), there are some unusual winter activities and games in this area. For daredevils there is the Cresta sled run, which is restricted to men. The participant lies on his stomach on a sled "skeleton"—little more than a long metal tray—and hurtles down a chute of ice. On the frozen lake of St. Moritz people ride horseback and play polo and also golf; horse and greyhound races are also held on the ice. Summer visitors come not only to hike and climb but also to sail on the lakes, or play golf or tennis.

St. Moritz is the westernmost terminus of the Rhätische Bahn (the Rhaetian railway), but there is bus service westward along the valley of the Upper En, past the lakes to Maloja and the Val Bregaglia.

Pages 160 and 161: The magnificent Morteratsch glacier lies amid the remote and peaceful ice-strewn peaks of the Val Roseg. Fortunately for the hotel and train station a kilometer below its toe, this wide and mighty glacier has receded in recent years.

Celerina and Samedan

Northeast of St. Moritz along the River En are Celerina and Samedan, smaller and quieter towns. The Cresta sled run from St. Moritz culminates in Celerina. From Punt Muragl, at the nearby entrance to the Val Bernina, a funicular ascends to Muottas Muragl (2,450 m/8,038 ft), affording a view of many of the Bernina mountains including the Piz Bernina, Piz Tschierva, Piz Rosatsch, and Piz Surlej, and the chain of lakes in the Upper Engadine Valley. Both towns are on the railway.

Pass Routes

Several passes over the spine of the Rhaetian Alps link the Engadine with central and eastern Switzerland. The Septimer and Julier passes over the Rhaetian Alps north of the lakes of the Upper Engadine are routes with origins at least as old as the Roman Empire.

Septimer Pass. From Maloja or Casaccio, below the Maloja Pass, you can start or finish a route that was used in Roman times, the Septimer Pass (in Romansch, the Pass da Sett). In ancient and medieval times, this was a pass route for foot and horse travel; it has never been paved, and today only a few hikers ramble along the route. This trail strikes out northwest and then north over the edge of the Rhaetian Alps, climbing above meadows and a waterfall to a stony shelf. Here the deep blue Lunghin Lake lies below grand walls of rock. If you are coming from Maloja, before reaching the Septimer Pass you must cross the higher Lunghin Pass (2,645 m/8,678 ft), which is the watershed for three seas: from here, the En flows into the Black Sea, the Maira (Mera) into the Adriatic, and the Julia Wasser into the North Sea. The trail then crosses the lower Pass da Sett (2,310 m/7,579 ft); there are fine views of the Bernina group. In the mountains above the Septimer Pass, to the northwest, is Juf (2,126 m/6,975 ft), said to be the highest farm settlement in Europe. From the pass, the trail descends to the little town of Bivio, where it joins the Julier Pass road from Silvaplana. From Bivio you can take a bus back to Silvaplana and the En Valley lakes, or north to Chur, capital of the canton.

Julier Pass. From Silvaplana, a paved road, with bus service, extends over the Julier Pass (Pass dal Güglia) to Bivio. At the pass (2,284 m/7,493 ft) are two fragments of Roman pillars, a testament to the time when imperial legions marched here. The pass is dominated by the Piz Julier or Piz Güglia (3,380 m/11,089 ft), and the view embraces a great sweep of Upper Engadine scenery, including Piz Bernina and the surrounding peaks, and the lakes to either side of Silvaplana. Beyond Bivio the road follows the Julia (Gelgia) River north toward Chur, passing the artificial lake of Marmorera on the way.

PONTRESINA AND THE VAL ROSEG

Smaller than neighboring St. Moritz and less luxurious, Pontresina is a village of considerable charm and style, with some lovely traditional Engadine houses decorated with sgraffito (see Lower Engadine). It is a year-round resort, an important ski center that also attracts climbers and hikers in the summer. Pontresina is the main departure point for the two great glaciers that spread northward from the Bernina group, the Roseg and Morteratsch.

The Val Roseg opens almost directly opposite Pontresina and leads to the glaciers west of Piz Bernina. About 8 km/4.8 mi up the valley is the isolated Hotel Roseggletscher, a big country inn more elaborate than the typical *Berghotel*. A popular excursion from Pontresina is to take the Pferde Omnibus, a little horse-drawn carriage, to Roseggletscher for lunch. From the hotel terrace there is a stunning view of the cirque of glaciers at the upper end of the valley.

Beyond the Roseggletscher the Ova da Roseg stream becomes intricately braided, a network of pale blue brooks weaving through the gravel beds deposited by the glacial melt. At the bridge near the hotel, hikers have two choices. The trail on the left bank of the stream leads to a hut below the Roseg glacier; the trail on the right bank, across the bridge, climbs to a hut below the Tschierva glacier. (A third trail, behind Hotel Roseggletscher, climbs to Fuorcla Surlej.)

The Coazhütte (Chamanna da Coaz). From Hotel Roseggletscher, the trail toward this hut continues to the southwest. This is one of the easiest of all alpine club huts to reach: the ascent is gradual and the difference in altitude moderate. The hut, at 2,610 m/8,563 ft, is located on a little promontory overlooking the Vadret ("glacier" in Romansch) da Roseg; another glacier, the Vadret de la Sella, joins the Roseg on the other side of a small island in this vast river of ice. The glaciers are enfolded on three sides by mountain walls, with the Piz Roseg (3,937 m/12,917 ft) dominating the scene to the east, and the Piz Glüschaint (3,594 m/11,791 ft) to the south. Within these walls is a grand sweep of glacier, so wide that it looks like a sea.

Another way to reach the Coaz hut is via Fuorcla Surlej, a notch in the mountainous ridge separating the Val Roseg from the main valley of the Upper Engadine, to the west. A cable car from Surlej, across the lake from Silvaplana, ascends to within 150 m/490 ft of the summit of the Piz Corvatsch; from the intermediate station at 2,699 m/8,859 ft, a trail ascends to Fuorcla Surlej (2,755 m/9,039 ft), where there is a *Berghotel*. From Fuorcla Surlej, a trail descends to join the one between Hotel Roseggletscher and the Coaz hut.

ORANGE ALPINE POPPY

Papaver rhaeticum

This mountain poppy almost glows with its clear, bright yellow color; the flowers become orange when dried. One of several subspecies of alpine poppies, it is relatively rare, found only in the central and southern Alps and the Swiss Engadine, in lime-rich, slightly dry areas. It grows among boulders, using an oblique root to cling to the slope, thus fastening itself against slides. The stem, which is covered with white hairs, reaches a height of 20 cm/8 in and bears only one flower. Shaggy, feathery, and finely lobed leaves are clustered at the base of the plant. The flower is shaped like a bowl, with four petals. It blooms in July and August, at altitudes of 1,500 to 3,000 m/4,921 to 9,842 ft.

The Tschiervahütte (Chamanna da Tschierva). The Tschierva and Coaz huts offer such different scenery that it is worth visiting both. The walk to the Tschierva is slightly shorter but a little steeper. It ascends along the east side of the Val Roseg, then up the right bank of the Tschierva glacier (Vadret da Tschierva) to the hut at 2,583 m/8,474 ft. The location of the hut is magnificent, under four of the major peaks in the area: the Piz Morteratsch (3,751 m/ 12,306 ft) is just above the hut; the Piz Bernina (4,049 m/13,284 ft) is at the head of the glacier, next to the Piz Scerscen (3,971 m/13,028 ft) and the Piz Roseg (3,937 m/12,917 ft).

The Tschierva glacier plunges wildly down to the valley below; huge séracs stand above like gigantic pyramids of ice. From the Tschierva hut, however,

Cows enjoy the classic alpine scenery in the Val Roseg. For centuries herdsmen have moved their animals to high pastures for summer grazing.

the great cirque of glaciers at the end of the Val Roseg is mostly cut off from view. The Tschierva glacier is enclosed in a much narrower space (less than half the width of the upper Roseg and Sella glaciers), but you are much closer to the mountains, and they are considerably higher and more impressive.

Morteratsch Glacier

Pontresina is also at the head of the Val Bernina. The Morteratsch glacier (Vadret da Morteratsch) enters this valley about 5 km/3.1 mi southeast of Pontresina. This glacier is longer than the Roseg and is very wide at its source.

Though the Morteratsch glacier can be viewed from either its left or right bank, the easiest way to see it is from Diavolezza, above its right bank. There is a small station at Bernina, a few kilometers from Pontresina on the rail line to Italy. Across the road from the Bernina station, a cable car climbs to the Chamanna da Diavolezza; you can also walk up. The "hut" is actually a hotel with a sun terrace, and since it is so easy to reach, there are often many people here. Yet the view is tremendous, and it is worth coming up despite the crowds. The hut is situated on the edge of a high terrace overlooking the Pers glacier.

The view from the Diavolezza hut also embraces the two sections of the Morteratsch glacier, the Vadret da Morteratsch on the west and the Vadret Pers on the south. These two steep icefalls drop from a crown of mountains, with a massive island of rock, the Isla Persa, dividing them; below it, they join to form the Morteratsch, a broad valley glacier. The huge, snowy mass of Piz Bernina spreads itself above the Morteratsch glacier, with a crest of mountains extending on both sides, along the Italian border; these peaks include the Piz Argent (3,945 m/12,943 ft), the Piz Zupò (3,996 m/13,110 ft), and the many-pronged Piz Palü (3,905 m/12,812 ft), which stands like a rampart, its rock walls crusted with ice and snow, above the Pers glacier. Rising above the left bank of the Morteratsch glacier are the Piz Morteratsch and Piz Boval (3,353 m/11,001 ft).

The trail to the Chamanna da Boval, on the left bank of the glacier, begins at the Morteratsch stop on the rail line between Pontresina and Bernina. This hut is lower than the Diavolezza, but it is positioned at the very edge of the Morteratsch glacier, with a superb view straight up the ice toward the Piz Bernina and the border ridge.

From the Diavolezza hut there are guided excursions between mid-June and October across the glacier to the Boval hut. Along with boots, dark glasses and sunblock are essential equipment for this trip.

Piz Languard

Pontresina is the base for excursions to Piz Languard (3,262 m/10,702 ft), a small mountain facing the great Bernina peaks and glaciers. The view from the top is spectacular, and as the Piz Languard is isolated, the unobstructed view is a true panorama. Piz Languard belongs to the class of relatively low mountains with comprehensive, panoramic views of the kind that Victorian travelers loved. Their ascents were mainly hikes, as no technical climbing is involved. Whenever possible they set out before dawn, so they could watch the sunrise from the peak. From Pontresina, a lift goes partway up the mountain, to Alp Languard. From here, a path climbs steeply to the Georgyhütte, perched on a narrow ledge a mere 86 m/282 ft below the summit. The hut faces the Bernina range, giving a spectacular view of the Piz Palü and Piz Bernina and serried ranges of mountains. On the summit, there is a 360-degree view of Swiss, Austrian, and Italian Alps—wave upon wave of mountains, rolling away on every side as far as the eye can see, extending to the Italian Dolomites.

The Lower Engadine

The Lower Engadine is one of the most distinctive regions in Switzerland, though it does not share the grand glaciers of the Upper Engadine nor peaks quite as high. But this is a delightful area for hiking, skiing, and touring, with alpine country on both sides of the En River. The only Swiss National Park is located in this area.

The Lower Engadine, or Engiadina Bassa, is a center of Romansch culture; you feel that you are in a world apart here. It has villages of astonishing charm, composed of traditional Engadine houses, whose façades are boldly and gaily decorated, sometimes with fanciful creatures such as mermaids, dragons, and griffins, or with abstract geometrical patterns. Some of the figures are painted, but many are made by sgraffito, a Renaissance technique: the figures are incised through an overlying coat of plaster so that the images contrast with the white façade. Although there are painted houses in Bavaria and in some villages in northern Austria, their style is completely different, much more embellished and sophisticated. Engadine houses display the whimsy of folk art, while their geometrical sgraffiti patterns are both simple and elegant.

The Romansch language, moreover, has survived in the Lower Engadine, where one hears it nearly everywhere. Pockets of Romansch culture remain in less tourist-frequented sections of the Upper Engadine, but the language is scarcely heard in that region's chic international resorts.

A pleasant hike passes along the Clemgia River, which flows between grassy banks in a wide and peaceful valley flanked by pine forests. Facing page: Along the river's upper portion, jagged rocky Dolomites contrast sharply with the gentle undulating landscape below.

THE LOWER EN VALLEY

The Lower Engadine extends between Susch in the west and the Austrian border in the east. While the land along the south bank of the En slopes abruptly upward, the rise above the north bank is more gradual, making space for villages, alps, and pastureland. Above these, however, are mountains even higher than those south of the river, as well as broader and more extensive glaciers. Here the Rhaetian Alps overleap the Austrian border, where they are known as the Rätikon Alps and Silvretta Alps.

Ardez, Guarda, and Scuol

Along the Lower En Valley is a string of unspoiled, pretty villages, including two of the jewels of the region, Ardez and Guarda, in which are some of the finest Engadine decorated houses. Scuol (*Schuls* in German), in effect the capital of the Lower Engadine, is a small town of much charm, displaying

many handsome old Engadine houses in its old quarter. A few miles west of Scuol is the walled castle of Tarasp atop a steep, conical hill with a commanding view of the En Valley and surrounding mountains. Scuol and nearby Tarasp and Vulpera constitute an important spa center. There are paths linking many of the Lower Engadine villages; an especially pleasant trail through flowery meadows connects Ftan (above Scuol), Ardez, and Guarda. There are several ski lifts near Scuol; the area attracts skiers seeking a quiet, unhurried winter sports center with the regional flavor of the Engadine. These villages are connected by the Rhätische Bahn; the railway ends at Scuol, but there is bus service east from Scuol to the Austrian border. Guarda, 50 m/160 ft above the railway, is linked to its station by bus.

S-charl. The scenery south of the En is often a combination of the soft and the rugged, marked by pine woods and fresh green meadows that contrast sharply with the clusters of jagged gray mountains that rise throughout the region. From Scuol, a road (with bus service) southward climbs steeply up the gorge of the Clemgia to one of the choicest spots in the region, the quiet, very pretty hamlet of S-charl, beautifully located at the edge of a meadow, with striking views of the peaks at each end of the valley. From S-charl, there are trails in several directions, some leading into the National Park. The path through Val Sesvenna climbs through pastures to high alpine scenery at the Pass (*Fuorcla* in Romansch) Sesvenna, below the Piz Sesvenna (3,204 m/ 10,512 ft) and its glacier.

Another route from S-charl follows the Clemgia River southward. This route leads over the pass, the Fuorcla Funtana da S-charl, to the inn at Süsom Givè (bus service available), which is on the Pass dal Fuorn (Ofenpass) at the edge of the National Park. Just below S-charl, at the Val Mingèr bus stop, there is a trail to Il Foss in the National Park, with views of the big gray tooth of the Piz Plavna Dadaint (3,166 m/10,387 ft). From Il Foss you can continue north through the Val Plavna to Tarasp, or cross the Val dal Botsch Pass to reach the road in the National Park, or retrace your steps back to Val Mingèr.

Muot da l'Hom and Fuorcla Champatsch

Several trails traverse the slope north of the En along a sort of natural balcony. One section extends between Ftan and the Val Tasna, through Alp Laret. Experienced hikers may take a variation and proceed higher, on a less well-marked route, through wild, empty, beautiful meadows toward Muot da l'Hom. Piz Minschun (3,068 m/10,066 ft) dominates the landscape of this high country. Lifts descend to the valley at Prui and Motta Naluns, above Scuol. From Scuol, you can also use the Motta Naluns lift for a boost up the trail toward Fuorcla Champatsch, a pass slung between the Piz Champatsch (2,920 m/9,580 ft) and the Piz Nair (2,966 m/9,731 ft) leading to the Val Laver.

Piz Buin

A series of almost parallel valleys gives access to the high alpine country north of the En. The best-known mountain in this area is Piz Buin, over whose three summits (the highest is 3,312 m/10,866 ft) runs the Swiss-Austrian border. On the Swiss side, it is approached from the lovely Val Tuoi, which extends north from the village of Guarda. A pleasant trail climbs to Chamanna Tuoi, the SAC hut used for climbing the south or Swiss face of the mountain.

Piz Linard

The highest mountain in the Silvretta group is the Piz Linard (3,411 m/ 11,191 ft), which is entirely within Swiss borders. Lacking the expansive glaciers of Piz Buin, it is not as famous as that mountain, yet the scenery around it is wild and grand. It is north of the attractive village of Lavin, between Susch and Guarda. From Lavin, a steep trail leads up to the Chamanna dal Linard (2,327 m/7,635 ft), an SAC hut (no hut warden or service) at the mountain's base. A more gradual trail from the village ascends the scenic Val Lavinuoz; the stark, bold tower of Piz Linard rises to the west, while the valley is closed off by several hanging glaciers.

THE SWISS NATIONAL PARK

The Swiss National Park is unlike most European national parks, and also unlike American ones. Its land is strictly designated as a wilderness area. Nature is left alone: the forest in the park is not managed or groomed—dead trees and fallen branches are not cleared away. Hunting and grazing are forbidden. Typical alpine wildlife can be seen, and red deer are abundant, but this is one of the few mountain areas in Switzerland where there are no cows, sheep, or goats on the high meadows. It differs from most European parks because there is also no development for skiing and very limited facilities for

Pages 172 and 173: The Tschierva Hut offers a dramatic view of its namesake's tumultuous glacier, where séracs stand above the ice like giant pyramids.

tourists. And it differs from American parks in several ways: hikers must keep to the marked trails and picnic only at designated spots; they may not start fires or pitch a tent anywhere in the park; there is no campground. The only accommodations in the park are at the hotel at Il Fuorn on the road, or at the Chamanna Cluozza, a hut in the western region of the park. There are no other restaurants and no snack bars or shops. The only road in the park extends between Zernez eastward through the Pass dal Fuorn (2,149 m/7,051 ft).

The park is well laced with trails, and hiking is the best way to see it. The road through Il Fuorn, where most trails originate, has many parking areas for day hikers and is also served by bus. The highest point in the park is the Piz Quattervals (3,165 m/10,348 ft), in the park's southern section. The trail along the Val Sassa skirts the long ridge of this mountain to the east and south; the Valletta trail hugs the west side of its ridge. Another trail from Il Fuorn south to Alp la Schera and Buffalora circles a small mountain, Munt la Schera (2,587 m/8,488 ft), that hikers can ascend for a good view. Trails northward to the Fuorcla dal Val dal Botsch climb to a rocky crest, with views of the rugged mountains that form the park's northern border.

The chief entry point to the National Park is the small town of Zernez on the En River, a few miles upstream from Susch; there is an information center in the National Park House. Zernez can be reached by rail; there is bus service eastward through the park to the Italian border.

The Northern Rhaetian Alps

The three chief resorts of the northern Swiss Rhaetian Alps are Arosa, Davos, and Klosters; they are especially renowned for their skiing.

Arosa

The highest and most attractively located of the three is Arosa (1,775 m/ 5,823 ft), on a broad terrace at the upper end of the Plessur Valley, wrapped by mountains on three sides. Arosa is also the least densely built of these three resorts. Because it is at the end of its road, there is no through traffic; to further enhance the quiet, cars may not circulate in the village between midnight and 6 A.M.

The mountains above Arosa are of moderate height, the highest being the Aroser Rothorn (2,980 m/9,777 ft). One of the chief viewpoints is the summit of the Weisshorn (2,653 m/8,704 ft), which you can ascend by cable car; the view extends as far as the Bernina group. Two small lakes near the center of

Arosa are used for bathing and boating, an unusual feature at an alpine resort at such an altitude.

Arosa has fine alpine skiing and an extensive area of cross-country trails. It also maintains 29 km/18 mi of walking trails throughout the winter, and organizes snowshoe excursions. Among the winter activities are outdoor and indoor ice skating and curling, sleigh rides, and horse racing, greyhound racing, and golf on a frozen lake.

Arosa can be reached from Chur by car or narrow-gauge railway. The road is very steep (chains are recommended for winter driving), so many guests come instead by train.

Davos

Davos is at the northern end of the Flüela Pass in the center of the northern Graubünden. It is an elegant, built-up, and fairly large resort, with the aspect of a town rather than a village. It is divided into two sections, Dorf and Platz, which now flow into each other. Here, too, the chief season is winter. Davos has the largest skating rink in Europe, open in summer as well as winter. But it is best known as a ski center, with very extensive slopes and an almost equal balance of easy, intermediate, and difficult runs; it is also known for some very long runs. From the Weissfluhjoch (2,693 m/8,835 ft) to the town there is a run of 1,100 m/3,600 ft, and the Parsenn course drops 1,992 m/6,535 ft. In summer you can also ride up the Parsenn system, consisting of a funicular to the Weissfluhjoch and then a cable car to the Weissfluhgipfel (2,844 m/9,331 ft), with good views.

Klosters

Klosters, in the Prättigau Valley, is only a short distance north of Davos and shares with it the Parsenn ski area, with which it is connected by the Gotschnagrat cable-car system. Klosters is one of the fashionable Swiss ski resorts, though smaller and less opulent than Davos. Like Davos, it has two sections—Dorf and Platz. It is close to the Austrian border, and in spring there are organized ski mountaineering tours over the border to the Montafon Valley in Austria; in summer, hikers and climbers cross these same mountains.

The Austrian Alps

A map of Austria seems to indicate that the country is bristling with different chains of mountains: the Otztal Alps, the Stubai Alps, the Zillertal Alps, and so on. In reality, these are merely names that local people have given to the mountains of their valleys; these Alpine segments are parts of larger groups that in Switzerland would be considered one range. The Austrian Alps essentially consist of two great bands of mountains stretching across much of the country in a west-to-east direction. The band of mountains lying across northern Austria is generally limestone, while the mountains extending across southern Austria are mainly crystalline, made of igneous rock and metamorphic rock such as gneiss and schist. In western Austria, the Inn River divides the northern from the southern mountains; in eastern Austria, the Salzach and other rivers form this division.

These two mountain chains present a very different appearance: in the northern limestone Alps the rock is light gray, eroded into jagged peaks, with much exposed rock because of the general absence of snow cover; in the south there

Fall colors stand against an early snow at the north end of Austria's Grossglockner Highway.

are higher peaks, often snow-covered and surrounded by glaciers, creating a landscape more typically "Alpine."

The Austrian Alps are sprinkled with huts so numerous and accessible that in some sections a day's hike will bring you past two or three of them, allowing you to stop for lunch at one, for tea at another. The ratio of hikers to climbers is very high, much higher than in Switzerland. Austrian huts, moreover, are often more elaborate than Swiss huts; some have warm water and even showers, and some have cafeteria-style dining rooms, or more varied menus. In terms of amenities, they correspond to the Swiss *Berghotels,* although being club run the Austrian huts are more standardized than the family-run *Berghotels.* Many Austrian huts are supplied by a special lift line, a *Materialseilbahn,* and it is sometimes possible to have rucksacks ferried up on this; some also have jeep service.

Addresses: For information on Austria contact the Austrian National Tourist Office. In the U.S.: 500 Fifth Avenue, Suite 2009, New York, NY 10110; (212) 944-6880. 500 North Michigan Avenue, Suite 1950, Chicago, IL 60611; (312) 644-8029. 1300 Post Oak Boulevard, Suite 960, Houston, TX 77056; (713) 850-9999. 11601 Wilshire Boulevard, Suite 2480, Los Angeles, CA 90025; (213) 477-3332.

In Canada: 1010 Ouest Rue Sherbrooke, Suite 1410, Montreal, Que. H3A 2R7; (514) 849-3709. 2 Bloor Street East, Suite 3330, Toronto, Ont. M4W 1A8; (416) 967-3381. Suite 1380 Granville Square, 200 Granville Street, Vancouver, B.C. V6C 1S4; (604) 683-5808.

In Great Britain: 30 St. George Street, London W1R OAL; (44) 1-629 0461.

Application forms for membership in the Austrian Alpine Club may be obtained from the New York office of the Austrian National Tourist Office. The completed application must be sent to: Osterreichischer Alpenverein (OAV), Wilhelm-Greil-Strasse 15, A-6010 Innsbruck; (43) 512-58 41 07.

The Rätikon and Silvretta Alps

THE VORARLBERG, THE WESTERNMOST of Austria's nine federal states, borders the Swiss Engadine to the south and Liechtenstein to the west. A generally mountainous region, its highest peaks are along the Swiss frontier, in the ranges known as the Rätikon and Silvretta, and its connection with what is now Swiss territory is ancient. In the third century A.D., Rhaetian tribes arrived in the Vorarlberg and a thousand years later, in the thirteenth and fourteenth centuries, Valaisians (Walser in German) from the Swiss Valais immigrated here, settling in the higher valleys. The local people speak the Montafon dialect, a mixture of Romansch and Walliser (and in the turmoil following the collapse of the Austro-Hungarian empire, expressed interest in union with Switzerland). This rich cultural mixture, as well as its relative remoteness from the center of Austria, endows the region with a distinctive character and charm.

The crisp, sharp profile of the Rätikon peaks forms a striking battlement along the Swiss border; the scenery reaches visual splendor with the mass of rugged peaks and beautiful glaciers surrounding Piz Buin, in the center of the Silvretta range.

Although the Rätikon and Silvretta Alps form an almost continuous line of mountains, the Rätikon is a limestone group, while the Silvretta mountains are mainly crystalline: igneous and metamorphic rock, mainly gneiss, mica schist, and—in this region—amphibolite. The Silvretta is thus the western edge of the band of crystalline mountains extending across much of southern Austria near the Italian border.

The Rätikon Alps

THE MONTAFON VALLEY

The best way to see the Austrian side of the Rätikon Alps is from the Montafon Valley, which contours along the northern slope of the Rätikon and the western edge of the Silvretta range. The Ill River springs from the glaciers of the Silvretta group and flows northwest to join the Rhine.

From Bludenz on the west, the Montafon Valley rises southeastward, narrowing as it climbs to its source near the Bielerhöhe. Several tributary valleys, principally the Gauertal and Gargellental, penetrate the mountains to the south, while the Silbertal extends eastward toward the Verwall group.

Schruns

Schruns, at the northwestern end of the valley, is the major town, almost adjoined by Tschagguns, directly across the Ill River. Set in a broad basin, Schruns is a small market town, surrounded by pastures and farms. Ernest Hemingway spent what he called some of the happiest winters of his life (1925 and 1926) in Schruns, working on *The Sun Also Rises* and learning to ski in the Montafon Valley. East of Schruns is the Hochjoch (2,520 m/8,268 ft), whose slopes serve as the town's main ski area. The Hochjochbahn cable car connects Schruns to this mountain, with additional chair lifts toward the summit and the ski areas near the Kapelljoch. There is good skiing for beginner and intermediate levels.

Bartholomäberg. This quiet village occupies a sunny balcony on the slope north of Schruns. It affords a good though distant view of the Rätikon, which appears as a long line of peaks, and of the Zimba (2,643 m/8,671 ft), known as the "Montafoner Matterhorn," because of its pointed top.

Silbertal. This tiny, peaceful village is near the mouth of the valley of the same name. At the valley's eastern end is the Verwall group of mountains. From Silbertal you can take the Kristberg cable car up the slope north of the village, and then walk east to Wasserstuben-Alpe, on the western edge of the mountains. From Silbertal you can also walk upstream along the Litz River to the little restaurant at Fellimännle, and then continue up the valley to the Untere Gafluna-Alpe, where there is a junction. The main trail continues to the right (east), to the Obere Freschhütte at the southern base of the Verwall mountains. The trail to the left (northeast) rises up the Gaflunatal, a narrow valley that cuts into the Verwall mountains, climbing to the Reutlinger Hütte below the Reutlinger Turm (2,601 m/8,533 ft). South of Silbertal village is the Hochjoch, the mountain seen from Schruns. You can climb from Silbertal to Kapellalpe on this mountain and then to a little lake, the Schwarzsee, below the summit. The trail continues southward to the Wormser Hütte.

Rätikon-Höhenweg Nord

From the Montafon, several tributary valleys rise southward into the Rätikon mountains. A trail known as the Rätikon-Höhenweg Nord extends along the base of the north slope of the mountains. Hikers can follow this trail for a few

From Bielerhöhe, a path to the Wiesbadener Hütte follows the east side of the lake and then climbs steadily upward, passing a gurgling river splashing over smooth stones. The scenery is outstanding. The hut is virtually surrounded by glaciers and mountains, including the Piz Buin, the highest peak in Austria's Silvretta Alps.

days, staying at alpine club huts along the route, or they can select one segment of the trail to walk on a day's excursion. (A parallel route on the Swiss side of the same mountains is called the Rätikon-Höhenweg Sud.)

Lünersee. This lake, almost encircled by mountains, sits below the eastern flank of the Schesaplana (2,965 m/9,728 ft), the highest peak of the Rätikon. The lake is accessible from the Brandnertal, a valley south of Bludenz. From the upper end of the valley, a cable car rises to the top of the dam wall, where the Douglasshütte is located; there is a path around the lake. Another approach to the Lünersee is from the Rellstal, a valley east of the Brandnertal. From Vandans, northwest of Schruns, an unpaved road ascends southwest up this valley to Alpe Lün, beyond which a trail continues southwest to the Lünersee. The route affords a good view of the Zimba.

Lindauerhütte. At the upper end of the Gauertal, this hut looks out on the Drei Türme, a group of three rock towers set close together (highest point: 2,830 m/9,285 ft). From Tschagguns, it is a quick drive by bus or car to the Golmerbahn chair lift in nearby Latschau, west of the town. Starting at the upper lift station a trail climbs mainly southward to the Lindauerhütte. You can continue from here to the Lünersee by a trail that leads directly west over the Ofapass and Verajöchle. This walk follows the line of the Rätikon peaks, offering a fine view of the Drei Türme and the Drusenfluh (2,827 m/ 9,275 ft). At the Verajöchle the Schesaplana comes into view to the west.

Tilisunahütte. This hut, at the upper end of the Gampadelstal, overlooks the small Tilisunasee. A trail from Tschagguns leads south to Tilisuna-Alpe, and then west to the hut. You can also reach this hut from the Lindauer hut to the west, on a segment of the Rätikon-Höhenweg Nord trail that passes between the dark igneous-metamorphic rock of the Schwarzhorn (2,460 m/ 8,071 ft) to the north, and the pale limestone of the Sulzfluh (2,818 m/9,245 ft) to the south. From Tschagguns you can also make a loop trip, passing the hut and then turning northwest past the tiny Tobelsee to Alpila, then back to Tschagguns.

The Gargellental

The narrow and densely wooded Gargellental is the longest tributary of the Montafon, an important valley for skiing and summer hiking, yet it is little developed. The valley's upper end divides the Rätikon on the west from the Silvretta group on the east, providing a visible contrast between the former's grayish white limestone and the darker igneous and metamorphic rock of the latter. An especially notable geologic feature here is the Gargellener Fenster, or "window," where erosion has exposed a section of the Pennine nappe beneath the overlying Austro-Alpine crystalline cover.

The village of Gargellen is a center for mountaineering and skiing, with several options for hikers. Although one of the region's chief resorts, with several gracious hotels, Gargellen is small and very quiet—a place without neon. The village is at the end of the valley road, so there is no through traffic. The valley here is quite narrow, with rock towers visible above. Gargellen enjoys an advantageous location, with mountains to the west, south, and east of the village. Several of the hiking trails climb to notches in the long mountainous ridge that wraps halfway around the village.

St. Antönier Joch. The largest mountain near Gargellen is the Madrisa (2,826 m/9,272 ft), whose triangular rock peak is on the Swiss side of the border (south of the mountain is the Swiss resort of Klosters). A two-section chair lift from the village climbs partway up the slope of the Schafberg, from which there is a good view of the Madrisa. Accessible from both the middle and top stations of the chair lift, a path leads north and then west to the St. Antönier Joch, a notch in the mountainous ridge that here forms the Swiss-Austrian border. (From this pass, a trail descends into Switzerland.) A mountain route continues northward from the St. Antönier Joch along the narrow ridge toward the Riedkopf, a small mountain from which there is a fine view northwest to the Sulzfluh and other peaks of the western Rätikon. You can return to Gargellen by taking the path eastward into a large bowl, the Täscher, and then descending northeast through Rongg-Alpe. Or you can return to the middle station of the Schafberg chair lift and ride down to Gargellen. From the upper lift station you can also walk south to the little Gandasee, a lake under the Madrisa's north wall.

Sarotla Pass. North of the St. Antönier Joch is the Sarotla Pass, another notch in the border ridge. From Gargellen you can walk northwest past the jagged teeth of the Röbispitzen to the pass, from which there is a view of both the Rätikon and the Silvretta.

Schlappiner Joch. The Schlappiner Joch is directly south of Gargellen, reached by a trail that follows the Valzifenzer stream before climbing to the ridge. To the south is the Swiss hamlet of Schlappin and then Klosters. This pass marks the border between the Rätikon group in the west and the Silvretta in the east; it was formerly much used by local people for crossing the border.

Gargellen has very good skiing for beginners and intermediates, and also cross-country skiing. Organized ski-mountaineering tours over the passes into Switzerland are popular excursions in late winter and early spring.

Pages 184 and 185: Near Bielerhöhe, the landscape is made up of grassy moorland interrupted occasionally by pine woods on the sides of the long valley. This is good walking country for fit, well equipped people of all ages.

The Silvretta Alps

This range is the highest section of the border between Austria and Switzerland. It has several substantial glaciers, whereas there are none in the Rätikon. The Verwall group, a set of lower mountains, closes off the valley to the north.

The Silvretta Hochalpenstrasse (Silvretta Alpine Highway), a very scenic, 25-km/15-mi toll road, provides the closest motor access to the Silvretta peaks. It links the two great valleys of the southern Vorarlberg: the Montafon Valley at the western end of the Silvretta and the Paznauntal at the range's eastern end. The road is open from approximately the end of May to late October, depending on seasonal conditions.

Toward the upper end of the Montafon Valley are two small, attractive resort villages, Gaschurn and Partenen. These villages have good skiing for all grades and cross-country skiing; they are also used as starting points for ski-mountaineering trips into the Silvretta range. The Silvretta Hochalpenstrasse begins just beyond Partenen, and extends to Galtür in the Paznaun Valley. The road climbs steeply, with many hairpin turns, above tree line to the Vermunt Valley. There the road passes two artificial lakes, the Vermunt Stausee and the Silvretta Stausee at Bielerhöhe, which is the most scenic point of the route.

The Bielerhöhe

The Bielerhöhe is the watershed between the North Sea and Black Sea, and also the border between the Austrian federal states of Vorarlberg and Tyrol. There is a restaurant and hotel, and a large parking area. Upon the lake, you can take the only boat trip in Europe above 2,000 m/6,560 ft. From the edge of the dam, there is a view of the Piz Buin (3,312 m/10,866 ft) and Silvrettahorn (3,244 m/10,643 ft) rising above their glaciers. A trail around the lake provides increasingly fine views as you approach its southern end, closer to the mountains.

The Wiesbadener Hütte. For a truly spectacular view, however, you should follow the trail beyond the lake to the Wiesbadener hut, southeast of the lake. Facing the hut is a fine sweep of mountains and glaciers, in the center of which is the Piz Buin, the highest peak in the Austrian Silvretta Alps (the highest peak in the whole chain, Piz Linard—3,411 m/11,191 ft—is entirely on the Swiss side of the border). The Swiss border extends over the summit of the Piz Buin, but this mountain presents its most dramatic face on the northern, Austrian side. The view from the Wiesbadener Hütte also includes the Silvrettahorn, Signalhorn (3,207 m/10,522 ft), and Dreiländer

Spitze (3,197 m/10,489 ft), with the Vermunt, Ochsentaler, and Schnee-glocken glaciers. There is an interesting contrast between the Ochsentaler, a hanging glacier torn into crevasses, and the smoother Vermunt-Gletscher. As this hut is quite easy to reach and the view from it excellent, it is very popular. Instead of retracing your steps to the Bielerhöhe, you can climb to the Radsattel, a very fine viewpoint northeast of the hut (on which there is often snow), then descend northeastward to the wild, lovely Bieltal and return to the Bielerhöhe.

Bieler Spitze. A path behind the hotel at Bielerhöhe climbs the grassy slope northeastward; traces of a path continue west toward the Bieler Spitze (2,506 m/8,222 ft), from which there is a panoramic view of the Silvretta Stausee framed by the Hohes Rad (2,934 m/9,626 ft) on the left and the Lobspitze (2,873 m/9,426 ft) on the right, with the Silvretta ridge and glaciers in the background.

Saarbrücker Hütte. From Bielerhöhe you can also take the trail west from the Madlenerhaus (directly west of the dam) to the Saarbrücker hut, at 2,538 m/8,327 ft the highest hut in the Silvretta group and in a very scenic location. Above the hut the Litzner glacier descends steeply from the Grosse Seehorn (3,121 m/10,240 ft) and the Grosslitzner (3,109 m/10,200 ft). From the hut you can either retrace your steps to the Bielerhöhe, or follow the jeep road directly north to the Vermunt Stausee and return by bus from there to Bielerhöhe.

The Paznauntal

Along the Paznauntal, which extends from the Vermunt northeastward to Landeck, are three small, pretty resorts: Galtür, Mathon, and Ischgl. These are neat, compact villages whose wooden houses display richly carved balconies. From the upper end of the valley there are views of the snow-streaked Silvretta, although the mountains close to the center of the Paznauntal are low. The valley contracts to a narrow gorge before emerging at Landeck and the Inn River.

Galtür and Ischgl have good cross-country skiing along the valley floor and also good alpine skiing, especially for intermediate grades. Galtür is also a starting point for ski-mountaineering tours into the Silvretta range.

Jamtal Hütte. From this hut, south of Galtür, there is a superb view south to the Jamtal Ferner, the biggest glacier in the Silvretta, and a number of peaks including the Dreiländer Spitze and, to the east, the Fluchthorn (3,399 m/11,152 ft), the second highest peak in the Silvretta. Hikers may scramble up the much lower Westlichen Gamshorn (2,987 m/9,800 ft), northeast of the hut, for a splendid panorama. From Galtür in the upper Paznaun-

A pleasant footpath wanders through alpine grassland on the hike from Bielerhöhe to the Wiesbadener Hütte.

tal you can drive up the Jamtal as far as Scheibenalpe (the road, however, is closed between 8:30 A.M. and 5 P.M.) and then follow the trail to the Jamtal hut; there is also jeep service.

Heidelberger Hütte. This hut, just across the border in Switzerland (yet owned by the German Alpine Club), is northeast of the Fluchthorn, in a scenic location. The easier approach to the hut is up the Fimbertal from Ischgl (there is also jeep service), but it can also be reached via the Laraintal, from Mathon, a village west of Ischgl. Although somewhat longer and more difficult, the Laraintal route offers a scenic view of the Larainferner, a glacier dominated by the Fluchthorn. In summer, when conditions are good, you can drive up the Fimbertal as far as Bodenalpe (the road is closed between 9 A.M. and 5 P.M.).

The Verwall Group near the Paznauntal

These mountains, lower than the Silvretta Alps, form the north wall of the Paznauntal. From Ischgl you can take the trail northwest to Madleinsee, a little tarn, for good views of the Verwall group.

As you head west from Galtür, about 1 km/0.6 mi from the Silvretta Hochalpenstrasse tollbooth, the Kopserstrasse road branches off for the Zeinisjochhaus on the Kops-Stausee. You can also hike from Galtür past the Gasthaus Kleinzeinis to this point. Alternatively, a hike eastward leads from Partenen to the Zeinisjochhaus. The Zeinisjoch is the watershed between the North and Black seas, and site of a rare geographic phenomenon. The Zeinisbach, flowing from the north, splits just before the *joch:* one branch of this brook flows into the Danube, which flows into the Black Sea; the other flows into the Rhine and then into the North Sea. From the *joch* there is a good view westward to the Versalspitze (2,462 m/8,077 ft), northward to the Fluhspitze (2,617 m/8,586 ft), and southward to the Ballunspitze (2,671 m/8,763 ft). Beyond the *joch,* the trail curves around the western edge of the Fluhspitze to Verbella-Alpe and then the Verbellener Winterjochli. A little farther is the Neue Heilbronner hut, near the little twin Scheid lakes, in which is reflected the impressive Patteriol (3,056 m/10,026 ft), one of the best-known mountains in the Verwall group, with a summit of jagged points.

ALPINE PASQUE FLOWER
Pulsatilla alpina alpina and *Pulsatilla alpina sulphurea*

There are two subspecies of this wild pasque flower that illustrate the botanical phenomenon of ecotypes. Although very closely related, the two subspecies grow on different types of soil. Subspecies *alpina*, which has a white flower whose petals may be tinged with violet on the exterior, requires a lime-rich soil and is found in the northern and southern limestone Alps; subspecies *sulphurea* (also known as *apiifolia*), which has a yellow flower, avoids limestone. These alpine pasque flowers are tufted, with short stems and feathery, dissected leaves of the sort botanists call "pinnately-compound." The flowers are solitary, white or yellow according to the subspecies, with six or seven flat petals around wide yellow centers. Their height is between 10 and 40 cm/12 and 16 in.

Top: Pulsatilla alpina alpina; *bottom:* Pulsatilla alpina sulphurea.

The Lechtal Alps

THE LECHTAL ALPS ARE the western edge of the band of limestone mountains extending across northern Austria. These gigantic forms of bare rock thrust suddenly upward from the woods and meadows, creating the contrasts of color and texture typically seen in areas of limestone mountains: silvery gray stone above green vegetation, scored surfaces and jagged edges rising from the gentler contours of fields and pastures. Richly nourished with lime, the soil produces a profusion of wildflowers. The villages of the untouristed and relatively remote Lower Lechtal share the character and charm of the Vorarlberg.

To the south is the Arlberg massif, in the center of the lower Vorarlberg. The Arlberg Pass across this massif separates the Lechtal Alps from the higher, crystalline Silvretta and Verwall groups to the south. This pass is also the watershed between the Rhine and Danube rivers. The Arlberg tunnel, under the central part of the route, allows passage across the region in winter.

There are several important ski resorts in the Arlberg area: St. Anton am Arlberg, St. Christoph am Arlberg, Zürs, and Lech. Skiers from the Arlberg played an important part in the 1920s in the development of downhill techniques; St. Anton still has a famous ski school. It is quite built-up, extending at some length along the valley. St. Christoph and Zürs, higher above the valley, are both small—each more a cluster of hotels than a village.

St. Anton

From St. Anton, the three-section Valluga cable car rises to the Valluga (2,809 m/9,216 ft)—the highest mountain of the Arlberg and Upper Lechtal Alps, with a splendid view of the region.

Leutkircher Hütte. From St. Anton, you can also take the chair lift to Kapallkopf; the trail to this hut continues north and then east, passing below the steep, rocky walls of the Weiss Schrofenspitze (2,752 m/9,029 ft). Above the hut to the northeast is the Stanskogel (2,757 m/9,045 ft), which gives the Stanzertal, the valley below, its name. From Nasserein, on the eastern edge of St. Anton, there is a different path to the same hut.

Ansbacher Hütte. From Schnann, a village near the eastern end of the Stanzertal, a steep climb northeastward brings you to the Ansbacher Hütte, at the foot of the Samspitze (2,625 m/8,612 ft). The hut, the highest in the Lechtal Alps, sits on a terrace and offers a fine view of the Verwall group.

The road north from Arlberg to Lech climbs over the Flexen Pass. Built high above the valley, the road is cut into the rock through tunnels and galleries that are open on one side.

The Upper Lechtal

Lech is an engaging year-round resort set in a broad grassy basin amid the rugged forms of the Lechtal Alps. A small river, the Lech, flows through the center of the village, bordered by a promenade decked with flowers in summer. Of all the ski resorts in the Arlberg area, Lech, although prosperous and busy, best preserves the character of a village. Its strict building code has prevented the construction of concrete boxes and six-story hotels. Most structures are built chalet-style, and some of the cable-car stations are even installed in partly wooden buildings with pitched, chalet-style roofs. Lawns and small fields still remain between hotels and houses, and meadows edge the village. In comparison, St. Anton is larger and much more densely built, while Zürs is an artificial community consisting mainly of hotels, lacking any appearance of village life. Zürs and St. Christoph are ski resorts, deserted in summer. The ski areas of Lech and Zürs are linked by lifts (this area is connected also with St. Anton by ski buses), with good skiing for all grades.

Once used merely for summer pastures, Lech was settled by the Walliser people in the thirteenth century, and strains of the Walliser dialect remain in the local speech. Its church, on which several ancient frescoes remain, was built in 1390. Lech remained a small dairy-farm community, reached only by cart roads and frequently cut off by avalanches in winter, until the construction of the Flexen Pass road between 1895 and 1900. Even then, Lech could be reached in winter only by horse-drawn sleighs; it was not until the 1930s, when powerful snowplows became available, that Lech became really accessible.

The mountains around Lech belong to a range known as the Lechquellengebirge. As is characteristic of limestone mountains, these massive outcrops of rock are scattered rather than connected in a chain. They are comparatively low, none being over 3,000 m/9,840 ft. Several lift systems provide views of the mountains and access to trails. The main cable cars are the Rüfikopfbahn and Bergbahn Oberlech (the latter climbs toward the Mohnenfluh), and the Schlegelkopf chair lift, which also rises toward the Mohnenfluh.

Lecher Gipslöcher. From Oberlech, the hamlet above Lech to the north, a trail leads up to a nature preserve and the "Lecher Gipslöcher," a strange area of conical, funnel-shaped holes caused by erosion of underlying gypsum.

Rüfikopf. The mountain directly southeast of Lech is the Rüfispitze (2,632 m/8,635 ft). From the village, a cable car rises to the Rüfikopf, a knob nearly at the top of the mountain, offering a panoramic view of the district. To the south is the Rüfispitze, its precipitous, bare gray walls eroded into towers. This is a good point from which to observe the broad, shallow, U-shaped valleys with their smooth contours, the result of successive glaciations. From

the upper cable-car station, you can walk southeast to the tiny Monzabonsee. From there it is an easy walk downhill through the meadows to Trittalpe and then to Zürs, from which you can return to Lech by bus.

Stuttgarter Hütte. This more extensive tour loops in a clockwise direction around the summit of the Rüfispitze. From the cable-car station, walk to the Monzabonjoch, near the little lake, then east to Ochsengümplemulde. The trail continues southward over a notch in the ridge called the Rauhekopfscharte to the Krabachjoch and the Stuttgarter Hütte. From the hut, descend westward through the Pazüeltal to Zürs.

Freiburger Hütte. A small road leads west of Lech through the village of Zug (toll beyond Zug), through Spullers Wald to the Formarinsee, source of the River Lech. From the lake, a trail climbs to the Freiburger Hütte, with a good view of the Rote Wand (2,704 m/8,871 ft). For a broader view, continue eastward and climb to the top of the nearby Formaletsch (2,292 m/7,520 ft). Below its southeast ridge is the Steinerne Meer, a large karst area.

Göppinger Hütte. From Zug, the village west of Lech, take the road west to Unteren Alpele (a supply lift hoists provisions and also hikers' rucksacks to the hut). The trail climbs steeply northward to the Laubegg (good view) and then northwest to the hut, in a scenic location just below the Hochlichtspitze (2,600 m/8,530 ft).

Butzensee. From Oberlech, above the west bank of the river, a path climbs past Tanegg to Unter and then Ober Gaisbühelalpe, then westward to the Mohnensattel, the notch between the Zuger Hochlicht and the Mohnenfluh (2,544 m/8,346 ft). West of this notch is the little Butzensee. From the western edge of this pretty lake, a path descends southeast past Kriegeralpe and returns to Oberlech.

Ravensburger Hütte and Spullersee. From Omesberg, at the southwestern edge of Lech, a trail leads southwest to Brazer Stafel and the Ravensburger Hütte. This hut is located between the Schafberg (2,679 m/ 8,789 ft) and the Roggalspitze (2,673 m/8,767 ft), a favorite peak for rock climbing. A little farther along this trail is the Spullersee; from the southern side of this artificial lake you may see the Silvretta peaks and glaciers. You can make this a loop trip by circling the Schafberg; from the Spullersee, continue northwest up the valley of the Spulleralpe, then join the trail eastward to Zug and Lech.

From the village of Schnann, a steep climb leads hikers to the Ansbacher Hütte, which has fine views of the Verwall mountains above the valley. Huge, almost-bare rocks rising from meadows are typical of the Lechtal Alps.

A high jagged peak presides over the valley below the trail from the Ansbacher Hütte to Flirsch.

The Lower Lechtal

Beyond Lech the valley continues northeast to the little village of Warth, then turns east and finally northeast, descending to Reutte. The lower valley is broad, gentle, and very quiet, with scattered farms and small villages little affected by tourism. These include the villages of Holzgau, Bach, and Elbigenalp, whose houses are decorated with painted scenes and baroque ornamental flourishes. The mountains seen from the valley floor are low.

Parseierspitze. At 3,036 m/9,961 ft, this is the highest point in the northern limestone Alps. It can be approached from Madau, south of the road between Holzgau and Elbigenalp. Take the trail southward up the Parseiertal past Seelealpe, with a good view of the Parseierspitze. The trail continues to the Memminger Hütte near the northern face of the mountain. From here climb to the Seekogel for a fine view to the northwest. To make this a loop trip, return by the trail that circles around the Seekogel, leading first southwest and then north to Madau.

Wetterspitze. This mountain (2,895 m/9,498 ft) is northwest of the Parseierspitze. It is reached from Sulzlbach, directly east of Holzgau. Follow the trail south to Ronigalm and then to the Frederik-Simms-Hütte at the base of the mountain.

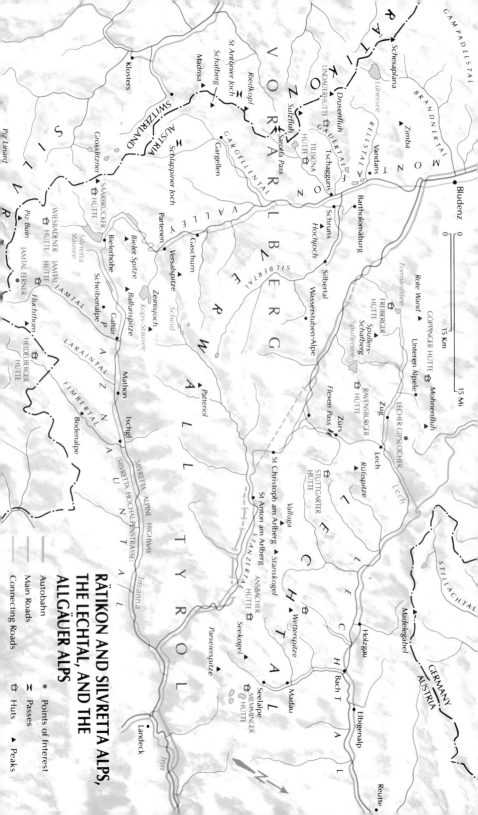

RÄTIKON AND SILVRETTA ALPS, THE LECHTAL, AND THE ALLGÄUER ALPS

Autobahn
Main Roads
Connecting Roads

• Points of Interest
✕ Passes
⛉ Huts

• Points of Interest
✕ Passes
▲ Peaks

GAMPADELSTAL
Schesaplana
BRANDNERTAL
Zimba
Lünersee
BRANDNER MONT
Bludenz
GÖPPINGER HUTTE
RELLSTAL
Vandans
Bartholomäberg
Schruns
Hochjoch
Silbertal
Wasserstuben-Alpe
SILBERBERG
Formannsee
Rote Wand
Mohnenfluh
Unteren Alpele
FREIBERGER HUTTE
Spullers-Schafberg
Spullersee
RAVENSBURGER HUTTE
LECHER GIPSLOCHER
Zug
Lech
Zürs
Rüfispitze
Flexen Pass
St Christoph am Arlberg
St Anton am Arlberg
Valluga
Stanskogel
ANSBACHER HUTTE
STUTTGARTER HUTTE
Wetterspitze
Seekogel
LECHTAL
Madelegabel
Holzgau
Bach T
Elbigenalp
GERMANY
AUSTRIA
STILLACHTAL
Madau
Seelalpe
MEMMINGER HUTTE
Parseierspitze
Reute
Inn
Landeck
Trisanna
Bodenalpe
FIMBERTAL
HEIDELBERGER HUTTE
Fluchthorn
Piz Linard
Piz Buin
WIESBADENER HUTTE
JAMTAL FERNER
JAMTAL HUTTE
LARAINTAL
Bielerhöhe
Galtür
Mathon
Ischgl
Paterrol
Scheibenalpe
Ballunspitze
Bieler Spitze
Zeinisjoch
Kops-Stausee
Silvretta Stausee
SAARBRÜCKER HUTTE
Grosslitzner
Schlappiner Joch
Partenen
Gaschurn
Versalspitze
Scheid
SILVRETTA ALPINE HIGHWAY
(SILVRETTA HOCHALPENSTRASSE)
MONTAFON
GARGELLENTAL VALLEY
Gargellen
Madrisa
Schafberg
St Antönier Joch
Rieckopf
Sulzfluh
Saroda Pass
TILISUNA HUTTE
Tschagguns
Drusenfluh
GAUERTAL
LINDAUERHUTTE
SWITZERLAND
AUSTRIA
VORARLBERG
Kloster
Klosters
VALAIS
ENGADIN
0
15 Km
15 Mi
N

The Otztal Alps

THOUGH SEVERAL PEAKS OF the Hohe Tauern are higher, the Otztal range offers the most extensive high-alpine scenery in Austria—a lavish spread of spectacular glaciers, above which rise several of Austria's best-loved mountains. At numerous viewpoints, such as the one at Hohe Mut above Obergurgl, the eye is delighted by the sparkle of snow-covered glaciers poised above lush meadows. Each of the three major valleys that penetrate these mountains offers spectacular views, as do their tributaries.

The Otztal Alps are part of the igneous-metamorphic range, Austria's highest mountains, extending across southern Austria along or near the Italian border. The region contains the greatest concentration of high mountains and glaciers in Austria. Some 200 sq km/77 sq mi are covered by glaciers—one-third of the surface area—and over 280 peaks reach 3,000 m/9,843 ft. The second highest peak in Austria, the Wildspitze, is in this group, as well as the Weisskugel, the third highest peak partly on Austrian territory (the Grossvenediger is the third highest entirely within Austrian borders).

These mountains are mostly dark, rocky pyramids that do not rise to a very great height above the glaciers that surround them, so that an alpinist may be able to climb more than one "three thousander" in a day—something generally impossible in the higher western Alps. From these mountains, the streams run northward, draining into the Inn River. Several great Tyrolean valleys—the Pitztal, Kaunertal, and Otztal—are the chief access routes into the Otztal Alps.

THE KAUNERTAL

The entrance to the Kaunertal Valley is at Prutz, along the road south of Landeck. The last village, Feichten, is only halfway up the valley. The upper end of the valley is undeveloped, culminating in the Gepatsch Stausee (or Speicher), a long artificial lake. The Gepatschhaus, at the lake's far end, faces the Gepatschferner; this is the biggest glacier of the Otztal Alps, covering an area of 29 sq km/11 sq mi, and the second largest in Austria (only the Pasterze is more extensive, although both are the same length, 9.5 km/5.9 mi). The Gletscher-Panoramastrasse (a toll road) continues to the edge of the Weiss-Seeferner, a glacier on which there is summer skiing. (There is also bus service up the road.) Above this broad expanse of ice are such peaks as the Weiss-Seespitze (3,518 m/11,542 ft), the Hinter Hintereis Spitze (3,485 m/11,434 ft), and the Hochvernagt Spitze (3,535 m/11,598 ft). Concealed behind these mountains is the Weisskugel (3,738 m/12,264 ft), over whose summit runs the Italian border.

From the Gepatschhaus, a walk southeast yields a close view of the tongue of the Gepatschferner. A much longer trail climbs steeply eastward to the Olgrubenjoch, offering a superb view over the Sexegertenferner toward the Wildspitze, Hochvernagt Spitze, and other peaks.

THE PITZTAL

The Pitztal leads to some of the finest alpine scenery in Austria. The Wildspitze (3,772 m/12,375 ft), the country's second highest mountain (also the highest in the Tyrol), is at the end of the valley, above some of its biggest glaciers.

The lower part of the valley (the Ausser Pitztal) is broad at first, with numerous villages; the principal ones are Arzl, Wenns, and Jerzens. Then the valley narrows and the slopes grow higher and steeper. The main village of the Upper or "inner" Pitztal is St. Leonhard, only slightly more than halfway up the valley. Besides its superb scenery, an attraction of the Pitztal is that the upper valley is quite undeveloped and unspoiled (except for the Wildspitze Bahn), with no large resort. Yet there are hotels, some very gracious, at several hamlets at the upper end of the valley, including Plangeross, Tieflehn, and Mandarfen.

Wildspitze

The chief tourist attraction of the Pitztal is the Wildspitze, which is now accessible via the Pitztaler Gletscherbahn. This underground funicular climbs from Mittelberg, at the end of the valley road, to the edge of the Mittelbergferner, the big glacier below the summit—a huge "snow bowl." This area is used for summer and, of course, winter skiing, offering not only alpine but also cross-country skiing almost year-round, an unusual option at an Alpine summer ski resort. At the upper funicular station there is a large restaurant with a panoramic view of the massif and its glaciers, though not of the entire chain of the Pitztal mountains. From there you can continue by cable car to the Hinterer Brunnenkogel (3,438 m/11,280 ft) near the Wildspitze summit. At this upper station there is only a tiny platform upon the glacier, but no restaurant or comfort station, the construction of which were blocked by Austrian environmentalists. The view includes the snowy mound of the nearby Wildspitze, and extends in clear weather to the Dolomites, Mont Blanc, and the mountains of northern Austria.

The Taschachtal and the Pitztal

The best way to enjoy the full panorama of mountains and beautiful glaciers above the Pitztal is to hike. There are two approaches to this high-alpine country, either southwest up the valley of the Taschach Bach, or southeast up the valley of the Pitze.

The Taschachhaus. The Taschachhaus is an alpine club hut in a spectacular location, on a grassy shoulder overlooking the sinuous Taschachferner. Two approaches lead to this hut at the upper end of the Taschachtal. One begins near the end of the Pitztal road where a broad trail, at first a jeep road, follows the course of the Taschach stream southwest through its long, U-shaped, green, and gentle valley. This is a beautiful place to see the alpenroses when they bloom in July, covering the long green slopes with masses of brilliant pink. The trail rises more steeply when it reaches the lateral moraine at the upper end of the valley, before arriving at the hut. From the Taschach-

RUSTY ALPENROSE
Rhododendron ferrugineum

The rusty alpenrose produces an effect like heather on the Scottish moors: when the shrub is in bloom, the alpine slopes burst into color. The flower of this small, wild rhododendron is a brilliant cherry-pink, which blazes against the bright green mead-ows. Because it grows in masses, sometimes covering large areas, the slopes appear dotted with vivid pink—an incomparable sight.

The plant's bell-shaped flowers have five petals and are almost at right angles to the stem. The small, oval leaves are shiny, smooth, and dark green above, yellowish-brown below.

The rusty alpenrose flowers mainly in July on high meadows and also in lightly wooded areas. They prefer a lime-free soil, and grow at altitudes between 1,000 and 2,500 m/ 3,280 and 8,202 ft. A very similar dwarf species, the hairy alpenrose *(Rhododendron hirsutum)*, is found on limestone-based soil.

Gentle weather in July brings the lovely blooms of the alpenrose to the Tyrolean meadows of the northern Otztal valley.

haus you can walk a little farther south to a point directly above the ice; climbers can descend to the glacier and continue toward the Wildspitze or one of the other mountains of the Weisskamm, the long ridge of which it forms a part: this includes the Hinter Broch Kogel (3,628 m/11,903 ft) and the Petersenspitze (3,482 m/11,424 ft). The close proximity of the mountains results in a very impressive view. The snout of the glacier, descending steeply to the upper valley, is torn into jagged crevasses and séracs.

Another approach to the Taschachhaus is via the Riffelsee, a little tarn above the western slope of the Pitztal. From Mandarfen a chair lift rises to the lake, in a hollow ringed by bare, steep slopes; the scene is dominated by the Seekogel (3,357 m/11,014 ft). The Riffelsee hut is above the lake, to the southeast. From here, hikers can pick up the Fuldaer Höhenweg, a trail that leads southwest to the Taschachhaus, following the folds of the slope, with several unbridged stream crossings.

Braunschweiger Hütte. From Mittelberg in the Pitztal, cross the bridge and take the trail along the right bank of the Pitze, southeastward through the narrowing valley. The trail ascends past a fine waterfall and over a steep, rocky step, in view of the icefall of the Mittelbergferner, then turns mainly east for the hut. The view is superb, extending across the great glacier to the Wildspitze and the Weisser Kogel (3,407 m/11,178 ft). Like the Taschach hut, the Braunschweiger is used for ascents of the Wildspitze, as well as for numerous glacier excursions.

There are also several fine hikes from the sides of the valley.

Kaunergrathütte. This is one of the highest huts in the region (it is sometimes possible to have your rucksack sent up on the supply lift). To reach it from the hamlet of Plangeross, follow a steep path westward along the left bank of the Lussbach. The route continues along the edge of the moraine and up a scree slope to the hut, in a splendid location close to the imposing Watzespitze (3,532 m/11,588 ft), which is nearly encircled by small glaciers.

Neue Chemnitzer Hütte. From Plangeross a trail climbs eastward along the right bank of the Kitzlesbach to reach this hut, near the base of the Hohe Geige (3,393 m/11,132 ft). There is also a superb view of the crown of the Kaunergrat, the cluster consisting of the Watzespitze and Verpeilspitze (3,423 m/11,230 ft) and their glaciers, across the Pitztal.

THE OTZTAL

There is much more development in this valley than in the neighboring Pitztal, with several large resort villages, principally Umhausen, Längenfeld, Sölden, and Obergurgl.

Umhausen

South of Oetz is Umhausen. Directly southeast of the village, near the road to Niederthal, is the Stuiben waterfall, which drops 140 m/459 ft in two sections: this is the highest waterfall in the Tyrol.

Längenfeld

Längenfeld is both the largest village in the valley and the lowest one from which there is an approach into the high mountains. There are 40 km/25 mi of cross-country ski trails connecting Längenfeld with Huben to the south and Gries to the east. A special "Länglaufbus" transports cross-country skiers between Längenfeld and Sölden.

Gries

The hamlet of Gries is partway up the narrow Sulztal east of Längenfeld. You can drive or take the bus to Gries, from which there are several possibilities.

Gamskogel. Head south to Nisslalm and then southwest to reach the summit of the Gamskogel (2,813 m/9,229 ft). The last stretch involves scrambling over some boulders; however, the view is a fine one, including the nearby Schrankogel (3,497 m/11,473 ft), the Hohe Geige, across the Otztal to the west, and even the Wildspitze.

Amberger Hütte. From Gries, follow the trail southeast up the valley past Vordere Sulztalalm to Hintere Sulztalalm and the Amberger Hütte, above a small pool with warm sulfur water. The hut is below the west face of the Schrankogel; the mountain's glaciers, however, are on its eastern side. Another trail continues directly south from the hut past Lausbühel to the snout of the big Sulztalferner, below a cirque including the Wilde Leck (3,359 m/11,020 ft), Windacher Daunkogel (3,348 m/10,984 ft), and the Westlische Daunkogel (3,301 m/10,830 ft).

Winnebachseehütte. From Gries a trail leading northeast along the right bank of the Winnebach climbs steeply to the Winnebachseehütte. The hut is in a scenic location next to a small tarn at the edge of the Stubai Alps. In an arc surrounding it are the Breiter Grieskogel (3,287 m/10,784 ft), the Seeblaskogel (3,235 m/10,614 ft), and the Gaislehnkogel (3,216 m/10,551 ft), with several small glaciers.

Pages 202 and 203: Not far from Winkle, a seasonal waterfall cascades from a verdant ridge on the east side of the Otztal valley.

Sölden

A center for hikers and downhill and cross-country skiers, Sölden is linked by cable car to Hochsölden, a higher ski resort above the west slope of the valley (hotels only, no village). There is good skiing for all grades.

Gaislacher Kogel. This mountain (3,056 m/10,026 ft; spelled Geislacher on some maps) is the easternmost point of the Weisskamm, the grand ridge of mountains and glaciers of which the Wildspitze is the crown. From Sölden a two-section cable car travels to the summit of this mountain. Until the construction of the Pitztaler Gletscherbahn, this was Austria's highest cable car. The view shows the Stubai Alps, including the Zuckerhütl, as well as the big Otztal mountains to the south. Experienced hikers can also climb to the top of this mountain. From the southern edge of Sölden, and also from Bodenegg, in the lower Ventertal, there are paths to Gaislach Alm. From there a trail climbs west, then north and west again to the scenic little Gaislachersee.

Rettenbach Ferner. A drive from Sölden up the Rettenbachtal leads to the edge of the Rettenbach glacier, beneath the Pitztaler Jöchl. This road, which reaches 2,800 m/9,186 ft, is Austria's highest "Alpenstrasse." A 1.7-km/1.4-mi tunnel (at 2,800 m/9,186 ft, the highest road tunnel in Europe) connects the Rettenbach and Tiefenbach glaciers; the two glacier areas are also connected by ski lifts. There is skiing on the glacier (including cross-country) from May to December. Nonskiers can ride up to the Rettenbachjoch by chair lift for the view of the Wildspitze.

The Windachtal

East of Sölden the Windachtal rises into the Stubai Alps. Some of the finest of those Alps are accessible to climbers by going above the Windachtal north and east.

Hochstubai Hütte. From Granbichl, on the eastern edge of Sölden, follow the path that first leads eastward up the Windachtal, but turn off soon to the northeast for Kleble Alm. The trail climbs steeply northward to the pretty Laubkarsee. From the Laubkarscharte, a notch in the ridge, it continues eastward (there may be snow here), rising over a stretch of boulders to the Hochstubai Hütte. Facing the hut are the Wütenkarferner and Windacher Daunkogel. Another short climb of only 40 m/131 ft to the south brings you to the top of the Höhen Nebelkogel (3,213 m/10,541 ft), a good viewpoint for the Stubai and Otztal Alps.

Hildesheimer Hütte. From Granbichl, take the path that leads up the Windachtal along the right bank of the stream, past the Fieglhütte. (Or you can get a ride by jeep from Sölden to Fiegl.) At the junction that follows, turn left (northeast) and climb the steep Aschenbrenner Weg for the Hildesheimer hut (rucksacks can be transported via the supply lift). The hut is beautifully sited—it faces the Pfaffen glacier and the Zuckerhütl—and is used for ascents of this mountain.

Below Sölden, at Zwieselstein, the valley forks. The Gurglertal heads almost directly south, while the Ventertal takes a more southwesterly course.

THE VENTERTAL

The Ventertal is cut below the eastern wall of the Weisskamm, the grand massif that includes the Wildspitze. This lovely valley is distinguished not only for its proximity to some of the great mountains and glaciers of the Otztal Alps, but also for its undeveloped, unspoiled condition. It has none of the major cable-car systems that often attract tourists for a day's outing, nor is there a single large resort in the valley, although comfortable accommodations are available. At the valley's upper end is the quiet, simple village of Vent, a center for mountaineering, hiking, and ski-mountaineering tours. At Vent the valley forks again—southwest to the Rofental, and south to the Niedertal (also called the Spiegeltal). Near the entrance to the Rofental is the hamlet of Rofenhöfe. Some of the most scenic huts in the Otztal Alps are found above the Ventertal.

Vent is associated with the memory of Franz Senn, the "glacier priest," a native of the Otztal who served as curate of Vent from 1860 to 1872. A founder of the German Alpine Club, Senn fostered the development of Alpine climbing in many ways. He encouraged local farmers to become Alpine guides (in which he resembled an earlier alpinist-priest, the Swiss Johann Josef Imseng), and he was also instrumental in the building of many huts. Before any hotels existed in the valley, alpinists who came to climb in the Otztal Alps were welcomed at his house.

Breslauer Hütte and Vernagthütte.   These two huts are both above the north slope of the Rofental, and the hike to them may be combined. To reach the Breslauer Hütte, you can begin by using the chair lift from Vent to Stablein (rucksacks may be transported from Rofen). From there, the trail climbs mainly westward, traversing the steep slope of the Rofenkar, with a dramatic view of the steep, crevassed Rofenkar glacier. The Breslauer Hütte, at the base of the Otztaler Urkund (3,554 m/11,660 ft), is used for ascents of the Wildspitze and other nearby peaks. From the hut, there is a superb view of the Ramolkamm, the ridge of mountains and glaciers separating the Ventertal and Gurgltal. To continue to the Vernagthütte, take the lower of the two routes that proceed beyond the Breslauer Hütte (the upper one leads

A modest hike in the Pitztal mountains leads to Taschachhaus and the nearby Taschachferner (glacier) and ice-fall. Facing page: Stone steps form part of the path to Taschachhaus, which was originally built in 1874, the third German Alpine Club hut built in Austria.

to the Wildspitze). This trail heads mainly southwest, following the folded contours of the slope, before climbing to the Vernagthütte. On the north side of the hut is the splendid, broad Grosser Vernagtferner; on the west is the Guslarferner. The major peaks above these glaciers are the Fluchtkogel (3,497 m/11,473 ft) and the Hochvernagt Spitze (3,535 m/11,598 ft); the hut is used for climbs of these peaks, among others (rucksacks may be sent up from Rofenalpe).

To descend to Vent, it is not necessary to return to the Breslauer Hütte. Where the trail to that hut crosses the Vernagtbach, you can take a trail down to Rofenhöfe, then walk back to Vent.

Hochjochhospiz. A path from Vent through Rofenhöfe continues up to the end of the Rofental, along the left bank of the Rofenache. The Hochjoch-hospiz is above this bank of the stream, with very fine views of the snowy mass of the Weisskugel (3,738 m/12,264 ft; the second highest peak in the Otztal Alps), the Langtauferer Spitze (3,528 m/11,575 ft), and the Hinter Hintereis Spitze, all on the Italian border.

Martin-Busch-Haus (Samoarhütte). From Vent, the path to this hut leads up the Niedertal, along the left bank of the Niedertalbach. The hut has a very scenic location below the tongues of three glaciers—the Marzell, Mutmal, and Schalf. Above the hut to the east is the Schalfkogel (3,537 m/11,604 ft); to the south is the Mutmal Spitze (3,522 m/11,555 ft), and behind it the border ridge, topped by the Hintere Schwärze (3,624 m/11,890 ft) and the Similaun (3,599 m/11,808 ft), among other peaks. The Niederjoch, a notch in this ridge, is an old pass route. Farmers across the border in Italy, in what was formerly the South Tyrol, still have grazing rights in the Ventertal and in the spring may drive their sheep across the Niederjoch to the meadows of Vent, then drive them home again in autumn. To the west of the Martin-Busch-Haus, near the track to the Kreuz Spitze, is the little Brizzisee (Samoar See), a lake with a beautiful view of mountains and glaciers.

THE GURGLERTAL

Below Zwieselstein, this upper end of the Otztal continues almost directly south into the mountains and glaciers of the eastern edge of the Otztal Alps. There are three resorts in the Gurglertal. Midway up the valley is the moderately priced Untergurgl, offering a concentration of vacation apartments. Obergurgl, near the upper end of the valley, is an important ski resort, smaller than Sölden and with excellent hotels. On its main street is a large silvery ball, a model of the "Stratosphere," a high-altitude research balloon flown by the physicist Auguste Piccard, who made an emergency landing on the Gurgler glacier above the village in 1931. Hochgurgl, fairly high above the eastern slope of the valley, consists entirely of hotels. Above Hochgurgl is the toll road to the Timmelsjoch, a pass to Italy (closed in winter).

Ramolhaus. From the southern end of Obergurgl, the trail to this hut leads southwest up the valley, above the left bank of the Gurgler Ache. The route traverses the slope, winding around its many folds. The hut is perched on a rocky shoulder above the tongue of the Gurgler Ferner, with a commanding view of this great glacier and the mountains around it. Above the hut are the three peaks of the Ramolkogel (3,549 m/11,643 ft) and to the south is the Schalfkogel.

Hohe Mut. This is one of the finest viewpoints above Obergurgl. From the southern end of the village, you can walk or take the two-stage chair lift to Hohe Mut, the high crest of land extending between the Gaisbergtal and the Rotmoostal, southeast of the village. From this point there is a view of two almost contiguous but quite different glaciers, the Gaisberg, narrower and steeper, with a high snowy wall at its back, and the wider, gentler Rotmoos. Above the Gaisbergferner are the Liebener Spitze (3,399 m/11,152 ft) and the Hochfirst (3,403 m/11,165 ft), while those above the Rotmoosferner include the Heuflerkogel (3,238 m/10,623 ft) and Scheiberkogl (3,133 m/10,279 ft). The Rotmoostal is a deep, wide, U-shaped valley. In summer, herds of Otztaler Haflinger, ponies in shades of chestnut with blond manes and tails,

Long grassy slopes descend to cliffs above the rushing waters of a gorge near Vent in the Otztal mountains.

are set loose to graze in its meadows. From Obergurgl (between the two sections of the chair lift) you can walk southeastward up the Gaisbergtal to the edge of the Gaisbergferner. To the east is the Granatenkogel, a mountain on which garnets have been found. From the Hohe Mut you can walk down to that point, or southeast to the moraine above the Rotmoosferner. From the Schönweishütte you can also walk southeast along the Rotmoostal to reach the same point.

Schönweishütte and Langtalareckhütte (Karlsruher Hütte). You can walk from Obergurgl south to the Schönwieshütte by following the path up the Rotmoostal and then turning right (west); using the Gaisberg chair lift shortens this walk a little. You can also take the upper chair lift to Hohe Mut, then walk down. From the Schönwies, continue southwest to the Langtalareckhütte (Karlsruher Hütte) and a view of the Gurgler Ferner.

Hochwildehaus. To reach this hut, take the route past the Schönwies to the Langtalareck hut. Then cross the bridge over the stream from the Langtalerferner, one of the glaciers descending from the Hohe Wilde (3,480 m/ 11,417 ft) on the Italian border. The route continues steeply up a rocky rib— there are passages with a few fixed cables requiring some care—to reach the lateral moraine of the Gurgler Ferner. The Hochwildehaus is magnificently located directly above this long, broad glacier, facing the Schalfkogel across the opposite bank; the peaks of the border ridge rise to the south.

The Stubai Alps

THE STUBAI ALPS, which adjoin the eastern edge of the Otztaler Alps, are part of the long range of the Austrian central Alps extending across the southern part of the country. Like their neighbors in the Otztal, they embody a high-alpine landscape, with tumbling glaciers wedged between dark, rugged peaks. The Stubaital is a tributary valley of the Wipptal, which connects the valley of the Inn River with the Brenner Pass, Austria's main link with Italy. An additional attraction of the Stubaital is this very convenient location: it can be reached within an hour from Innsbruck, the capital of the Tyrol. Indeed, many skiers and hikers use this magnificent old town of baroque houses and gabled roofs, fine restaurants and charming wine cellars, as a base for day excursions into the Stubai Alps. At Innsbruck's Alpine Zoo, you can observe at leisure many of the rare birds it may be difficult to sight in the mountains, as well as the major alpine animals.

The Stubai Alps are big mountains, like the other sections of the Austrian central Alps, mainly over 3,000 m/9,840 ft high. They are composed of igneous and metamorphic rocks such as granite, schist, and gneiss; however, some of the mountains near the eastern end of the valley (the Elfer, Serles, and Kalkkögel) are limestone. The near conjunction of these two major kinds of rock in one valley is unusual.

There are five villages along the Stubaital. Heading southwest up the valley, these are Schönberg, Milders, Telfes, Fulpmes, and Neustift. None is a flashy resort; all are neat, comfortable villages. Franz Senn, the "glacier priest" who introduced and promoted alpinism in these mountains, spent his last years in Neustift, still a pretty place with traditional wood chalets set amid little farms. He died there in 1884 and is buried next to the village church.

Farther up the valley, at the hamlet of Milders, there is a junction. The branch to the north is the Oberbergtal; the major branch, on the south, is the Unterbergtal, which climbs past Ranalt to the base of the great Stubai glacier and the station for the Stubaier Gletscherbahn.

The Oberbergtal

Franz-Senn-Hütte. From Milders, the road goes as far as Oberissalm and the Oberisshütte. You can drive to this point, or take a taxi-bus from Neustift. From Oberiss, you can have your rucksack sent up to the hut by the supply lift, though the ascent to the hut is short and easy. It follows the left bank of the Alpeiner Bach, across meadows and then over a steeper, rocky stretch.

From the Franz-Senn-Hütte it is possible to follow the same trail farther upstream, southwest, to the moraine of the Alpeiner Ferner, southwest of the hut. This substantial glacier is enfolded within a mountainous crest including the Schwarzenbergspitze Westliche (3,378 m/11,083 ft) and the Ruderhofspitze (3,474 m/11,398 ft). Another trail from the hut leads directly west to the Rinnensee, a small tarn set among great boulders, with a view of the Ruderhofspitze. Beyond the lake, a steep, rocky trail climbs to the Rinnennieder, a notch in the ridge bordering the Lüsenser Ferner. Another route from the Rinnensee, slightly to the north and involving some scrambling, climbs the Rinnenspitze (3,000 m/9,840 ft), overlooking the same glacier.

The Unterbergtal

A number of huts are positioned at the base of the mountains that wrap around this valley, the heart of the Stubaital.

Neue Regensburger Hütte. The trail starts behind Cafe Knoflach at Falbeson, just before Ranalt as you head up the valley. The route climbs very steeply northwest up the Falbesontal. Splendidly positioned in a high, wild valley between the long Pfandlspitze ridge and the Kraülspitze and Knotenspitze peaks, the hut offers views up the valley toward the Hochmoos glacier, the Ruderhof, Kraülspitze (3,416 m/11,207 ft), and Knotenspitze (3,292 m/10,801 ft). For a closer perspective, continue southwest past the hut to the little Falbesoner See, keeping above the boggy area near the stream. This small lake is below the rock walls of the east side of the Kraülspitze, near the edge of the moraine of the Hochmoosferner, with the Ruderhofspitze at its back.

Experienced hikers can make a two-day tour linking the Regensburger Hütte and the Franz-Senn-Hütte. A bus from Neustift stops at the trail to the Regensburger Hütte; from this hut the trail climbs steeply northeast and then north over ledges to Schrimmennieder. The route continues over this notch, descending to the north through a narrow fold called the Platzengrube, with only traces of path, and finally turns westward, rounding the spur of the Gschwenzgrat. This section of the trail, not steep but rather exposed, descends to the Franz-Senn-Hütte.

Stubaier Gletscherbahn. This two-stage cable-car system begins at the end of the Unterbergtal road. The first stage rises to the Dresdner Hütte just below the glacier; the view here is limited. The second stage travels to the Eisgrat at the edge of the Schaufelferner, the glacier that spreads in front of the Stubaier Wildspitze (3,340 m/10,958 ft) and the Schaufelspitze (3,333 m/10,935 ft). There is summer skiing on this broad glacier. It is also possible to walk up toward the Eisjoch (3,149 m/10,331 ft), a notch between the two

mountains mentioned just above; the route, next to the ski slopes, is marked by ropes. The top station is on the glacier where the view of the mountains opens out. The most extensive view is from the Eisjoch; the nearby snow-covered summit of the Schaufelspitze dominates the view to the east, the Schussgrubenkogel (3,211 m/10,535 ft) is close by to the south, and the Zuckerhütl rises to the southeast. In the distance is a great spread of mountains and valleys.

Peiljoch. From the Dresdner Hütte there is a very scenic but strenuous route over the Peiljoch to the Sulzenauhütte. It climbs steeply eastward along a scree slope, on which there are some fixed cables. At a junction, bear right—south and then southeast rather than east—to reach the Peiljoch (Beiljoch on some maps), a notch in the long, rocky ridge closing off the Fernautal to the east. A superb view opens up of the Sulzenauferner, a big swell of ice dramatically ripped into crevasses as it tilts downhill in a pronounced icefall. Above the Sulzenau glacier is the Zuckerhütl (3,505 m/ 11,499 ft), the biggest mountain in the Stubai Alps entirely upon Austrian territory. The next peak to the east is the Wilder Pfaff (3,457 m/11,342 ft)—the "wild priest," one of several features here bearing a clerical tag (the Pfaffenferner and Pfaffensattel are two other examples). The trail traverses

Sentinels in a land of bleak moraines, rock markers at the top of the hike to the Sulzenauhütte look down to a magnificent sweep of glacier. Facing page: Several pretty lakes can be found on the hike from the Sulzenauhütte to the Nürnberger Hütte. The trail is rocky and difficult, but the views are spectacular.

a knife-edge ridge of the moraine and descends steeply to a grassy terrace and the Sulzenauhütte.

Sulzenauhütte. About 6 km/3.8 mi up the valley beyond Ranalt, on the south side of the road, is Graba (Grawa on some maps) Alm, near the Graba waterfall. The trail climbs mainly south to the Sulzenau Alm, where the valley widens to a broad meadow around a braided stream. At the end of the meadow is a big rock cirque, streaked with waterfalls. There is a striking contrast between the alpine scene above the cliff, a monochromatic world of black rock and snow, and the soft green slopes below, especially lovely in July when blooming with pink alpenroses. The trail bends west for a final steep climb around this cliff to reach the hut. Continue a short distance west and south to reach the Blaue Lacke, a blue tarn near the edge of the Sulzenauferner.

East of the hut, on the way to Niederl, the lovely Grünausee faces the Wilde Freiger Ferner; above this glacier to the south is the snow-topped Wilde Freiger (3,419 m/11,217 ft), one of the highest mountains of the Stubai Alps.

Nürnberger Hütte. The trail begins about 1 km/0.6 mi up the valley beyond Ranalt and heads south up the Langental. It passes the Besuchalm, climbing steadily and sometimes steeply up the west slope of the valley to reach the hut. To the west is a long ridge topped by the Urfallsspitze (2,808 m/9,213 ft) and the Maierspitze (2,781 m/9,124 ft); to the south is the Grüblerferner, a broad glacier descending from the peaks along the Italian border: the greatest of these are the Roter Grat (3,098 m/10,164 ft), Hochgrindl (3,035 m/9,957 ft), and the Feuerstein peaks (3,267 m/10,719 ft).

The Stubaier Höhenweg

This is a classic Austrian hut-to-hut tour (for very experienced and properly equipped hikers) around the Stubai Alps: Day 1. From Fulpmes or Neustift to the Starkenburger-Hütte and Franz-Senn-Hütte. 2. Franz-Senn-Hütte—Dresdner Hütte. 3. Dresdner Hütte—Sulzenauhütte—Nürnberger Hütte. 4. Nürnberger Hütte—Bremer Hütte—Innsbrucker Hütte. From Pinnistal return to Neustift. (The route is the reverse of the one described below for reaching the Innsbrucker Hütte.) Much of this route is covered during the Stubaital International Alpen Relay Marathon. The distance for men's teams is 120 km/75 mi; the shorter course for women is 60 km/38 mi.

Habicht and Serleskamm

The Stubaital is the only valley in the Tyrol with both crystalline (igneous and metamorphic) and limestone mountains. This unusual conjunction is found in two nearby groups of mountains along the south side of the valley. The

Serleskamm is a ridge of limestone mountains including the peaks of the Serles (Waldrastspitze), Kirchdachspitze, and Ilmspitze, while the nearby Habicht and its group are mostly granite and gneiss. Yet the Elferspitze, at the northern edge of the Habicht group, is limestone.

The Serleskamm and the Habicht group separate the Stubaital from the Gschnitztal, the valley directly to the south. There is access to these mountains from both the Stubaital and Gschnitztal. The Pinnistal rises southwest from the Stubaital, forming the cleft between the Habicht group and the Serleskamm.

Innsbrucker Hütte. This hut can be reached from either the Stubaital or from the Gschnitztal (see below). From Neder, between Fulpmes and Neustift, walk or take a taxi-bus to Pinnisalm at Kirchschoassen, near the upper end of the Pinnistal. You can also reach this point by taking the Elfer chair lift from Neustift and walking south to reach Pinnisalm. From there, a trail heads southwest past Karalm to the hut, located at the Pinnisjoch, the saddle between the massive Habicht (3,277 m/10,751 ft) and the Kalkwand (2,564 m/8,412 ft), at the southern tip of the Serleskamm. Above the hut is the eastern face of the Habicht, topped by the Mischbachferner—this is the steepest glacier climb in the eastern Alps. There is also a good view of the Tribulaun (3,096 m/10,157 ft) to the south.

To reach this hut from the Gschnitztal, take the trail about 0.5 km/0.3 mi west of the village of Gschnitz. It climbs steeply west and northwest over the meadows, then contours along the south wall of the Kalkwand, at a gentler gradient, to reach the hut.

Bremer Hütte. The route begins at the end of the Gschnitztal road, near Gasthof Feuerstein. From there, walk southwest farther up the valley (or take a taxi-bus) to Laponesalm. The path continues southwest; to the right (north) are the ridges of the Rötenspitze (2,982 m/9,783 ft) and the Ausser Wetterspitze (3,072 m/10,079 ft); to the left are the mountains along the Italian border, including the Pflerscher Pinggl (2,766 m/9,075 ft), Weisswandspitze (3,018 m/9,902 ft), and Schafkampspitze (3,010 m/9,875 ft). The trail continues past the little Simmingsee to the hut, which lies between the Inner Wetterspitze (3,064 m/10,052 ft) and the Simmingerferner. A short distance north is the pretty Lauterer See, between the two Wetterspitze peaks.

Kalkkögel

This is a kidney-shaped ridge of limestone mountains on the north side of the Stubaital, between Neustift and Fulpmes.

Schlicker Seespitze. From Fulpmes take the Froneben chair lift, then walk westward to Schlicker Alm. Continue southwest to the Schlicker Scharte,

The Nederbach flows through the small village of Wald toward Kühtai and into the Längental reservoir.

a saddle between the Hoher Burgstall (2,611 m/8,566 ft) and the larger mountainous ridge that includes the Schlicker Seespitze. The southernmost peak of the Kalkkögel, its silvery gray, craggy rock walls are typical of limestone mountains. At a junction here turn right (northwest) to approach the base of the Schlicker Seespitze (2,804 m/9,199 ft) and the Seejöchl. A left turn at the aforementioned junction leads south past the Hoher Burgstall to the Starkenburger Hütte.

Starkenburger Hütte. This hut is close to Neustift, on the high meadows northwest of the village, and near the base of the Hoher Burgstall. It is often used as the starting or end point of a tour of the huts that half encircle the Stubaital.

There is cross-country skiing along the valley between Neustift and Falbeson. Besides the glacier ski area on the Schaufelferner, there are downhill slopes near Fulpmes.

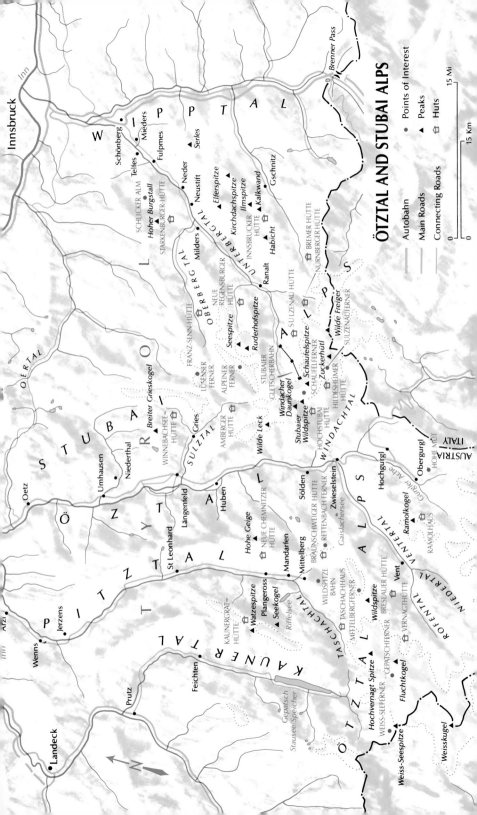

The Karwendel Group

THIS SECTION OF THE northern limestone Alps consists of four mountainous ridges, extending west to east between the Inn River and the German border. A fifth, smaller cluster lies a few kilometers within German territory. The Karwendel group shares the characteristics of the great band of limestone mountains stretching across northern Austria and parts of southern Germany: these pale gray mountains are steep and rugged, with a notched, pointed profile. Although lower than the Alps of southern Austria and lacking glaciers and snowcaps, their jagged outline and large surfaces of exposed, scored, and fissured rock are impressive and contrast pleasingly with the green forests and meadows in the valleys below.

Innsbruck

The long wall towering above Innsbruck, the famous "Nordkette," is actually the southern strip of the Karwendel group. In successive bands toward the north are the Gleirsch-Halltalkette, the Hinterautal-Vomperkette (the highest of the four chains), and the Nördliche Karwendelkette (the German border runs along its spine). The smaller Soiern group is on the German side of the border. The Karwendel rock is primarily Wetterstein limestone.

Mittenwald and the Karwendelspitze. To reach the edge of the Nordkette from Innsbruck, take the two-stage Hafelekar cable car. Walking at the top is limited, however, as you are soon in the zone of rock. The most attractive entrances to the Karwendel are from its western or northern side. On the west, Mittenwald (in Germany) is a charming little town with a spectacular location. Above its baroque houses, whose façades are painted with tableaux of both religious and secular scenes, towers the western Karwendelspitze (2,385 m/7,825 ft). A cable car swings visitors nearly to the summit, the ride itself giving dramatic close-up views of the great silver-gray wall, the limestone eroded into pillars and fissures. The vista from the top looks along the jagged ridgeline of the Nördliche Karwendel group and into the deep valley of the Karwendeltal. In places you can see how the rock strata were pushed into an almost vertical position.

Eng

Another approach from Germany takes you into the heart of the Karwendel. A secondary road extends between Wallgau, a small town north of Mittenwald, and the Sylvenstein Stausee, a reservoir just off the road between

Bad Tolz and the Austrian border. About midway between Wallgau and the lake is the hamlet of Vorderiss, from which a road extends southward up the Risstal to Hinteriss and the Karwendel region. Between Wallgau and Vorderiss the road is private (toll); another toll must be paid to drive south from Hinteriss. The road continues alongside the lovely Rissbach to Eng, a beautifully located hamlet in broad meadows below a curving wall of pale gray, rugged mountains. From the Risstal several valleys rise into the mountains, so that there are walking routes from various points along this road, on which there is also bus service. From west to east, these valleys are the Rohntal, Tortal, Johannestal, Laliderertal, and Engtal; the last three connect with the Karwendeltal, so you can link two walks together or walk to Scharnitz (see below).

The Rohntal and Rappenspitze. From Hinteriss, a track leads westward up the valley to Rohntalalm, with a good view of the Ostliche Karwendelspitze. You can continue westward up a stony ridge to the summit of the Rappenspitze (1,835 m/6,120 ft) for a fine view of the northern Karwendel chain and of the Soiern group northward over the border.

The Tortal. The trail starts about 0.5 km/0.3 mi south of Hinteriss, proceeding southward up the valley to Tortal Niederleger. Above is the Torwände, the cliffs at the base of the Lackenkarkopf (2,413 m/7,917 ft). You can continue mainly westward toward the Tortal Hochleger, near the base of the Ostliche Karwendelspitze.

The Johannestal and the Laliderertal. The walks up these two neighboring valleys can easily be linked. The entrance to the Johannestal Valley is about 3 km/1.9 mi along the road south of Hinteriss. Cross the bridge and head south up the valley along the Johannesbach to the meadows of the Kleiner Ahornboden, beautifully situated at the foot of the Birkkar (2,749 m/9,019 ft; the highest mountain in the Karwendel group) and Kaltwasserkar Spitzen (2,733 m/8,967 ft). To reach the Laliderertal turn left (southeast); this very scenic trail leads past Ladizalm to the Falkenhütte, providing a fine view of the Laliderer Spitze (2,582 m/8,471 ft). The path continues to Hohljoch, passing below the Lalidererwände, the splendid rock wall linking the Laliderer and the Dreizinken-Spitze (2,602 m/8,537 ft). From Hohljoch, follow the trail to Laliders-Niederleger, and then northward up the Laliderertal to the main road, about 4 km/2.5 mi east of the starting point up the Johannestal.

The Engtal. From Engalm, at the upper end of the Engtal road, an easy path leads west to Hohljoch. Retrace your steps home or return via the Laliderertal. From Engalm you can also take the trail southeast to the Lamsenjochhütte, in a narrow gap between the Lamsenspitze (2,508 m/ 8,228 ft) and the wall of the Schafjöchl.

The pleasant Karwendel walk from Engalm to Hohljoch passes through lush green forests below bare rocky mountains.

Scharnitz

Scharnitz is a small Austrian town near the German border, south of Mittenwald. It is the entry point for two of the major valleys of the Karwendel region, both leading eastward. The northernmost of the two is the Karwendeltal; to the south is the Hinterautal. The Karwendeltal separates the Northern from the Hinterautal Karwendel group; the Hinterautal separates the group of that name from the Gleirsch (Gleierisch on some maps) one.

Karwendelhaus. From Scharnitz, you can walk up the Karwendeltal as far as you wish. Follow the small road eastward out of town, along the Isar River, and turn left (northeast) at the junction for the Karwendeltal, Larchetalm and Karwendelhaus. Past the Karwendelhaus, this trail connects with the one to the Johannestal; continuing still farther eastward it merges with the trails to the Laliderertal or to the Engtal. The Karwendelhaus is magnificently sited on a rocky spur above the valley meadows: above the hut rise the Odkarspitze (2,743 m/8,999 ft) and the west face of the Birkkarspitze (2,749 m/9,019 ft); on the opposite side of the valley is the Ostliche Karwendelspitze.

The Hinterautal. Walk eastward from Scharnitz as for the Karwendeltal, but at the junction continue to the right (east) for Scharnitzalm and Gasthof Wiesenhof. You can continue eastward up this valley along the right bank of the Isar stream. The midsection of the valley is broader than the Karwendeltal, but a long ridge divides the eastern end of the valley into two narrow strips. From Kasten you can continue up either one. The valley to the north, the Rossloch, terminates in a big cirque of rock and scree, scooped out below the Hochkanzel (2,575 m/8,448 ft) and the Lalider, Dreizinken, and Grubenkar Spitzen (2,661 m/8,730 ft). The valley to the south is the Lafatschertal; midway up this valley is the Hallerangerhaus, scenically located below the towering rock masses of the Speckkarspitze (2,621 m/8,599 ft). Farther eastward up this valley is the Bettelwurf (2,725 m/8,940 ft), the highest mountain in the Gleirsch-Haltalkette.

The Gleirschtal. These walks approach the northern edge of the Nordkette, the southernmost chain of the Karwendel group. From Scharnitz, begin as for the Hinterautal, as far as Scharnitzalm. Cross to the left bank of the Isar, then cross another bridge over the gorge of the Gleirschbach and continue up the valley along the right bank of the Gleirschbach. At the junction, there are several choices. To the right (southwest) is the Grosses Kristental, in which the Solsteinhaus is located between the Erlspitze (2,405 m/7,890 ft) and the Grosser Solstein (2,541 m/8,337 ft). (This point can also be reached from Zirl, the town west of Innsbruck.) Or, proceed straight ahead to Möslalm, at the head of the narrower, shorter Klein Kristental, which leads to the northern edge of the Nordkette. At Möslalm you can also bear left to enter the Mandltal, below the Hafelekarspitze, on the south side of which is Innsbruck.

A lake flanked by evergreens sparkles in the northern Karwendel Alps, an area named after a legendary medieval huntsman.

The Zillertal Alps

IN MAYRHOFEN, THE GREAT RESORT at the foot of the Zillertal Alps, is the climbing school run by Peter Habeler. Among his other achievements, this famous mountaineer, with Reinhold Messner as his partner, climbed Mount Everest without using supplemental oxygen. Habeler, a deceptively slight, unassuming man, says that as a youth he did all the training that later led him to conquer the 8,000-m/26,246-ft peaks of the Himalayas here in the mountains around his native valley.

Among the rugged peaks above the Zillertal are several with climbs of such high quality, such as the north face of the Hochfeiler, that they can still challenge a Peter Habeler. These high peaks make for a spectacular high-alpine landscape, much of which you can enjoy without being a mountain climber.

With a length of 45 km/28 mi, the Zillertal is the longest and the major tributary valley of the Inn River. The lower Zillertal is unusually broad and flat; from the mouth of the valley up to Mayrhofen the valley rises only about 100 m/328 ft. Beyond Mayrhofen, however, are the Zillertal Alps, part of the band of mainly igneous and metamorphic high mountains that spreads across southwestern Austria.

The Zillertal is heavily settled as far as Mayrhofen. Partway up the valley is Zell am Ziller, a noted resort. Mayerhofen, however, is the valley's most important center for skiing, hiking, and mountaineering. Flowing from the Tuxer Alps to the west and the Zillertal Alps to the south, a number of tributary streams conjoin to form the Ziller. With Mayrhofen at the center, these valleys spread out like a fan, and rise into the mountains: the chief of these are the Tuxertal, Zemmgrund, Stillupgrund, and Zillergrund (the Zemmgrund itself has several tributaries). In local dialect, "grund" means valley. This complex topography creates many possibilities for the outdoor traveler.

The core of these mountains consists of gneiss. Both the Zillertal Hauptkamm (high ridge), which forms the main range, and the lesser Tuxer Hauptkamm consist of this gneiss. The erosion of softer rock left the high, knife-edge gneiss peaks that characterize the region. Surrounding these two ridges are bands of schist, the type of rock that also forms the area between the ridges. The Zillertal Alps have other rich mineral deposits, including garnets.

The closeness of the Zillertal to the province of Salzburg accounts for the difference of color of the church towers in the valley, which are green on the east side of the valley and red on the west. By tradition, churches under the dominion of the archbishop of Innsbruck had red towers, while those under the archbishop of Salzburg had green ones.

Mayrhofen

This large and popular resort is no longer a village but more like a small town, with a dense concentration of shops instead of open green spaces on the main street. It has a very low altitude for an Alpine resort, only 630 m/2,060 ft, but several cable-car systems provide access to ski slopes.

Peter Habeler claims that these mountains are more rugged than the Stubai Alps, with many challenging climbs, especially that of the north face of the Hochfeiler.

Penken and Wanglspitze. You may start this route from Mayrhofen, taking the Penken cable car and the chair lift to Penkenalm, or from Finkenberg, with the Finkenberger Almbahn. From Penken take the trail northwest to the Penkenjoch, then continue past Wanglalm to the Wanglspitze (2,420 m/ 7,940 ft) for a good view. You can return on a path called the Finkenberger Zirbenweg to the top station of the cable car.

The Tuxertal

This valley, southwest of Mayrhofen, is dominated by the Tuxer Hauptkamm, a glaciated, mountainous ridge to the south. To the north are the lower Tuxer Voralpen. Of the various tributary valleys above the upper end of the Zillertal, this is the most populated, due to the development of its glaciers for year-round skiing. Beyond Finkenberg are the villages of Vorderlanersbach and Lanersbach; Hintertux is the last village of the valley.

The Gefrorene-Wand-Kees dominates the valley (*Gefrorene-Wand* means "frozen wall"; *Kees* is a local dialect word meaning "glacier"). It is used for summer as well as winter skiing. Spread out in a broad arc above the glacier are the Olperer (3,476 m/11,404 ft)—the highest mountain of the Tuxer Alps—as well as the Kaserer peaks (Grosser Kaserer: 3,266 m/10,715 ft), and the Gefrorene-Wand-Spitzen (3,288 m/10,787 ft). The Hintertux Gletscherbahn cable-car system serves this glacier. A path southward from the valley station leads to several fine waterfalls, of which the highest is the Schraubenfälle.

Tuxer Jochhaus and the Weitental. Take the Hintertux Gletscherbahn to the first intermediate station and then the chair lift to the Tuxer Jochhaus for a good view of the big Gefrorene-Wand glacier. A trail to the south climbs to the top of the Frauenwand (2,541 m/8,337 ft), a viewpoint for the glacier of the Gefrorene-Wand, the Grosser Kaserer, and the Gefrorene-Wand-Spitzen. From the Jochhaus, you can return to Hintertux via the Weitental, on the edge of the Tuxer Voralpen. The trail at first leads north, then east, passing the Schleier waterfall and descending to Hintertux.

Tuxer-Ferner-Haus and Spannagelhaus. The Hintertux Gletscherbahn rises to the Tuxer-Ferner-Haus, at the very edge of the Gefrorene-Wand-Ferner, with an excellent view of the Olperer. From the nearby Spannagel-haus, there is a trail down to Hintertux.

Zamsertal and Zemmgrund

The road to these valleys (route 169) passes through Ginzling, south of Mayr-hofen, then through a tunnel to reach Breitlahner, beyond which the road is private (toll). From Breitlahner you can continue on the right (west) by road to the Zamsertal and the big Schlegeisspeicher dam, or continue on foot to the left (south) for the Zemmgrund.

The Zamsertal is dominated by the Schlegeisspeicher, a long reservoir, and the broad Schlegeiskees above it.

Furtschaglhaus. It is possible to drive or take a bus as far as the Dominikus Hütte, at the northern end of the Schlegeisspeicher. A road and then a path extend along the western side of the lake. From the southern end of the lake, the trail continues southeast on the right side of the stream, then climbs steeply to the Furtschaglhaus. There is a superb view of the Furtschaglkees merged with the broad Schlegeiskees to form a sweeping curve of glaciers, surmounted by the north face of the Hochfeiler (3,510 m/11,516 ft)—the highest mountain of the Zillertal Alps—and the Grosser Möseler (3,478 m/11,411 ft), both on the Italian border.

Pfitscher Jochhaus. From the western side of the Schlegeisspeicher, a trail (marked 524) diverges to the southwest along the right bank of the Zamserbach; this swings southward and climbs steeply to the Italian border and the road to the Pfitscher Jochhaus, above the little Jochsee. North of the hut is the Stampflkees, touching the Italian border; above it, on Austrian territory, are the Sagwandspitze (3,227 m/10,587 ft) and the Schrammacher (3,411 m/11,191 ft). These mountains and the Stampflkees below them form the western edge of the Zillertal Alps. The ridge southeast of the Jochsee has a fine view of a group of hanging glaciers—the Weiss-Spitzenferner, Hochferner, and Griessferner.

Olperer Hütte. From the western side of the Schlegeisspeicher (before reaching the trail to the Pfitscher Jochhaus), turn right onto the trail for this hut. It climbs steeply to the north and northwest. The hut is positioned below the Grosses Riepenkees, the glacier on the east flank of the Olperer, and serves climbers ascending this mountain. There is a fine view across the lake.

A rushing river cuts through the misty land just north of the Berliner Hütte. Pages 226 and 227: The long, fjord-like Schlegeis reservoir in the Zillertal mountains, built in the 1960s, is the start of several pleasant alpine walks.

(east) and climbs steeply in switchbacks to the Greizer Hütte, with a grand view of the Floitenkees. This glacier extends between the two great pillars of the Grosser Mörchner, directly southwest, and the Grosser Löffler (3,376 m/ 11,076 ft) to the east. Behind the glacier to the south is the Floitenspitze (3,194 m/10,479 ft); that and the Grosser Löffler are on the Italian border.

Stillupgrund

To reach this valley, take the middle road south from Mayrhofen to Kumbichl. The road (toll) turns west and then south again to enter the Stillupgrund. You may drive as far as the Speicher Stillup, a reservoir that dominates the lower part of the valley. There is bus service from Mayrhofen to Gasthof Wasserfall, along the side of the reservoir, and a minibus goes to the Grüne-Wand-Hütte farther up the valley. (An alternative approach is by the Ahornbahn cable car from Mayrhofen; from its upper station on a ridge above the Stillup Valley, you can walk down to the Stillup reservoir.) The hut is on lovely meadows amid splendid, steep slopes. From here, continue southeast toward the end of the valley, then turn left (east) for the steeper climb to the Kasseler Hütte. The hut lies below the Hinter Stangen Spitze (3,227 m/10,587 ft), directly to the east. The view to the south is of the Stillupkees and the Wollbach Spitze (3,210 m/10,531 ft); to the southwest is the sharply pointed Grosser Löffler above the Löfflerkees. The Löffler and Wollbach peaks are on the Italian border.

The Zillergrund

This is the longest of the tributary valleys that enter the main Ziller Valley. Its junction is at the southern edge of Mayrhofen. The valley at first leads east, then angles gently southeast to the Zillergründl reservoir. (There is minibus service to Bärenbad, just before the reservoir.) The most notable mountains here are the Gerlos group, centering around the Wild-Gerlos-Spitze (3,278 m/10,755 ft) and the Reichenspitze (3,303 m/10,833 ft), surrounded by glaciers; overhanging the Zillergrund are the Zillerkees and the Kuchelmooskees. A path runs along the northern side of the reservoir; halfway along this shore a trail diverges to the left (north and east) to the Plauener Hütte, dramatically sited on a rocky ledge below the Kuchelmoos glacier.

Gerlos Pass

The Gerlos group is at the eastern edge of the Zillertal Alps. A scenic road over the Gerlos Pass leads from the Zillertal eastward to the Upper Pinzgau

MONKSHOOD
Aconitum napellus

Many alpine wildflowers were gathered in medieval times for their reputed medicinal or aphrodisiac properties; some were known to be toxic. Highly poisonous (even to the touch) alpine plants include monkshood and other members of the *Aconitum* genus. Wolfsbane (*Aconitum vulparia* or *lycoctonum*), for example, was once used to poison such predators as wolves and foxes, and was also applied to arrowheads.

Like other flowers of this genus, those of monkshood have the shape of helmets. The plant flowers from June to August in moist pastures and

woods, on lime-free or sometimes neutral soil, up to 2,900 m/9,514 ft.

Valley. West of the pass is Gerlos, a small ski resort. From the pass there is a fine view to the south over the Durlassboden reservoir to the Wild-Gerloskees, with the Wild-Gerlos and Reichen Spitzen behind this glacier. Between the Gerlos Pass and Krimml the road is private (toll) and very scenic. Some beautiful waterfalls are visible from the road, including a glimpse of the impressive series of the Krimml Falls.

Krimml Falls. These waterfalls are among the highest in Europe — collectively, the falls drop 380 m/1,247 ft. At Krimml, at one end of the toll road, there is a parking lot for the falls. From there a path leads to the base of the falls and then climbs through the woods alongside the three sections of the falls, with various viewpoints. The finest views are higher up. The whole tour can take several hours, and a parka or raincoat is advisable for protection from the spray.

Zittauer Hütte. A hike to the Zittauer Hütte brings you close to the Gerlos group. To reach the hut, drive partway along the Durlassboden reservoir to the parking area at Finkau; from there a path leads south up the Wild-Gerlostal, along the right bank of the stream. At the upper end of the valley the trail turns east to climb to the hut, at the edge of a lake. From here there is a superb, close view of the Wild-Gerloskees and the Gerlos group above.

Facing page: A deep lush carpet of green covers the forest floor on the trail to the Berliner Hütte, an ornate Victorian rest-stop.

The Hohe Tauern

SEEN FROM THE NORTH, the Hohe Tauern appear as a high, white wall spread across the horizon. Among this grand span of peaks and glaciers, which stretches across the East Tyrol, is Austria's highest peak and longest glacier. This range straddles the Tauerntal, the valley between Mittersill and Lienz. To the west of the valley is the Venediger group; to the east is the Grossglockner group. Both are among Austria's finest Alpine regions. The mountains of the Venediger group reserve much of their beauty for the hiker; the valleys below are home to some of Austria's loveliest farm villages. The Grossglockner group can be enjoyed by all, via the magnificent Grossglockner Alpine Highway, the finest drive in the Alps.

The East Tyrol was a rather isolated region until the completion in 1967 of the Felbertauern road and tunnel in the Tauerntal, linking the eastern and northern Tyrol. Before then, motorists from Innsbruck or other points in northern Austria had to make a wide detour around both the Hohe Tauern and the Zillertal Alps to approach the valleys of the East Tyrol. The area directly west of this region (the South Tyrol) was part of Austria until 1919, when it was ceded to Italy. Except for the much-visited Grossglockner area, this is a generally quiet region of pastures and beautiful old wooden farmhouses. Though the houses themselves are attractively simple, many have balconies so charmingly carved that you might think there are local competitions for ingenuity of design.

The Drau River divides the East Tyrol into two geologic zones: south of the river are limestone Alps (Dolomites), while north of it are the higher mountains of the central Alpine zone. The latter appear in the Tauern Fenster, a geologic "window," where Pennine rock underlying the Austro-Alpine cover is exposed. The Venediger group is chiefly gneiss and schist; the mountains of the Grossglockner group, mainly mica schist.

The Pinzgau, the valley along the northern edge of the Hohe Tauern, is very rich in minerals: the Habachtal has the only emerald deposit in the Alps. The stones are especially precious because of their rich and varied shades of green; a 42-carat Habacher emerald is among the British crown jewels. Aquamarine is also found in this valley.

In the Zillertal Alps and the Hohe Tauern, the word *Kees* appears, meaning "glacier" (in German, *Gletscher,* sometimes *Ferner*). This is from Old High German *Ches,* meaning "cold" or "ice." The Venediger group has the largest covering of ice in the eastern Alps.

THE VENEDIGER GROUP

The Upper Pinzgau

From the Upper Pinzgau Valley, at the northern side of the Venediger group, several valleys (particularly the Habachtal and Obersulzbachtal) climb south into the mountains, providing access for hikers and climbers.

Neue Thüringer Hütte. This hut is reached from the Habachtal, between Neukirchen and Bramberg (you can park south of the main road at Wirtshaus Habachklause). The trail leads up the valley to the south, passing Wirtshaus Enzian and Gasthof Alpenrose. South of Moaralm the broad valley narrows to a gorge, streaked with numerous waterfalls. The trail climbs steeply eastward on switchbacks to the hut. Spread before the hut in a broad curve is the Habachkees; the crest behind the glacier rises to the Hohe Fürlegg (3,244 m/10,643 ft).

Kürsinger Hütte. From Neukirchen or Wald drive south along a gravel road to a parking area at Hopffeldboden in the Obersulzbachtal. Walk up the valley, turning right at a junction, and climb to Seebachalm. A little farther is the lovely Seebachsee. Continue up the valley to Berndlalm (near the turbulent Seebachfall), and climb steeply over the lateral moraine to reach the hut. It is in a superb location overlooking the glacier, with the Gross and Kleinvenediger peaks rising above the ice to the southeast. The icefall of the glacier is picturesquely called the "Türkische Zeltstadt"—Turkish tent city.

The Upper Tauerntal

The road to the upper branch of the Tauerntal diverges northwest from the main road, directly south of the Felbertauern tunnel. Two km/1.2 mi past the junction is the tiny hamlet of Matrei im Tauern, consisting of a few plain, old wooden houses, some barns, and a simple inn, the Matreier Tauernhaus. From here, the Venedigerblick chair lift climbs the east slope of the Tauerntal for a good view of the Grossvenediger (3,674 m/12,054 ft)—the third highest mountain wholly on Austrian territory—and of the great spread of glaciers to the west. For a much closer view of the mountain from the upper Tauerntal, drive to Aussergschlöss, or walk there by crossing the bridge at Matrei and taking the path northwest, along the right bank of the Tauernbach.

Innergschlöss and Neue Prager Hütte. This route yields an even closer, superlative view of the Grossvenediger. From Aussergschlöss continue to Innergschlöss and then hike westward to the Neue Prager Hütte. (You can take a taxi-bus to Innergschlöss, or drive there on a toll road, open only in the

early morning or evening.) From Innergschlöss, continue on the path along the left bank of the Gschlössbach, cross the second bridge, and climb the switchbacks past the Alte (old) Prager Hütte to the new one, in a superb location on the Kesselkopf, a great knob surrounded on three sides by glaciers. To the north is the Viltragenkees, to the west and south the Schlatenkees, with the Grossvenediger and the Kleinvenediger (3,477 m/11,407 ft) at its back.

Badener Hütte. This route starts at Innergschlöss and follows the Venediger Höhenweg to the hut. Cross the first bridge beyond Innergschlöss and take the trail heading south. It passes the little Salzboden lake; to the right (west) is the impressive Schlatenkees. The trail climbs to the Löbbentörl Pass, with spectacular views of the Kristallwand (3,329 m/10,922 ft) and the icefalls of the Schlaten and Kristallwand glaciers. After contouring along the lateral moraine, the trail descends to the hut, in a scenic location facing the Frossnitzkees. Some care is necessary on exposed sections (fixed cable) near the hut.

Another approach to this hut is from Gruben, to the south. This village is at the mouth of the Frossnitztal, on the Felbertauern road between the tunnel and Matrei in Osttirol. The trail leads mainly northwest up the left bank of the Frossnitzbach, passing several alps (Katal, Mitteldorf, and Zedlach) to

The upper section of the Grossglockner Highway snakes its way through wilderness and, after a snowfall, offers a silently majestic route through the Hohe Tauern area. Facing page: From the Franz-Josefs-Höhe, non-climbers can enjoy a panoramic view of the Grossglockner mountain and the splendid Pasterze glacier.

reach the Badener Hütte. This is an easier route than the one from Innerg-schlöss, but the grandest scenery is north of the hut, approaching Löbbentörl.

Below Gruben, the main road continues south to Matrei in Osttirol, the chief resort of the region, lying between the Grossvenediger and the Gross-glockner groups. It has a skiing area on the slopes above the east side of the Tauerntal, served by the Goldried lift system. Matrei is at the junction for the Virgental.

The Virgental

This valley is the main approach for the Grossvenediger group. The curious name of the region's major peak derives from a bit of Austrian folklore about a strange man (ostensibly Venetian) who came to the mountains to dig for gold: bad luck follows anyone who takes him by surprise or makes fun of him. The legend of the "Venedigermanndl" is found in other Austrian valleys, but no other mountain is named for him.

The Virgental is a very handsome valley with pretty villages. It is one of Austria's best-kept secrets: an unspoiled, undeveloped valley near superb alpine scenery. No travel agent will ever send a client here because there are no gracious or luxury hotels. There is not a single large resort in the Virgen-tal—no major cable-car line for downhill skiing or summer viewing, though both winter and summer alpine sports are practiced here. Fine as the scenery above the valley is, much of it cannot be seen from the Virgental itself, but only from its upper slopes. Travelers who want to see the beauty of the glaciers and mountains in the Venediger group must rely on their own legs.

The chief villages in the valley are Virgen, near the mouth of the valley, and Prägraten near its upper end. Virgen is the larger of the two, with more facilities for tourists, including a swimming pool and tennis courts. Prägraten, however, is closer to many of the best hiking routes. The houses of this unspoiled farm village are scattered over the valley floor, separated by pas-tures and fields. Throughout the village there are barns with hay sticking through the cracks or out of the windows, and lofts open to receive the hay wagons in summer; you can see people haying in the village meadows, and you may see lambs in the farmyards. Amid this pastoral charm there are a few simple hotels and shops. Although—or perhaps because—Prägraten is unspoiled and undeveloped, it is not entirely undiscovered. The village is a favorite destination for ramblers, hikers, and climbers, and visitors should reserve well in advance for hotel rooms or vacation apartments in the sum-mer. There are also accommodations in the hamlets, including Hinterbichl.

Umbal Wasserschaupfad. The Umbal glacier is the source of the Isel, the river that drains the Virgental. A path has been constructed along the upper end of the turbulent glacier stream and its various cascades. Signboards along the trail explain the process by which the waters of a glacier stream form the landscape, and point to appropriate features. You can drive here from Ströden (also spelled Streden), the last big parking area in the upper valley, or come by bus.

Essen-Rostocker-Hütte. You may take a bus or drive to one of the private parking areas near Ströden, west of Hinterbichl (paid parking beyond Hinterbichl). The trail climbs north and then slightly northwestward up the Maurertal, past Stoanalm: this is a beautiful deep valley cut between high walls. The hut is on a moraine facing a splendid scene: a long rock wall serving as the base for a line of peaks, many of which are snow-covered. The view includes the Simony Spitze (3,488 m/11,443 ft), the Maurerkees Kopf (3,323 m/10,902 ft), and the Grosser Geiger (3,360 m/11,024 ft)—all of which may be climbed from this hut. In the foreground are the imposing Simony and Maurer glaciers. (It is possible to have your rucksack sent up here on the supply lift.)

Johannishütte and Defreggerhaus. This long tour provides hikers with a superb view of the Grossvenediger. The Johannis hut is the oldest in the Venediger group; the Defreggerhaus (at 2,962 m/9,718 ft) is the highest. From Prägraten you can ride up to the Johannis hut by taxi-bus; reservations should be made at the tourist office. Alternatively, you can hike from Hinterbichl directly up the Dorfertal (northward) to the hut, which is charming, tiny, and almost quaint. Behind it is a mass of snow: the Dorfer, Rainer, and Mullwitz glaciers, with the Hohes Aderl (3,504 m/11,496 ft) and Rainerhorn (3,560 m/11,680 ft), and the peak of the Grossvenediger appearing to the northeast.

For a grander view, continue up the trail to the Defreggerhaus. From the Johannishütte, the trail heads northeast, at first moderately steeply over sloping meadows, and then more so onto a moraine overlooking the tongue of the Zettalunitzkees, and up switchbacks to the hut. For the finest view, walk behind the hut to the edge of the ridge, which overlooks a mass of glaciers, the Mullwitzkees and Rainerkees; beyond is the snow-covered summit of the Grossvenediger.

Clarahütte. Begin at Ströden, west of Prägraten (bus; paid parking). Take the path through the woods to Pebellalm, where the Umbal Wasserschaupfad begins. The trail follows the Umbaltal westward, along the Isel, gently at first and then more steeply to the hut. There is a fine view of

The trail from the Essen-Rostocker-Hütte to the Johannishütte is rough but marked. This beautiful and unspoiled area is relatively untouristed; the landscape offers pastoral slopes between breathtaking peaks and fascinating glaciated valleys.

the Rötspitze (3,495 m/11,467 ft) on the Italian border, and the Welitz-kees. The trail may be followed farther northwest for a view of the superb Umbal glacier.

For skiers in the Virgental, there are lifts at Virgen and Prägraten. At Prägraten, there are 25 km/15 mi of cross-country tracks along the valley floor from Bobojach to Stoanalm, and an illuminated track for night cross-country skiing. This is also a major center for ski mountaineering in spring.

THE GROSSGLOCKNER GROUP

The crown of this group of mountains is the Grossglockner (3,798 m/ 12,461 ft), the highest mountain in Austria, at the base of which flows the country's biggest glacier, the Pasterze. An unusual, man-made feature of this region is the Alpine highway that brings motorists to the edge of these splendid sights.

Grossglockner Alpine Highway
(Grossglockner Hochalpenstrasse)

The Grossglockner Alpine Highway is the most spectacular drive in the Alps. But while the existence of this great highway enables anyone to drive near great mountains and glaciers, it also introduces new and unwelcome elements into the Alpine world: paved roads, heavy traffic, and streaming crowds. Neither cable cars nor funiculars leave such an imprint on the landscape or open it to such mass visitation. The road was first proposed in 1924; construction was begun in 1930 during the Great Depression, partly as a sort of public works project, and it was completed in 1935. A toll road, it is 58 km/ 36 mi long, including its several scenic detours. It is usually open from May until late November, depending on seasonal conditions.

The route is an ancient one. Roman objects were found during construction of the Hochtor tunnel. The Romans themselves reported finding large gold deposits in these mountains and those to the east; gold mining continued here during the Middle Ages, when this became a trade route connecting southern Germany, Bohemia, and Venice. During the seventeenth century, prisoners sentenced to the galleys were chained together and driven to Venice over this pass. At several points along the present road, signs indicate the *Romerweg* (Roman road), remnants of an ancient path.

The road extends between Zell am See at its northern end and Heiligenblut at its southern end; it can be driven from either direction. There are two important detours from the main highway: to the Franz-Josefs-Höhe terrace, from which there is a view of the Grossglockner and the Pasterze glacier, and to the Edelweiss-Spitze, a superb viewpoint. These two detours offer the grandest vistas of the entire route. (To be sure of a parking space, try to arrive before midday.) There is also bus service along the road, from Zell am See to Lienz, and there are restaurants and several hotels along the route.

From Bruck, just south of Zell am See, the road at first rises gradually southward up the Fuschertal to Fusch. The road's northern tollhouse is at Ferleiten, beyond the Bärenschlucht (gorge). Above the Schleier waterfall there are increasingly good views of the snowy mountains ahead.

From the Pifflalpe and Hochmaiss parking places, as the road climbs, there are fine vistas to the southwest of the Gross Wiesbachhorn (3,564 m/ 11,693 ft), the Fuscherkarkopf, and the Sinnewelleck group. At Fuscher Törl there is a very splendid overlook of these mountains. From here you may take a short branch road northeast and then walk up to the Edelweiss-Spitze (2,577 m/8,455 ft), a small peak along the ridge east of the Ferleitental. From the Edelweiss terrace and observation tower, the view is panoramic, presenting a grand sweep of mountains interspersed with glaciers, rising above a base of green meadows. Especially attractive are the Fuscherkarkopf (3,331 m/10,928 ft) and its neighbor, the Sinnewelleck (Sonnenwelleck on some maps; 3,261 m/10,699 ft); these mountains are almost twins in shape but not in color: the former is snow-covered and the latter has a summit of bare rock, so that one is white and the other black. Among the multitude of peaks seen from the Fuscher Törl and Edelweiss viewpoints are the imposing Gross Wiesbachhorn and Gross Bärenkopf (3,401 m/11,158 ft); the summit of the Grossglockner appears behind this wall of mountains.

The road reaches its highest point at the Hochtor Pass (2,575 m/8,448 ft), where there is a tunnel. This is the border between Salzburg and Carinthia. At Tauerneck you round a curve and get a first glimpse of the Grossglockner. The road turns west into the narrow Guttal ravine; from there you can take the branch road, the "Gletscherstrasse," which contours around the Wasserradkopf as it climbs to the Franz-Josefs-Höhe (see below). There are parking areas along the approach.

THE LARCH
Larix decidua

One of the trees best-loved by the people of the Alps, the larch provides lovely masses of color on Alpine slopes when its needles turn golden yellow in the fall. The larch is also unusual in being the only alpine conifer that sheds its needles in winter—an adaptation that may help it survive winter temperatures. During spring and summer, the needles are light green.

The larch can be easily identified by the growth of its needles. Instead of being distributed evenly along a branch, they grow in tufts on tiny stubs protruding from the branch.

The boughs that litter the forest floor under the base of these trees have knobs on them, the spurs from which the needle clusters grew. The cones are quite small and rather oval.

In outline the tree is slender with a tapered crown. The trunk has few branches near the bottom; on the upper part, the branches are not dense. Because of this, the tree casts only light shade, so grass and shrubs may grow beneath it. When young, its bark is grayish-brown, but when mature, the bark is reddish-brown, cracked, and scaly.

Pages 242 and 243: An early fall snowstorm dusts larch trees on the northern end of the Grossglockner Highway, the highest and most spectacular public road in Europe.

Pasterze Glacier and Grossglockner

The Franz-Josefs-Höhe is a long terrace with a panoramic view above the eastern edge of the Pasterze glacier and facing the Grossglockner. The name of this beautiful mountain means "big bellringer" (or "sexton"). From most viewpoints it appears as a shapely, rather slender cone with a sharp point, like a well-crafted arrowhead. From here, however, you can see its two peaks, joined very closely, with steeply hanging glaciers at their base. To the left (south) of the Grossglockner are the Adlersruhe (3,454 m/11,332 ft), Hohenwartkopf (3,308 m/10,853 ft), Kellersberg (3,265 m/10,712 ft), and Schwerteck (3,247 m/10,653 m); to the right (north) is the Glocknerwand, a black, ribbed wall, followed by the Hoffmans-Spitze (3,713 m/12,182 ft), Teufelskamp (3,511 m/11,519 ft), Romariswandkopf (3,511 m/11,519 ft), Schneewinkelkopf (3,478 m/11,411 ft), and Eiskögele (3,434 m/11,266 ft). Above the glacier are the Odenwinkelschartenkopf (3,267 m/10,719 ft) and the snowy head of the Johannisberg (3,460 m/11,352 ft).

The Pasterze glacier is 9.5 km/5.9 mi long and covers an area of 22 sq km/ 8.5 sq mi. The Franz-Josefs-Höhe overlooks the lower section of the Mittleres Pasterzenkees, a valley glacier, long and broad with deep crevasses. At the glacier's upper end there is a steep rise, above which a higher section (Oberster Pasterzenboden) of the Pasterze is visible. From the Freiwandeck area along the Franz-Josefs-Höhe, the "Gletscherbahn," a funicular, descends to the edge of the glacier, where you can walk on the ice within a specially marked area. Below the snout of the glacier is the Margaritze Stausee, a reservoir.

The view from the Franz-Josefs-Höhe may be compared with several other premier Alpine panoramas accessible to nonclimbers. It most immediately calls to mind the Mer de Glace at Chamonix, where the traveler also has a lateral view of a single great glacier and the mountains behind it. The Mer de Glace is longer than the Pasterze and has a more sinuous shape, with a great S-curve (in this respect resembling the Swiss Grosser Aletsch glacier, as seen from the Eggishorn and nearby points). The Gornergrat panorama above Zermatt overlooks a more complex series of glaciers, with many iceflows pouring into the main valley glacier. But you cannot easily descend from the Gornergrat onto the ice. The unique feature at the Franz-Josefs-Höhe is the funicular that allows you to descend and walk on the glacier. At the Mer de Glace, the funicular descends to a cave within the glacier, rather than permitting you to walk upon the glacier's surface.

Gamsgrubenweg and Hofmannshütte. From the Franz-Josefs-Höhe, hikers can take the Gamsgrubenweg, a path above the glacier. From the kiosk at Franz-Josefs-Höhe, a tunnel leads to the beginning of the Gamsgrubenweg. Though the path is wide, there is a steep drop on one side to the Pasterze glacier. It soon reaches the Hofmanns hut near the snout of the Wasserfallwinkel glacier, in view of the Grossglockner.

Continuing south after the Gletscherstrasse detour, the main road descends past Kasereck and the Heiligenblut tollbooth to the village of Heiligenblut in the Mölltal. From there the road continues southeast to Lienz.

The Grossglockner area is an important one for climbing, and there are mountain guides' offices at Heiligenblut and at Kals in the Kalsertal (see below). Hiking, however, is much more limited here than around the Grossvenediger group, as many more routes involve glacier crossings.

Gleiwitzer Hütte. From Fusch the trail leads west, at first along the right bank of the Hirzbach. Then it crosses over the stream to reach Hirzbachalm, with the Hoher Tenn looming up to the south. After a short turn to the south, the trail climbs steeply to the hut, with its view of the Hoher Tenn and its satellite peaks to the south.

Käfertal. From Ferleiten, you can follow the small road on the west side of the valley toward the Käfertal. This is on the left bank of the Fuscher Ache stream. At a junction turn right (west) and climb to Altjudenalm (or the Innere Judenalm). To the south is the splendid upper end of the Käfertal, with waterfalls descending below the Fuscherkar glacier, and the gleaming slopes of the Fuscherkarkopf above. The trail up the right bank of the stream to the Traunerhütte offers another superb view of the upper Fuschertal from a different perspective.

The Kalsertal

This valley approaches the Grossglockner from the southwest, whereas the Grossglockner Alpine Highway is to the east of the mountain. The Kalsertal is reached from the Iseltal, on the southern part of the Felbertauern road. The junction for the Kalsertal is at Huben on the main road (route 108). The road follows the Kalserbach northeast to the attractive little resort village of Kals. Here the road branches: right up the Ködnitztal on the Kalser Glocknerstrasse (toll, except in winter) for the Neues Lucknerhaus and Lucknerhütte, or left up the Dorfertal for the Kalser Tauernhaus.

Lucknerhütte. The Neues Lucknerhaus offers a view of the southern side of the Grossglockner. From the parking lot, a path continues to the Lucknerhütte for an even closer look at the mountain, which appears from this viewpoint more like a sharp-edged pyramid than a cone. Climbers continue up the steep, rocky slope to the Stüdlhütte, a popular base from which to climb the peak.

Trees line a ridge in the valley below Essen-Rostocker-Hütte. Facing page: Colorful rock formations decorate the trail from Essen-Rostocker-Hütte to Johannishütte. The hike also provides a marvelous view of the Grossvenediger peak. Tired hikers may travel to the Johannishütte by taxi-bus from the charming village of Prägraten.

The Dorfertal and Dorfersee. A path heads north up this valley, which is much longer than the Ködnitztal. At the outset the route passes through the narrow gorge of the Dabaklamm, where the trail has been blasted out of the rock; it then emerges into a broad valley. From the Kalser Tauernhaus there is a panoramic view eastward of the long, steep glaciers sweeping down from the ridge of the Grossglockner, with its line of peaks including the Eiskögele, Romariswandkopf, and Teufelskamp. The trail continues to the Dorfersee, a small lake, and then to the Kalser Tauern, a pass leading northward.

At Grossdorf, near Kals, is the Glocknerblick chair lift, the only one in the valley, offering a good view of the mountain.

Kals-Matreier-Törlhaus. From the upper end of the Glocknerblick chair lift you can also hike westward toward Ganotzalm, then turn southwest for the Kals-Matreier-Törlhaus, on the ridge separating the Kalsertal and the Iseltal, for a view of the Grossglockner. From here you can descend by the Goldried chair lift to Matrei in Osttirol, and return to Kals by bus.

The Kitzbühel Alps

THE GENTLE KITZBÜHEL ALPS ARE known as the "Grasberge," the grassy mountains. These low, rounded mountains and their broad valleys create a mainly pastoral landscape. Although this region offers only a moderate grade of walking, it is more challenging for skiers and is the setting for some of Austria's leading ski resorts. Chief among them is fashionable Kitzbühel, which has an international reputation.

Kitzbühel is neither a traditional Alpine village nor a wholly modern resort specially constructed for skiing, but something quite different—a small baroque town, surrounded by hills, that is also a major ski resort. Within its old walls are seventeenth-century houses with gabled roofs and façades painted canary yellow, lime green, raspberry, and blue. As in other baroque settings, such as Salzburg and Innsbruck, shops, restaurants, and wine cellars display elaborate baroque wrought-iron signs.

Above Kitzbühel, on the eastern side of the valley, is the Kitzbüheler Horn (1,996 m/6,549 ft), whose summit can be reached by hiking trail or by a two-stage cable car. Visible from the top is a perfect example, like a geological illustration, of the two types of mountains characteristic of the Austrian Alps. To the north are the crisp, jagged, gray forms of the limestone Kaisergebirge, while to the south a great snowy wall glistens in the distance—the crystalline gneiss and schist zones of the Hohe Tauern, with its high peaks and glaciers. Just below the summit spreads an alpine garden, with a large display of alpine wildflowers. From the Kitzbüheler Horn, a hiking trail extends along the slopes on the eastern side of the valley. Most of these mountains are about 2,000 m/6,560 ft high.

Just southwest of Kitzbühel is the famous Hahnenkamm ski run. The ski race here, part of the World Cup series, consists of both a downhill and slalom run. Summer visitors can ride up the slope on the Hahnenkamm cable car and then hike along a gentle trail past the Ehrenbachhöhe to the Steinbergkogel (1,971 m/6,466 ft), a summit with a good view. A hiking trail continues along the ridge to Pengelstein (1,938 m/6,358 ft), where there is a small restaurant.

The town offers four guided walking tours a week from June until mid-August.

Directly north of the town is the Schwarzsee, a pretty, shaded lake used for bathing and boating. Nearby is one of the few 18-hole golf courses in the Alps. In winter, besides downhill skiing, Kitzbühel offers 30 km of cross-country ski trails, curling, and skating.

The Kaisergebirge

THE KAISERGEBIRGE IS A FAIRLY small group, part of the northern limestone Alps, but it offers some of the loveliest scenery of this entire band of mountains as it stretches across northern Austria and southern Germany. Though the outer walls of these sheer-sided, jagged gray peaks can be seen from the roads around the Kaisergebirge, the best views are obtained from the hiking trails that penetrate to the base of these highly impressive mountains. The Kaisergebirge, or Emperor mountains, consist of two parallel groups, facing each other across the Kaisertal. On the south side is the Wilder (wild) Kaiser; on the north side, the Zahmer (tame) Kaiser. One of the charms of the region is that the inner valley between these groups, pastoral and undeveloped, is like a sanctuary, with gentle green meadows and woods that seem incongruously close to the savage towers of rock. Another attraction of the Kaisergebirge is that there is no famous resort in the area, and thus it is quite undeveloped and unspoiled.

The nearest gateway to these mountains is Kufstein, a small, interesting old city on the Inn River—a pleasant contrast to those Alpine villages that now are solely resorts, living only on tourism. A thirteenth-century fortress, commanding the Inn River, stands high above the city; it is said that during the Middle Ages, whoever held the Kufstein fortress controlled the Tyrol. Below the castle is the Heldenorgel, the world's largest organ, which is played every day of the year a few minutes after noon, and in the summer also at 6 P.M.

Although these mountains are comparatively low, their appearance makes them look deceptively big; the limestone has eroded into characteristically jagged forms, and the mountain sides are often sheared away, leaving nearly vertical faces and exposed ribs. Extreme climbers are attracted here by the challenge of sheer rock faces and an exceptionally firm kind of limestone (Wetterstein). There is a curious contrast here: though the hiking is not especially difficult, the climbs are extremely tough, and occur above a landscape much softer and gentler than the realm of ice and snow usually found near the most demanding Alpine climbs. There are numerous hiking trails along both the Wilder Kaiser and Zahmer Kaiser.

Wilder Kaiser

Stripsenjoch. This lovely walk goes up the Kaisertal, between the Wilder and Zahmer Kaiser. There is a pay-parking lot at the northeast end of

The stark stone peaks of the Kaisergebirge create romantically wild and almost theatrical scenery. The area offers an assortment of walks; the trail to Stripsenjoch leads past a number of cliff-like mountain faces. Facing page: Visitors may hike or ride the cable-car up the Kitzbüheler Horn, from which the views are extensive on a clear day. Nearby is Kitzbühel, once a silver and copper mining center and now a small resort town with many baroque buildings.

Kufstein for hikers. Across the road, a long series of steps are cut beside the small, dark gorge of the Kaiserbach (also called the Sparchenbach); above this steep initial section, however, are broad, gentle meadows. The charming little Antonius-Kapelle, a baroque chapel with white walls and a red roof, is set in a verdant pasture against a backdrop of the rugged gray mountains. The upper end of the walk is steeper, with views of the rugged, cliff-like faces along the northern edge of the Wilder Kaiser. The Stripsenjochhaus, at the Stripsenjoch saddle, has an impressive location at the base of the Totenkirchl (2,190 m/7,185 ft), a big, sheer, gray wall towering above, with some of the most difficult climbing routes in Austria.

Instead of returning to Kufstein from the Stripsenjoch, you can continue eastward down the Kaiserbachtal to the village of Griesenau, on the east side of the Wilder Kaiser. Another way to reach Griesenau is by taking the path northeast from Stripsenjoch to Feldberg, on a ridge facing the Mitterkaiser (2,001 m/6,565 ft) and other peaks along the eastern end of the Wilder Kaiser. This trail continues eastward to Obere and Untere Schiebenbühelalm before descending to Griesenau.

Gamskogel. From Kufstein, take the Wilder Kaiser chair lift to Brentenjoch, from which you can take a short tour to view the western edge of the Wilder Kaiser. Or take the Kaiser chair lift, closer to the center of town, to Berghaus Aschenbrenner, then walk up the path to Brentenjoch. From the chair-lift station here, follow the path eastward to the Gamskogel viewpoint, an elevation with good views of the Zahmer Kaiser and also the northwestern Wilder Kaiser. The path curves around below the Bettlersteigsattel, southeast and then west, to reach the Kaindlhütte, from which you can return to the chair lift.

Gruttenhütte, Gaudeamushütte, and Ackerlhütte. These are a series of huts in scenic locations below the south side of the Wilder Kaiser. From Ellmau, a village on the road south of the Wilder Kaiser (route 312), you can drive on a small road (toll) north to Wochenbrunner Alm to park. The path to the left leads north to the Gruttenhütte, near the base of the Ellmauer Halt (2,344 m/7,690 ft), the highest mountain in the Kaisergebirge. From Wochenbrunner Alm, the path to the right (northeast) takes you to the Gaudeamushütte, close to the Regalpspitze (2,253 m/7,392 ft). The Ackerlhütte is at the foot of the Ackerl Spitze (2,329 m/7,641 ft), one of the highest peaks of the Wilder Kaiser. To reach it, continue eastward from the Gaudeamushütte past the Baumgartenkopf.

Zahmer Kaiser

To walk to the Zahmer Kaiser, begin as for the Stripsenjoch walk above. At the first junction, bear left (northeast). The trail climbs gently to Rietzalm; stay to the left (east) at the next junction to reach the Vorderkaiserfeldenhütte, which overlooks the Kaisertal and the Wilder Kaiser across it.

Petersköpfli. Walk behind the hut for this trail to the crest of the Zahmer Kaiser. A short climb through the woods brings you up to an interesting limestone plateau where broken white rock is strewn among dwarf pines. From this height there is a very good view across the valley to the somber gray towers of the Wilder Kaiser. You can also see the Inn River to the west; the limestone mountains rise so abruptly from the broad valley floor that they resemble a row of tumblers placed upside down on a green cloth.

Stripsenjoch. From the Vorderkaiserfeldenhütte, take the *Höhenweg*, a high, scenic trail, southeast to the Kaiserquelle. Continue eastward high above the Bärental, a tributary valley, to Hochalm. To reach the Stripsenjoch turn southward, through the Feldalmsattel, and then descend to the hut at Stripsenjoch.

There is downhill and cross-country skiing above Kufstein, in the area of the Brentenjoch and Kaindlhütte.

The Niedere Tauern

THIS RANGE IS AN eastern extension of the Hohe Tauern, the great band of igneous-metamorphic mountains across south-central Austria. While the Hohe Tauern is a region of great peaks and glaciers, including Austria's highest mountain and biggest glacier, the mountains of the Niedere (or lower) Tauern are much lower. The highest is the Hoch Golling (2,863 m/9,393 ft); most others are much lower—between 2,200 m/7,220 ft and 2,600 m/8,530 ft. Yet the landscape is rugged, with bare, rocky peaks appearing above wooded slopes. Instead of glaciers, lakes predominate.

The Niedere Tauern comprise several groups: from west to east, the Radstädter, Schladminger, Wölzer, and Rottenmanner Tauern, according to the Austrian custom of naming mountains according to a nearby feature such as a valley, river, or town. The highest mountains of the range are in the Schladminger Tauern in the west.

A number of parallel valleys, rising south from the Ennstal, provide access to the mountains, and there is bus service up each valley. You can take day trips, hiking into the mountains from the upper ends of the valleys, or link the walks together by traversing the mountains from west to east (or the reverse), staying at huts along the way. (This west-east route appears as the "Tauern Höhenweg" on maps.) Because of the lower terrain and absence of glacier barriers, much of the Niedere Tauern is accessible to hikers; a walking trip here can be rigorous, however, requiring continual ascent and descent because of the numerous valleys that furrow the mountains. Since ski development is found only at the edges of this region, it remains quite unspoiled.

Ignaz-Mattis-Hütte and Keinprecht Hütte. From either the Preuneggtal, west of Schladming, or the Obertal, directly south of the town, you can reach the Ignaz-Mattis-Hütte at the edge of the Untere Giglach See. From the hut, a trail leads eastward to the Rotmannl-Scharte, a pass with fine views of the Dachstein group to the north. Follow the trail east and then south, contouring around a band of cliffs to reach the Keinprecht Hütte, from which you may head north for the Obertal and Schladming.

Landwiersee Hütte and Golling Hütte. East of the Keinprecht Hütte the route crosses another pass, the Trockenbrot-Scharte, to reach the Landwiersee Hütte above the two little Landwier lakes. The next section of the route, from the Landwiersee hut northeastward to the Golling Hütte, is one of the most scenic, passing to the north of the Hoch Golling. Its walls are rugged and steep, scooped into a shallow cirque on its northern face. Although rather lower than the grand western Alps, the vertical rise from the base of this mountain is substantial and impressive. The Golling Hütte is also reached from the Steinriesental, the upper end of the Untertal, which rises south from Schladming.

Preintaler Hütte. Beyond the Golling hut, the Tauern Höhenweg continues east and northeast to the Preintaler Hütte, through a rather wondrous landscape, the most interesting along the route. This is the area called the Klafferkessel, near the Greifenberg (2,618 m/8,589 ft). The terrain is strewn with small ponds, interspersed with great towers of rock that rise here and there like giant mushrooms. The trail twists around these little tarns and huge rock masses. At the northeastern end of the Klafferkessel is the Preintaler Hütte. The most direct way to Schladming from here is to take the path northwest from the Preintaler Hütte to the Riesachsee; directly west of the lake is the junction with the Untertal. To extend a tour through this region, you can continue northward from the Preintaler Hütte; this trail continues over the Neualm-Scharte, past the Obersee, Hüttensee (with the Hans-Wödl-Hütte on its shore), and Bodensee, at the upper end of the Seewigtal. This valley enters the Ennstal at Aich, east of Schladming.

The town of Schladming and the nearby village of Ramsau are centers for both alpine and cross-country skiing; Ramsau is also a starting point for ski-mountaineering tours.

EDELWEISS
Leontopodium alpinum

The edelweiss, a member of the daisy family, is almost the symbol of the Alps. Found between 1,600 and 3,500 m/5,249 and 11,482 ft, it is quite rare, but when you see one, others are usually nearby. What appear to be its petals are actually bracts (modified leaves), which are white, slightly fuzzy, and long and narrow; there are generally six to nine of them. Though each plant looks like a single star-shaped flower, it actually consists of several. A group of these real flowers, tiny and yellow, are packed tightly together in the center of the flower cluster. The stem is erect, round, green, and slightly downy; several stems may grow from the same base.

The plants are between 5 and 20 cm/ 2 and 8 in high.

Edelweiss flowers from July to August. It is found on high meadows or on stony, sunny slopes, often on thin, dry, limestone-rich soil.

Salzburg

Gmunden

Traun R.

UPPER

Mondsee

Attersee

AUSTRIA

Traunsee

Wolfgang See

Ebensee

Bad Ischl

Abtenau

Gosau

Bad Aussee

GOSAUTAL

KOPPENBRULLER

GABLONZER HÜTTE

Hallstatt

Hallstätter See

Obertraun

MAMMUTHÖHLE

Vorderer Gosau See

Hinterer Gosau See

ADAMEK HÜTTE

EISHÖHLE

Krippenstein

Bischofshofen

GROSSER GOSAUGLETSCHER

Hohes Kreuz

SIMONY HÜTTE

Mitterndorf

Tauplitz

Ach R.

Hoher Dachstein

SCHLADMINGER GLETSCHER

HALLSTÄTTER GLETSCHER

D A C H S T E I N

Radstadt

Ramsau

Schladming

Aich

Enns R.

E

N

N

S

T

A

L

PREUNEGTAL

UNTERTAL

SEEWIGTAL

N I E D E R E

T A U E R N

Riesachsee

▲ *Hochwildstelle*

STEINRIESENTAL

OBERTAL

IGNAZ-MATTIS-HÜTTE

PREINTALER HÜTTE

Radstätter Tauern Pass

Unterer Giglach See

GOLLING HÜTTE

▲ *Greifenberg*

Rotmannl-Scharte

KEINPRECHT HÜTTE

▲ *Hoch Golling*

LANDIERSEE HÜTTE

Landwiersee

NIEDERE TAUERN AND DACHSTEIN ALPS

▬▬ Autobahn	▲ Peaks
▬▬ Main Roads	Huts
▬▬ Connecting Roads	∩ Caves
● Points of Interest	

0 ————— 15 Mi

0 ————— 15 Km

The Dachstein

THIS IMMENSE LIMESTONE MASSIF is the most prominent mountain area east of Salzburg, with the only large glaciers in the eastern Alps. Although lower in altitude than the mountains of western and south-central Austria, its enormous proportions and rugged structure are very impressive. The Dachstein is something of a curiosity, honeycombed with vast caves—unusual features in such a large mountain group. The top of this mass of rock is partly a fascinating karst landscape, and partly covered by glacier.

The lower part of the Dachstein is mostly dolomite, a type of limestone that dissolves in water and easily cracks, breaks, and crumbles due to weathering and erosion. Above this lower section of dolomite are horizontal layers of Dachstein limestone, which are exposed on the plateau on top of the mountain, a barren, rock-strewn karst landscape. Karst occurs in areas of very soluble rock, where numerous sinks and basins form. Streams also disappear into the rock, leaving dry channels. The result is an uneven surface marked by hollows and furrows.

The Dachstein is large enough to be considered in two sections, its northern and southern sides; they have diverse aspects, and the approaches to them are different, though you can make a tour that loops completely around the Dachstein massif.

NORTH DACHSTEIN

The northern side of the Dachstein is at the edge of the Salzkammergut, the lovely region of lakes east of Salzburg. It may even be visited as a day excursion from Salzburg; there are, however, attractive towns and villages much closer to this mountain group.

Hallstatt. This very appealing little town is built on a narrow terrace on the shore of the Hallstätter See, and partly on the precipitous slope above the lake, a setting reminiscent of the Italian Riviera. The scenic lake is largely enclosed by cliffs and steep, wooded walls. The Dachstein massif rises above the southern end of the lake.

Hallstatt has a place in history: its name is used to denote the early Iron Age culture that archaeologists uncovered here. A small museum displays some of the excavated tools, ornaments, and weapons. There is also an ancient salt mine above the town—the oldest salt mine in the world still being worked. From Hallstatt you can take a small cable car up the steep slope for a guided tour of the mine.

Several other pleasant villages can be used as a base for exploring the north Dachstein. These include Abtenau and Gosau (a cross-country ski center), west of Hallstatt. Mitterndorf and Tauplitz are small resorts to the east.

Dachstein Caves (Dachstein Höhlen)

The existence of these vast caves is owing to the qualities of limestone, particularly its tendency to dissolve in water. Cracks developed in the limestone with movements of the earth caused by the shifting of tectonic plates and earthquakes. Over millions of years, rainwater widened the cracks into channels and sank through these channels into the mass of rock instead of remaining in surface basins as lakes. Streams, rivers, and even waterfalls flowed deep within the rock, creating internal passages and also great caverns where water had collected or backed up. Some of this was meltwater from the glaciers above.

The public may visit three caves on guided tours. The Mammuthöhle and the Eishöhle are both located midway up the Dachstein massif. To reach them, take the Dachstein cable car from Obertraun, at the southeastern end of the Hallstätter See, to the middle station (Schönbergalm). There is a small museum near this station, and both caves are nearby. The Koppenbrüller cave is at the edge of Obertraun, on the road toward Bad Aussee. It is chilly in the caves, so warm clothing is recommended.

The caves are extensive and visitors are shown only a limited section. The chambers vary from huge galleries to narrow passages. In some places, high cathedral ceilings were created where two subterranean rivers once flowed, one above the other, until the upper one wore through the rock to join the lower. As waterfalls scoured out big, round holes in the floor, sediments in the churning water ground pits into the rock, like the action of a mortar and pestle. Molded by water, the rock surfaces have fluid shapes interspersed with the needles and columns of stalactites and stalagmites.

The Mammuthöhle is the deepest cave in Austria, offering contrasts between immense spaces and narrow corridors. The Eishöhle is a sort of ice palace with walls and floors, stalactites and stalagmites, made of greenish white ice; some of the great frozen pillars look like modern sculpture. Boardwalks enable visitors to walk through these natural wonders. The remains of cave bears were found in the Eishöhle. The Koppenbrüller cave contains

Pages 258 and 259: An early morning fog hangs above the Obertraun Valley in the Dachstein mountains. This rugged and impressive limestone area features a number of vast caves that may be visited on guided tours.

streams of flowing water, so it is still in the process of creation; visitors may see examples of the cave-forming effect of water.

The Dachstein cable car rises in three sections from Obertraun. The first section is used for visiting the caves. The second rises to Krippenstein (with a large hotel, used for winter skiing), and the third to the plateau of Gjaidalm.

The Gjaidalm and Simony Hütte

Here you can view the karst landscape of the Dachstein plateau with its strange contrasts of color and texture. A large section of the plateau is covered with grasses, dwarf pines, and shrubs such as alpenroses. The Dachstein surface rock, nearly white, lies broken and tumbled about. The terrain is one of hillocks, humps, and hollows; the surface is so eroded that the trail does not steadily rise or drop as you head uphill or down; rather, it rises and falls every few meters. The little round hollows are full of grass, alpenroses, and such flowers as trumpet and spring gentians and daisies.

The same forces that created the strange landscape on the surface of the Dachstein—mainly the action of water upon limestone, eroding and sculpting the rock—also created the fantastical subterranean structures—its caves and channels, internal hollows and pillars. This makes for a landscape that is strange and wondrous both above the surface and below. From the Gjaidalm station you can walk mainly west and then southwest across this plateau to the Simony Hütte, in a superb location above the Hallstätter Gletscher, the biggest glacier on the Dachstein. Facing the hut across the glacier is the highest peak on the massif, the Hoher Dachstein (2,995 m/9,826 ft)—also referred to as "the Dachstein"—in a line of other peaks that look like rocky gray teeth.

The Gosautal and Gosaukamm

At the upper end of the Gosau Valley is a series of lovely lakes. The first and largest is the Vorderer Gosau See, with a very good view of the Dachstein, topped with glaciers, at the end of the lake. From this lake, you can take a cable car to the Gablonzer Hütte on the edge of the Gosaukamm, the western ridge of the Dachstein group; a path from the hut leads northward to the nearby Zwieselalm, facing the Dachstein and offering a fine view of the massif.

Adamek Hütte. From the Gosau lakes you can hike to the Adamek Hütte. The path extends past the first lake, continues through woods to the second lake (the Hinterer Gosau See), and then climbs steeply to the Dachstein limestone plateau. The hut is below a small glacier, the Grosser Gosaugletscher,

ALPINE FORGET-ME-NOT
Myosotis alpestris

Even among the more modest alpine flowers, the Alpine forget-me-not's bunches of tiny, baby-blue flowers have a look of simple, unaffected innocence. The flower is flat; five small petals with rounded edges grow around a tiny yellow or white center. The stem looks long for such tiny flowers, though the whole plant is only about 5 to 15 cm/2 to 6 in. The stems have small hairs and long, oval leaves.

It flowers from June to August in meadows, among boulders, and even on scree, on nearly any soil, from about 1,500 to 2,900 m/4,921 to 9,514 ft.

---

half encircled by jagged rock peaks, including the Hoher Dachstein. The view here is of the western side of the mountains between the Hoher Dachstein and the Hohes Kreuz, seen from the northeast at the Simony Hütte. In clear weather the Hohe Tauern may be visible in the distance.

South Dachstein

The south side of the Dachstein massif stands over the valley of the Enns River in the region known as the Dachstein-Tauern. On the opposite side of the river are the Niedere Tauern mountains.

The main base for visiting the south Dachstein is the market town of Schladming, in the center of the Enns Valley. On the north side of the river is the village of Ramsau, spread over gentle slopes. Above the green meadows and woods of Ramsau, the craggy, silvery walls of the Dachstein rise abruptly and massively, creating a striking contrast. From Ramsau, a cable car sweeps up the dramatic, vertical south wall of the Dachstein, right to the edge of the Schladminger glacier, which merges with the larger Hallstätter glacier. The view is extensive, not only across the Dachstein glaciers but also to distant ranges such as the Hohe Tauern and the mountains along the Yugoslav border. There is summer skiing on this glacier, both alpine and cross-country. You can also ride over the glacier in the "Gletschertaxi," a big Sno-Cat with open-air seats, or take a tour with a guide. Because the upper cable-car station is so close to the glaciers (the station itself is perched on a rock ledge), only these snow tours are possible; hikers should therefore approach the Dachstein from its north side.

There is alpine skiing in the Schladming–Ramsau area, and Ramsau has an extensive network of cross-country ski trails.

The German Alps

 he German Alps belong to the southernmost part of Germany, where the border bulges into the band of limestone Alps stretching across northern Austria. The three main German Alpine areas are the Allgäuer Alps, the Wetterstein Alps near Garmisch-Partenkirchen, and the Watzmann group around Berchtesgaden.

Addresses: For information on Germany, contact the German National Tourist Office.

In the U.S., there are two locations: 747 Third Avenue, New York, NY 10017-2852; (212) 308-3300. 444 South Flower Street, Suite 2230, Los Angeles, CA 90071; (213) 688-7332.

In Canada, the tourist office address is: 175 Bloor Street East, North Tower, Suite 604, Toronto, Ont. M4W 3R8; (416) 968-1570.

In Great Britain, the tourist office address is: Nightingale House, 65 Curzon Street, London W1Y 7PE; (44) 1-495-3990/91.

For information on joining the German Alpine Club, write to: Deutscher Alpenverein (DAV), Praterinsel 5, 8000 München 22; (49) 89-235 0900.

A ridge of mountains culminating in the Zugspitze stands mirrored in the calm waters of the Badersee in the Garmisch mountains, a favorite Bavarian resort area also offering a medieval castle and historic churches.

The Allgäuer Alps

THE ALLGAU PROTRUDES SOUTHWARD into Austria. The Allgäuer Alps, following the curve of the border, are close neighbors to the Austrian Lechtal Alps. These limestone mountains are comparatively low but rugged, with steep, exposed rock summits.

Oberstdorf

In the center of the Allgäu pocket is Oberstdorf, set on a broad, flat terrace, with the gray, triangular forms of the Allgäuer Alps rising to the east and the south. The southernmost town in Germany, Oberstdorf is pleasant, neat, and unpretentious. It is a market town as well as a small spa, with a *Kurhaus* (center for therapeutic baths) set in its public garden. It is also the chief resort of the region, a base for hikers and climbers in summer. In winter, it is the primary center for skiing and other winter sports in the Allgäuer mountains. It offers good and varied downhill runs, a famous ski jump, 80 km/ 50 mi of cross-country tracks, dog-sledding, and a modern ice stadium.

From Oberstdorf at 824 m/2,703 ft, a multisectioned lift system rises to the top of the Nebelhorn (2,224 m/7,297 ft), directly east of the town. This mountain, near the northern edge of the Allgäuer Alps, offers an interesting contrast: to the north, beyond a few low ridges, is a flatland spreading as far as the eye can see—the Bavarian plain. To the south, however, the view is entirely filled with mountains, a mass of peaks crowded together to the far horizon.

Stillachtal. The Stillachtal, the valley directly south of Oberstdorf, provides access to the Mädelegabel (2,645 m/8,678 ft), the highest peak in the Allgäu Alps. You can drive as far as Faistenoy, or take the bus to Birgsau, with a fine view of the Mädelegabel and other peaks along the border ridge. A path continues to Einödsbach, with an even finer view of this group. From there, a trail climbs mainly south past the Enzianhütte and then east to the Rappenseehütte. The hut overlooks a couple of small lakes, and is positioned close to the southern ridge of the Allgäu Alps, especially the Rappenseekopf (2,468 m/8,097 ft). From Einödsbach, a trail starting eastward (then south and east again) climbs to the Waltenbergerhütte, close to the Mädelegabel.

Oytal. Another valley, the Oytal, is east of Oberstdorf. An unpaved road leads up this valley to the Oytalhaus, a simple inn. From there, a trail continues southeast and then south to Käser Alpe, which offers a good view of the Höfats (2,258 m/7,408 ft) to the west and the Grosse Wilder (2,379 m/

7,805 ft) to the east. From here, you can make this a loop trip by climbing steeply southward to the Alpelesattel, then descending to Dietersbach Alpe; from there, turn northwest for Gerstruben Alpe and the road to Oberstdorf.

The Klein Walstertal. Though this valley is on Austrian territory, its only automobile access is by a road leading southwest from Oberstdorf. The valley has pretty views to the east, with the rugged gray Allgäuer Alps rising above grassy slopes; above the valley to the south is the rocky tower of the Widderstein (2,253 m/7,392 ft). The valley floor, however, has been spoiled by overbuilding, with a strip of hotels, restaurants, and even a casino along the road. Only the last village, Mittelberg, has escaped the worst of this development.

The Breitachklamm. From Tiefenbach, a village west of Oberstdorf, a road leads south to the edge of a deep gorge on the Breitach River, the Breitachklamm. You can drive or take a bus to the Breitachklamm, then walk through galleries that have been cut into the cliffs. The path through the gorge is also kept open during the winter, when great sheets of ice hang from the rocks. (Because of the spray, rain gear is advisable.)

Rubi, Reichenbach, and Schöllang. North of Oberstdorf are these three charming villages whose old houses are hung with flowers. From these villages there is a lovely view over the green fields of the Allgäuer Alps, whose rocky crowns seem close together because of the long perspective.

CHAMOIS
Rupicapra rupicapra

The grace and agility of the chamois are astonishing; it is a wondrous sight to watch groups of them leap along narrow rocky ledges with the precision of gymnasts. Chamois move easily on snow as well: they have a membrane between their toes that, when the toes are spread, creates the effect of a snowshoe.

The hallmark feature of the chamois is its horns, which are fairly short: they rise vertically from the head, then suddenly curl backward, like a hook. The horns of females usually appear more bent than curled. The chamois can reach a height of 70 to 85 cm/27 to 33 in at the shoulder, with a body length of about 100 to 130 cm/ 39 to 51 in.

The habitat of the chamois is mountain forests, rocky terrain, and alpine meadows; during the winter, the chamois may descend into the forested areas at the base of the mountains for shelter and food. Its cry consists of an occasional bleat or grunt; the alarm call is an aspirated cry created by blowing through the nostrils.

The Wetterstein Alps

THE REGION AROUND THE Wetterstein massif is known also as the Werdenfelser country, named for a medieval castle north of Garmisch. This group of limestone mountains hugs the Austrian border at another place where Germany protrudes slightly to the south. Its crowning peak, the Zugspitze (2,962 m/9,718 ft), is also the highest point in Germany.

The dominant component of this region is *Wettersteinkalk*, a very hard kind of limestone. Between the ridges are softer layers, *Partnachschichte*, containing clay. As is characteristic of the limestone Alps, steep, rocky walls rise abruptly from a base set amid meadows and woods. In the mountains, trails are often essentially climbing routes with fixed pitons, pegs, and cables, like the *Vie Ferrate* of the Dolomites. Hiking around the Zugspitze is therefore somewhat limited; there are more possibilities on the Wank and Kramer, lower mountains north of Garmisch-Partenkirchen.

The summit of the Zugspitze, Germany's highest peak, offers a splendid vista of the gray Garmisch mountains and into Austria, Switzerland, and Italy. A cog-wheel train takes visitors to the mountain's base at the Eibsee, a dark lake surrounded by trees; a cable-car continues to the top. The nearby town of Garmisch-Partenkirchen has a dramatic and musical heritage and many historic sites.

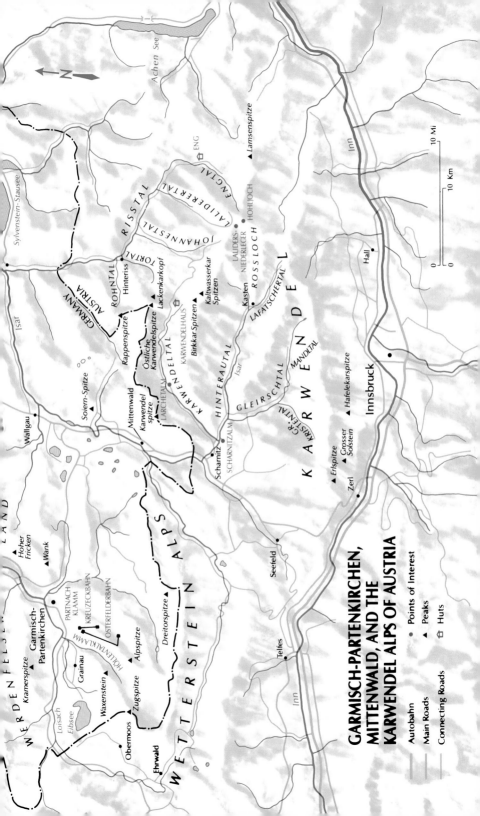

GARMISCH-PARTENKIRCHEN,
MITTENWALD, AND THE
KARWENDEL ALPS OF AUSTRIA

— Autobahn
— Main Roads
— Connecting Roads

• Points of Interest
▲ Peaks
⌂ Huts

Garmisch-Partenkirchen

These two adjoining towns, now virtually united, constitute Germany's most famous alpine resort. On the Loisach River, Garmisch-Partenkirchen is a rather large, sprawling place—the most populous of any alpine resort. The site of the 1936 Winter Olympics, it is Germany's major winter sports center, offering extensive downhill and cross-country skiing, and is especially well known for ice skating. Large stadiums for both skating and skiing were built for the 1936 Olympics. The Zugspitze is barely visible from Garmisch, being hidden behind the Alpspitze and Waxenstein. From the Austrian side, the view of the Zugspitze is closer and the mountain wall appears more vertical.

Near the base of the Zugspitze is the Eibsee, a lake set amid trees, with the tremendous apparition of the mountain's gray, craggy walls rising above. In summer, there is swimming at both this lake and the smaller Riessersee, directly south of Garmisch.

The Zugspitze. The greatest mountain of the Wetterstein massif straddles the Austro-German border, with a second peak on Austrian territory. It is a huge, pale gray rock mass, rising starkly upward from its base; the rock surface is scored and broken, as is typical of eroded limestone. From the summit you can see the Bavarian plain to the north and the mass of Tyrolean Alps to the south. The view ranges as far as the peaks and glaciers of the Hohe Tauern, and beyond into Italy and Switzerland. The effect when looking down from the summit is of long gray arms or tentacles spreading out—these are the various rock ridges that seem to buttress the central mass.

The Zugspitze can be approached from either Garmisch-Partenkirchen in Germany, or from Ehrwald, a pleasant town in Austria. From Garmisch, a cog railway, the Zugspitzbahn, goes to the Hotel Schneefernerhütte at the Zugspitzplatt. From there, a cable car rises to the mountain's summit in another ten minutes. A faster approach is to take the cog railway only as far as the Eibsee, near the base of the mountain, and then the cable car from the Eibsee to the summit.

On the Austrian side, from Obermoos, just outside of Ehrwald, a cable car climbs directly to the summit, where you can step over the border into Germany. There are restaurants on both the Austrian and German summits, and also a German post office; the German side tends to be much more crowded, with souvenir and refreshment stands as well as the summit restaurant. On the Austrian side there is a spacious, handsome restaurant with a glassed-in terrace.

The Höllentalklamm. From Hammersbach, a village southwest of Garmisch, there is access to the deep cleft of the Höllentalklamm—"the gorge of the valley of hell"—below the south wall of the Waxenstein. A path has been built through galleries and over bridges in this steep-sided, narrow gorge, and makes for a thrilling walk, with views of the turbulent, cascading stream of the Hammersbach in its constricted, rocky bed. (Because of the spray, rain gear is advisable for visits to this gorge or the Partnachklamm.)

Osterfelderbahn and Kreuzeckbahn. These two cable cars depart from Kreuzeckbahn, at the southwestern edge of Garmisch, and rise toward the Alpspitze (2,628 m/8,622 ft). They are fairly close together, allowing you to walk from the top station of the Osterfelderbahn down to the top station of the Kreuzeckbahn, while enjoying good views of the Alpspitze, Dreitorspitze, and other peaks.

The Partnachklamm. From the Olympic ski stadium south of Partenkirchen, you can walk through the gorge of the Partnachklamm; the lower of two paths is hewn through sheer walls of rock. Beyond the gorge, you can continue southward up the Reintal past Mitterklamm and Hinterklamm to the Bockhütte. The three peaks of the Dreitorspitze (2,633 m/8,638 ft at highest point) tower above, to the southeast. From this hut, a trail continues southwest through the Reintal, whose upper end is very narrow, enfolded between mountainous ridges. At the end of the valley is the Angerhütte (also called the Reintalangerhütte) where hikers stay overnight, as this is a very long walk from Partenkirchen.

Another possibility is to make a loop trip from the southern edge of the Partnachklamm by taking the trail southeast to the Schachenhaus, with an excellent view of the Dreitorspitze and the Hochblassen (2,707 m/8,881 ft), among other peaks. From the Schachenhaus you may descend to the Bockhütte to return to Partenkirchen.

The Wank. A low mountain (1,780 m/5,840 ft) east of Partenkirchen, the Wank offers views of the Wetterstein Alps from its summit, which can be reached by hiking trail or cable car from Partenkirchen. A trail leads around the Wank's north side to a broad saddle between it and the Hoher Fricken (1,940 m/6,365 ft), another low mountain to the north. From Esterberg at this saddle, you can continue northeastward to the Krottenkopfhütte, below the mountain of the same name (2,086 m/6,844 ft).

The Kramerspitze. West of Garmisch, this low mountain (1,985 m/ 6,512 ft) serves as a viewpoint for the Zugspitze and other Wetterstein Alps. A trail climbs steeply to the Kramer plateau and the Gasthaus St. Martin. The Stepbergalm, on a saddle between the Kramerspitze and the Hoher Ziegspitz (1,864 m/6,115 ft), can be reached by a trail between Garmisch and Grainau, a village west of the town.

Berchtesgaden Alpine Park

GERMANY'S SECOND-BEST-KNOWN Alpine resort is at the foot of the Watzmann (2,713 m/8,901 ft), the second highest mountain in Germany. The nearby Hochkalter (2,607 m/8,553 ft) bears Germany's only remaining glacier, the little Blaueisgletscher—the northernmost glacier in the Alps. These mountains are within the Berchtesgaden Alpine Park, which was established in 1978.

The park consists of three zones. The outer area of the park includes Berchtesgaden, Ramsau, and other nearby towns; the middle area is developed for outdoor activities such as skiing and hiking; the inner, nature-preservation area includes the Königssee, and the Watzmann, Hochkalter, and the other mountains around the lake, within the German border.

Berchtesgaden

The town of Berchtesgaden, with an attractive old quarter in its center, is set in a bowl half surrounded by limestone mountains. The distinctive configuration of the Watzmann, with its multiple peaks, dominates the town. The mountain is actually nearly split, with two sharply angled rock towers leaning toward each other over two broad, snowy gaps. The highest peak is the

The Königssee is a lake that visitors can cross by boat to visit a church with onion-top steeples. Facing page: Accessible by trail or cable-car, the view from the Jenner mountain offers a beautiful view down to the Königssee, nestled between rock peaks.

Mittelspitze (2,713 m/8,901 ft), "King Watzmann"; at an almost right angle to this is the Watzmann "wife" (Kleine Watzmann: 2,307 m/7,569 ft), with the five Watzmann "children" (Watzmann Kinder) between them. (According to legend, this king and his family ruled with an iron fist; in punishment, God turned them into stone.) To the east are the Hagengebirge, and to the south (in Austria), the Steinernes Meer.

Königssee and Obersee

Perhaps the loveliest of all German lakes is the Königssee, enclosed within almost vertical rock walls so that the effect is that of a fjord rather than a lake. The lakeside cliffs leave no room in many places for a path, but visitors can take a trip up the lake by almost silent launches. A favorite spot is the picturesque little baroque chapel of St. Bartholomä, with two red onion domes, on the west side of the lake. The chapel and a restaurant are on a grassy terrace, the only flat bank along the shores of the lake. Behind the chapel is the massive east wall of the Watzmann; the "Eiskapelle" trail leads through the woods to an opening at the foot of this imposing wall. At the end of the Königssee is Salletalm, from which a footpath leads to the Obersee, another very lovely but much smaller lake, also dramatically enclosed by cliffs. These two lakes, once connected, were separated by an ancient landslide.

Gotzenalm. To reach this scenic viewpoint over the Königssee, first take the boat to Kessel. From there, climb a steep path to the Gotzenthal-Alm and continue on past Seeaualm to Gotzenalm. A short path climbs up to the Warteck, descending slightly to Feuerpalfen for a superb view. Return to Kessel by the same route; alternatively, from Gotzenthal-Alm continue northward to Königsbachalm, where there is the option of continuing on to the middle station of the Jenner cable car or walking down to the Königssee.

The Jenner. The Jenner mountain (1,874 m/6,148 ft) rises to the east of the northern tip of the Königssee. A cable car ascends nearly to the summit (there is also a trail) from which there is a lovely view down to the lake, 1,200 m/3,937 ft below, enclosed within its rock walls. A trail continues eastward to the Stahlhaus on the border ridge with Austria. The Jenner mountain is the chief ski area near Berchtesgaden.

Grünstein and the Kürointhütte. The Grünstein is a very low mountain (1,304 m/4,278 ft) from which there is a good view of the Watzmann and Berchtesgaden; the Grünstein hut is just below the top. You can hike up from the north end of the Königssee or from Hinterschönau, west of Schönau (the town between Berchtesgaden and the Königssee). On the approach from the Königssee, you can also turn south at Klinger Alm for the Küroint hut, and then continue southward to a very fine viewpoint overlooking the lake.

Obersalzberg and Kehlstein

The lovely Berchtesgaden mountains are still shadowed by the memory of the Nazi period. Obersalzberg, east of Berchtesgaden, was the site of Hitler's country house (now destroyed, except for the bunkers). His "Eagle's Nest" was perched on the Kehlstein (1,881 m/6,171 ft), the mountain above Obersalzberg. Between May and October, special buses bring visitors up the winding, steep mountain road, almost to the summit. An elevator rises to the top, from which there is a panoramic view of the mountains around Berchtesgaden. There is a restaurant on the summit.

Untersberg

This mountain, on the Austrian border, separates Berchtesgaden from Salzburg to the north, and is as often climbed from Salzburg as from Berchtesgaden. Its German summit is the Berchtesgadener Hochthron (1,972 m/6,470 ft); the Austrian summit is the Salzburger Hochthron (1,853 m/6,079 ft). There are several ways up the Untersberg. From St. Leonhard, south of Grödig on the Austrian side, a cable car mounts nearly to the Austrian summit, from which a trail extends to the German summit. From Markt Schellenberg, a small German town just before the border, you can climb up a trail to the Schellenberg Eishöhle, a large ice cave (guided tours). Another approach starts at Hinter Gern (next to the village of Maria Gern, north of Berchtesgaden), from which a trail, the "Stöhrweg," climbs to Leiterl, the Stöhrhaus, and the summit.

Ramsau

A quiet alternative to Berchtesgaden is Ramsau, a pleasant resort village 9 km/5.6 mi west of the bigger town. The nearby Hintersee offers a good view of the Hochkalter and the Watzmann. From Ramsau you can take a trail southwest and then south past Schärtenalm, to the Blaueishütte near the small Blaueis glacier, below the summit of the Hochkalter. Another route from Ramsau leads more directly south to Eckaualm, then to Hochalm and Hochalpscharte, for a good view of the Blaueisspitze (2,481 m/8,140 ft) and the Watzmann. The Wimbachtal is a valley separating the Hochkalter and the Watzmann. At the head of the valley is a gorge, the Wimbachklamm. A trail climbs from the gorge southeastward past Stubenalm and Mitterkaseralm to the Watzmannhaus, scenically located below the mountain's north ridge.

The Italian Alps

T he Italian Alps are divided into two very different groups. The mountains in northwestern Italy, near Monte Bianco (Mont Blanc) and the Gran Paradiso, are snowcapped and surrounded by glaciers—characteristically grand alpine terrain. The Dolomites in northeastern Italy have an entirely different and unique appearance. These great masses and towers of rock are classified among the limestone Alps, although in composition they differ slightly from other limestone Alps, such as those in northern Austria. Also in northeastern Italy are the Adamello-Presanella and the Stelvio massifs, typically alpine mountains that contrast greatly with the nearby Dolomites.

Travelers in the Alps of northwestern Italy will find a few large resorts, primarily Courmayeur and Breuil-Cervinia, and a number of small and sometimes very simple, appealing villages. Aosta, at the hub of the region, is a large town that is too distant from the upper valleys to make a convenient base. By contrast, the Dolomites in the northeast are sprinkled with numerous resorts,

Near the top of Passo del Pordoi, between Canazei and Arabba, terraces of stone grace the rough-hewn Dolomite mountains above the hillside's deeply folded green ridges.

some very chic. Yet even in the Dolomites simple villages are found, as they are in the Adamello-Presanella and the Stelvio regions.

Since most Italians take their vacations during the month of August, advance booking for hotels in resort areas and even for Alpine Club huts is highly advisable.

Addresses: For information on Italy, contact the Italian Government Travel Office.

In the U.S., the addresses are: 630 Fifth Avenue, New York, NY 10111; (212) 245-4822. 500 North Michigan Avenue, Chicago, IL 60611; (312) 644-0990. 360 Post Street, San Francisco, CA 94108; (415) 392-6206.

In Canada, the travel office address is: 1 Place Ville Marie, Suite 1914, Montreal, Que. H38 3M9; (514) 866-7667.

In Great Britain, the travel office address is: Italian State Tourist Office (E.N.I.T.), Princes Street 1, London W1R 8AY; (44) 1-408 1254.

To join the Italian Alpine Club, contact: Club Alpino Italiano (CAI), Via Ugo Foscola 3, Milan; (39) 2-720 22 557.

The Alps of
Northwestern Italy

THE COMPLEX CHAIN OF mountains called the Alps was formed by Italy's collision with the southern edge of the European continent, and many of the greatest mountains created by this event now form the border between Italy and her neighbors. The eastern slopes of the Maritime, Cottian, and Graian Alps are in Italy, but the western slopes are in France; the southern slopes of the Pennine and Lepontine Alps are in Italy, but the northern slopes are in Switzerland. And the Mont Blanc massif is shared between France and Italy. Thus, the mountains of the Gran Paradiso massif belong to the same geological group as those of the French Vanoise; the mountains north of the Val d'Aosta (such as Monte Cervino and Monte Rosa) belong to the Pennine range and share the geological complexities of the Valaisian Alps; and Monte Bianco is the Italian slope of Mont Blanc.

Historically this region, part of the Piedmont, was linguistically and culturally French. Maps of the northwestern Italian Alps are sprinkled with villages, valleys, and mountains that have French names, and the traveler here discovers that the people speak French (and also a Provençal dialect) as well as Italian.

The Alps North of the Val d'Aosta

The Aosta Valley cuts diagonally across northwestern Italy, separating its two major alpine areas and providing access to the mountains of this region. The major town, Aosta, was originally Augusta Praetoria, named for Caesar Augustus, and Aosta was called "the Rome of the Alps." There are several Roman ruins, including a triumphal arch and the remains of an amphitheater, as well as medieval structures such as a fine Romanesque cloister at the Collegiate Church of San Orso. Aosta is now a fairly large, sprawling town with an industrial zone.

MONTE BIANCO (MONT BLANC)
AND COURMAYEUR

The French-Italian frontier extends over many of the greatest peaks on the Mont Blanc massif, though not directly over the summit of the highest one. Monte Bianco di Courmayeur, the Italian summit of Mont Blanc, however, is

indeed so high (4,748 m/15,577 ft) that it is the second tallest point in the Alps. The southern side of the Mont Blanc massif, which belongs to Italy, is quite different in appearance from the French side. Monte Bianco rises in the distance above the Val d'Aosta like a fantastic white apparition, monumental in size—a Himalayan effect. Yet when you draw near, this floating cloud of gleaming white resolves itself into a rugged wall of rock with glaciers plunging down its sides. Seen from the north, Mont Blanc is a snowy dome above long, comparatively smooth slopes of ice and snow. Its southern face looks rougher and more complex, displaying great ridges of exposed rock in which deep furrows are packed with the ice of precipitous glaciers. East of the summit, the celebrated Brenva glacier plummets from the curved wall of Mont Maudit. The ascent of Mont Blanc from the Italian side is generally a more demanding feat of mountaineering, and the Brenva route is a considerable challenge.

The long valley scooped out along the base of the massif is known by two names: its eastern side is the Val Ferret, fed by streams from Mont Dolent and the other mountains east of the Punta Helbronner; its western side is the Val Veny (Veni on some maps). The watercourses from these two valleys join at the village of Entrèves, creating the Dora Báltea, which flows southeastward down the Val d'Aosta, at right angles to the massif.

Courmayeur is the Italian counterpart to Chamonix, yet there are great differences between the two towns. From Chamonix you can look straight up to the snowy dome of Mont Blanc, but from Courmayeur—though the town faces a striking wall of icy, rocky towers—your view of Monte Bianco is blocked by nearby Mont Chétif (2,343 m/7,687 ft). A small, cosmopolitan resort town, Courmayeur is an agreeable combination of Italian elegance and alpine informality, with a cobbled main street on which traffic is prohibited. It is less congested and more relaxed than Chamonix, and less showy than the major Dolomite resorts. Courmayeur is a major center for skiing, climbing, and hiking.

Courmayeur is reached easily by the Petit St. Bernard Pass from France as well as by the Mont Blanc tunnel. From Courmayeur, the main road descends to Aosta.

Monte Bianco Cable Car. The chief cable car of the area is the Funivie Monte Bianco, the great system of connecting lifts that surmounts the entire massif. On the Italian side, the lift begins several kilometers from Courmayeur at La Palud near the village of Entrèves. It rises, with intermediate

A snow-capped ridge reaches into the clouds near Monte Bianco, the Italian side of Mont Blanc. Furrowed by glaciers, the southern side of the famous mountain is rougher and a more formidable challenge to mountaineers.

stops at Pavillon and Rifugio Torino, to Punta (Pointe) Helbronner on the border, and the views are spectacular. From this side, the Aiguille (also known as the Dent) du Géant looks more like a bony finger pointing up into the sky than a tooth. A connecting cable car then swings over the glacier to the Aiguille du Midi on the French side (bring your passport). You can hike up part of this route by a steep path to Mont Fréty; hikers in good condition can continue climbing to the Rifugio Torino.

Plan Chécrouit and Cresta d'Arp. A series of linked cable cars also rises from Courmayeur to the Plan Chécrouit and Cresta d'Arp, along the scenic ridge above the Val Veny. Many hikers following the Tour du Mont Blanc between the Col de la Seigne and Courmayeur take the trail along this ridge, past the pretty Lac de Chécrouit and the Col de Chécrouit, and use the Plan Chécrouit cable car to descend to Courmayeur. At the northeastern edge of the ridge is Mont Chétif, from the summit of which the view of the great mountain is superb. An excursion to the top of Mont Chétif may be made as a day trip from Courmayeur, or combined with the section of the Tour du Mont Blanc route through Plan Chécrouit.

Val Veny

At the southern base of Monte Bianco is the Val Veny (or Veni). The ridge above this valley is directly opposite the mountain's rugged south face, which has rocky ribs and steep glaciers, including the great Brenva. The view from the Val Veny extends northeast to the Aiguille du Géant and the Grandes Jorasses.

You may drive partway up the Val Veny toward the "Lac" di Combal (more like a braided stream than a lake), below the long, narrow Glacier du Miage. From there a path climbs to the Rifugio Elisabetta, an Italian Alpine Club hut scenically located below the impressive Glacier de la Lée (Lex on some maps) Blanche. To the northwest is the Aiguille de la Trélatête (3,892 m/12,769 ft), and to the northeast, Monte Bianco. The main trail, part of the Tour du Mont Blanc, climbs to the Col de la Seigne and the French border; from the col there is a view toward the Italian slope of Mont Blanc.

Val Ferret

The other section of the deep trench below the south face of the Mont Blanc massif extends northeast from Entrèves. Towering above to the north are the Aiguille du Géant, the Grandes Jorasses, the Aiguille de Triolet, and Mont Dolent, as well as other lesser *aiguilles* and *pointes.* You can drive up the valley as far as Arp Nouvaz (Arnuva on some maps), from which the Tour du

Mont Blanc continues over the Grand Col Ferret into Switzerland. This is one of the most attractive sections of the entire route, ascending through wild, empty country past the glaciers of Triolet, Pré-de-Bar, and Mont Dolent. The view extends down the Val Ferret and the Val Veny to the Col de la Seigne. There is cross-country skiing in Val Ferret.

MONTE CERVINO (MATTERHORN) AND BREUIL-CERVINIA

The Valtournenche climbs to the southern base of the Matterhorn, called Monte Cervino in Italian. Breuil-Cervinia, the resort at the upper end of the valley, is by virtue of its location the Italian counterpart of Zermatt.

Breuil-Cervinia is in a bowl, the bottom of an ancient cirque scooped out below Monte Cervino. From Breuil, the famous mountain has the simple shape of a couple of children's toy blocks, a cube above a triangle. Monte Cervino is the only big mountain visible from this resort, and thus it dominates the view. Above the west side of the valley are the two Jumeaux (or "twins": 3,872 m/12,703 ft), but they do not appear as very distinct from the wall below.

Breuil was first mentioned in literature in 1792 by Horace Benedict de Saussure, the Swiss naturalist who studied the Alps. In 1865, it was the base for the Italian team that was racing Edward Whymper's party to conquer the Matterhorn.

Though it is one of Italy's premier skiing resorts, Breuil is much smaller than Zermatt. It is not an alpine village, however; much of the place looks fairly new, with a number of five- and six-story buildings instead of old wooden chalets. Yet Breuil does not look as wholly impersonal and artificial as the contemporary ski resorts of France. Its central street is closed to traffic.

The Plateau Rosa cable car rises to 3,480 m/11,417 ft on the glacier east of Monte Cervino. This offers the best way to see the alpine scenery above Breuil, which consists of many of the same peaks visible from Zermatt, although seen here from a different side and perspective. The view includes the Dent d'Hérens, the east face of Monte Cervino, and the Klein Matterhorn. Beyond the glacier is the Zermatt Valley, with such mountains as the Ober Gabelhorn, Zinalrothorn, and Weisshorn to the northwest, and the Mischabel peaks to the northeast. On a clear day, you can see as far as Monte Bianco and the Jungfrau. On the Italian side of the border, to the south, is the Gran Tournalin (3,379 m/11,086 ft).

Monte Cervino is reflected in the clear water of the little Lago Bleu, a pretty lake just outside Breuil that is a popular picnic spot.

GOLDEN EAGLE
Aquila chrysaetos

It is a thrill to see a bird with a tremendous wingspan flash overhead, then disappear against a rocky face. The golden eagle may reach 75 to 90 cm/30 to 35 in in length and have a wingspan up to 2.5 m/7.5 ft; only vultures have a greater wingspan. Males may weigh as much as 4 kg/9 lbs; females up to 6 kg/13 lbs. The mature eagle is brown with gold tones on the neck, with a lighter area below the wings and at the base of the tail.

The golden eagle's alpine habitat extends from the upper limit of the forest to rocky regions up to 3,000 m/9,842 ft. Nests are usually above treeline, and eagles may be seen circling on ascending air currents above a nest.

Eagles are monogamous. Each pair controls a very large territory, where they hunt close together; on steep rocky walls within this domain, a couple establishes four or five berths, which they use in turn for nests. A factor limiting the altitude of the nests is the weight of the prey the eagles must lift to them, sometimes 8 kg/18 lbs, though probably most prey weighs about 1 kg/2 lbs. Only in favorable wind conditions can an eagle carry an animal as heavy as itself. There are reports of eagles having to drop young chamois and ibex after a few seconds of flight. In the summer they feed mostly upon marmots, but also on hares and other little mammals, as well as upon foxes, squirrels, ermine, and very young chamois and ibex. In winter they may eat domestic animals, including cats. Alpine stories of eagles carrying away human babies are considered to be folktales.

Because the eagle was considered a nuisance, it was hunted almost to extinction in some places. It is mostly silent, but may emit sounds resembling mewing or barking.

Facing page: From Belvedere, a cable-car ride from the Macugnaga area, the trail to Alpe Pedriola and the Rifugio Zamboni-Zappa is very scenic, with bright wildflowers lining the path and the face of Monte Rosa in the distance. Grand views continue beyond this hut on the path toward the Colletto Bortolan.

Breuil-Cervinia offers the highest and some of the best and most extensive (15–20 km/9–12 mi) summer skiing in the Alps, due to the breadth of the high glaciers that are the summer skiing ground. (The skiing is actually upon Swiss territory.) It is possible to ski across to the Klein Matterhorn or Trockener Steg cable cars and descend to Zermatt, then return the next day. Breuil-Cervinia is also an important mountaineering center, notably for ascents of Monte Cervino and the Dent d'Hérens. There is a guides' organization and climbing school. Breuil also has one of the world's fastest bobsled tracks. Hiking, however, is less extensive than at Zermatt because the topography of the upper Valtournenche limits the possible directions you can take. Hikers may take the cable car as far as Plan Maison, a grassy terrace above Breuil, and walk toward the walls that hem in the valley on the west and east. Some trails contour around the upper reaches of the basin. A route called the "Grande Balconata del Cervino" loops around Breuil and Valtournenche, the larger village to the south. This route links together various trails on the upper slopes of both sides of the valley, passing through some of the old farming villages.

Breuil-Cervinia is reached from Châtillon, east of Aosta in the Val d'Aosta.

VAL D'AYAS

This valley rises to a point below the Breithorn and the twin peaks of Castor and Pollux; climbers use the upper valley as a base for ascents of these mountains. It is broader and gentler than the Valtournenche. The chief resort near the upper end of the valley is Champoluc; the much smaller San Giacomo (St.-Jacques) is at the end of the road. Above the upper valley can be seen a shelf of glaciers, the southern slopes of Castor and Pollux. There is also an attractive view from Antagnod, a hamlet above the western side of the valley, from which you can look across to the glaciers. From San Giacomo, the hiking trails up the Vallone di Verra climb to the meadows at the foot of the moraines and glaciers. There are several ski lifts near Champoluc, as well as cross-country skiing. The Val d'Ayas is reached from Verrès in the Aosta Valley, east of Aosta.

VAL GRESSONEY

Whereas the Valtournenche ends in a wall of rock, the Val Gressoney ends in a wall of snow: the south face of the Liskamm, also visible from Zermatt. A curiosity of this valley is that there are still German-speaking communities among the mountain villages. Their inhabitants are Walser, people whose ancestors came from the Wallis (the Swiss Valais) and settled here centuries ago; their wooden chalets resemble those seen in the Valais. This valley is unspoiled, with no big developments to mar the pleasant alpine scenery: it is a place for quiet family vacations. There are several simple, pretty villages. At Fontainemore there is a medieval stone bridge over the River Lis (or Lys). The façade of the church at Issime vibrates with the colors of the Renaissance murals that cover it. At the upper end of the valley are Gressoney-St.-Jean and, higher still, Gressoney-la-Trinité, both picturesque villages with old wooden houses. From the upper end of the valley the steep Ghiacciaio (glacier) del Lis is visible, winding down from the great snowy hump of the Liskamm, source of the River Lis that waters this valley. From Gressoney-la-Trinité you can hike up to Lago Gabiet, for a fine view of the glaciers and the Piramide Vincent (4,215 m/13,829 ft), one of the multiple summits of Monte Rosa. Two smaller lakes, Lago Bleu and Lago Verde, are still closer to the snows. The trail to the Plateau de Lis ascends to the foot of the glacier. Gressoney is a mountaineering base for climbing the south face of the Liskamm and Monte Rosa. There are several ski lifts near Gressoney-la-Trinité and Gressoney-St.-Jean, and cross-country skiing along the valley.

The entrance to the Val Gressoney is at Pont-St.-Martin, near the southeastern end of the Val d'Aosta.

MACUGNAGA

Unlike the Val Gressoney approach to Monte Rosa, Macugnaga is reached from the Val d'Ossola to the east, not from the Val d'Aosta. Located at the upper end of the Val d'Anzasca, this resort enjoys a magnificent location below the east face of Monte Rosa (4,634 m/15,203 ft), one of the greatest mountains in the Alps. Macugnaga sits below this massive mountain, with several of its multiple summits spread in a line along the grand wall: from south to north, the Punta Gnifetti (Signalkuppe: 4,554 m/14,941 ft), Zumsteinspitze (4,563 m/14,970 ft), Punta Dufour (Dufourspitze; at 4,634 m/15,203 ft, the highest summit), and Nordend (4,609 m/15,121 ft). The Swiss border runs along the line of these summits, continuing beyond Monte Rosa over the peaks of the Jägerhorn (3,970 m/13,025 ft), Cima di Jazzi (3,804 m/12,480 ft), and Weissthor (Neue Weisstorspitze: 3,639 m/11,939 ft). The ascent of Monte Rosa from Macugnaga is extremely difficult.

Pages 286 and 287: A pond lies in a stony landscape looking south to Gran Paradiso mountain. The park is indeed a paradise for hikers and wildlife enthusiasts: once the hunting ground of Italian royalty, this is fine territory for viewing the elusive ibex and chamois.

Macugnaga actually consists of several villages set close together: principally, Borca, Staffa, and Pecetto. Though Macugnaga is an important mountaineering center and a ski resort, it remains quite unspoiled.

For centuries, Macugnaga has had close connections with Switzerland. The Moro Pass, north of Macugnaga, leads to the Saas Valley in the Swiss Valais. Before the Simplon road was built, the Moro Pass was the main Alpine pass route from Italy to the Swiss Valais. As in the Val Gressoney, a group of German-speaking Walser crossed the mountains from Switzerland and settled here during the thirteenth century. The wooden chalets of the old part of Macugnaga, with their flower-decked balconies, resemble those of the Valais.

The Belvedere chair lift from Pecetto rises nearly to the edge of the Belvedere glacier, from which there is a comprehensive view of the great amphitheater of mountains and hanging glaciers enclosing the upper end of the valley. A very scenic trail continues on a marked route across the glacier to the Rifugio Zamboni-Zappa, set amid beautiful meadows. From this remarkable viewpoint you can see at close range the most extreme difference in altitude of any Alpine mountain wall, about 2,500 m/8,200 ft. On warm afternoons, you can hear the roar of avalanches sweeping down the wall and see the white clouds of snow and pulverized ice.

The Moro Pass above Macugnaga can be reached by cable car or hiking trail. From the pass you can look toward Monte Rosa and also across the Saas Valley to the Mischabel range. There is a trail but no cable car on the Swiss side of the pass. The slope below the Moro Pass is used for skiing in winter, and there is cross-country skiing along the valley. From Switzerland, Macugnaga can also be reached from the Simplon Pass and Domodossola.

The Alps South of the Val d'Aosta

The mountains north of the Val d'Aosta belong to the Pennine Alps; those south of the valley belong to the Graian Alps. These mountains are the setting for one of Italy's greatest national parks, the Gran Paradiso, a region of magnificent snowcapped peaks and glaciers. Four great valleys on the south side of the Val d'Aosta climb into the mountains—the Valgrisenche, Val di Rhêmes, Valsavarenche, and Val di Cogne, of which the last three enter the park. Two more valleys enter the park from the east and south: the Valle Soana and the Valle dell'Orco. As French is the native language of the people in the valleys south as well as north of the Val d'Aosta, many place names appear on maps sometimes in French, and sometimes in Italian.

By mid-July in the meadows below Monte Rosa in Gran Paradiso National Park, pasque flowers (Pulsatilla) have gone to seed. Tiny hairs let the seeds be carried on wind currents far from the parent plant.

VALGRISENCHE

This is the most quiet of the valleys, since it is not actually part of the national park and there is very little development for skiing. The valley is in part very narrow, with a scant sprinkling of hamlets—tiny, simple, delightful places, none of which could be called an alpine resort, though several have a hotel. Planaval has a few old stone farmhouses with wooden balconies and slate roofs. Behind the hamlet is a cliff with a waterfall. West of Planaval is a cluster of glaciers, the big Ghiacciaio del Rutor and the smaller glaciers of Château Blanc and Morion. A trail departs near Planaval and leads over the cliffs to the foot of the Becca Blanche and Becca Noire, near the Col di Planaval, at the edge of the Ghiacciaio di Château Blanc. Another trail on this west side of the valley ascends to the edge of the Ghiacciaio di Morion, below the Testa del Rutor (3,486 m/11,437 ft).

Farther up the valley, where it widens a little, are the tiny villages of Valgrisenche and Bonne, two utterly simple communities consisting of a few stone buildings. From Bonne, steep trails mount the slopes below the Testa del Rutor as well as to the Forcla du Bre, a notch in the cliffs beyond which is the little Lac de St.-Grat, scenically positioned below the Gran Becca du Mont (3,214 m/10,545 ft) and the Becca du Lac (3,396 m/11,142 ft), with glaciers below.

Beyond Bonne is the artificial Lago di Beauregard, a long lake. You can drive across the dam wall and continue south for another 5 km/3 mi to the end of the public road, then continue on foot to the Rifugio Bezzi. The upper end of the valley is very wild, with many waterfalls. The view from the hut is of a wide, low cirque containing the Ghiacciaio di Vaudet and the Grande Sassière (3,751 m/12,306 ft), on the French border. The tallest peaks on the east are the Grande Traversière (3,496 m/11,470 ft) and the Grande Rousse (3,607 m/11,834 ft).

There are a few ski lifts near the village of Valgrisenche, and cross-country skiing along the valley floor.

GRAN PARADISO NATIONAL PARK

The Gran Paradiso is the only 4,000-m/13,123-ft mountain entirely upon Italian territory. The park named for it contains a multitude of other snow-swept mountains and glaciers. It is aptly named, for the park is a paradise for hikers, climbers, and lovers of wildlife. It was the first national park established within Italy (1922)—indeed, it was one of the first parks in all Europe—and it has a special historic significance as a sanctuary for the ibex, an alpine animal that Italian conservationists were instrumental in saving. This handsome member of the goat family was hunted to extinction in most of Europe, but the species was preserved and nurtured back in the Gran Paradiso and reintroduced from here into other alpine countries; today, large numbers roam the park.

In the spring, chamois and ibex come down and feed on the fresh grass in the valleys, occasionally within view of drivers on nearby roads. During most of the summer, however, they are well above tree line and you must hike up to about 2,000 m/6,560 ft or 2,500 m/8,200 ft to see them. Animals on slopes above a trail sometimes knock down stones, so hikers should be alert and watchful.

Visitors to the Gran Paradiso may not pick flowers or disturb the wildlife; they may camp and make fires only at authorized sites. Accommodations are available in villages and hamlets including Valsavarenche, Valnontey, and others.

Val di Rhêmes

The eastern but not the western slope of this valley is within the park. It is broader than the Valgrisenche, and there is a pleasing contrast between the broad meadows along the banks of the Dora di Rhêmes and the cliffs and pointed rock peaks above. Along the valley are several simple villages, with old stone houses as well as newer ones; the chief villages are Rhêmes-St.-Georges, near the entrance to the valley, and Rhêmes-Notre-Dame, near its middle. Several more hamlets are scattered along the road, the last and highest being Thumel. The upper valley is dominated by the triangular rock tower of the Granta Parei (3,387 m/11,112 ft), which divides the glaciers of Sotses and Golettaz. From the eastern side of the valley, toward the foot of the glaciers, the Punta Tsantalèynez (3,601 m/11,814 ft) comes into view. The road extends almost to the Rifugio Benevolo on the valley's eastern slope, from which there are fine views of these glaciers and the crest of mountains above them. At the top of the Ghiacciaio di Sotses is the Col di Rhêmes, on the French border, on the other side of which is the Vanoise National Park. Trails over the ridges on both slopes of the valley connect with the Valgrisenche (via the Col Fenêtre) to the west and the Valsavarenche (via the Col di l'Entrelor) to the east.

There is a ski lift near Rhêmes-Notre-Dame—accommodations can be found here as well—and two more near Chanavey, and cross-country skiing along the valley.

Valsavarenche

This is the wildest valley within the Gran Paradiso National Park, and the gateway to some of its grandest scenery. The crown of the entire park—the Gran Paradiso mountain, surrounded by other high peaks and the park's most extensive cluster of glaciers—is atop the valley's eastern slope. The Valsavarenche shares these treasures with the Valnontey, immediately to the east.

The valley is broad at first, so that the road lies beside the bed of the Savara stream. There are several small, unspoiled villages set amid meadows, including Dégioz and Eaux Rousses. Beyond Eaux Rousses, the stream has cut a small gorge with rocky sides. Then the valley widens again, and there are meadows beside the stream. Pont, with a couple of hotels and a campground, is at the end of the road. From this upper end of the valley, the great snowy mass of the Gran Paradiso is seen to the east and the Ghiacciaio del Grand Etrét below a narrow cirque to the south. From Pont, climbers set out for the Gran Paradiso. Since there are no mechanical lifts in the Valsavarenche, the only way to see the park here is to walk or climb.

COMMON HOUSELEEK
Sempervivum tectorum

The distinguishing feature of the various kinds of houseleeks found in the Alps is as much the stem as the flower; the stem is erect, comparatively long (often up to 20 cm/8 in) for an alpine flower, and appears to be braided. This is not the case. Actually the leaves, growing upright, encircle the stem and cling very close to it, creating the illusion of a braid. The leaves are succulent, narrow, and oval, with pointed tips. They are green, but may have a reddish tinge. Star-shaped flowers grow atop this curious stalk.

Houseleeks grow among rocks, on stony meadows, and on scree, in lime-free soil. This plant was once grown on roofs to keep the slates in place.

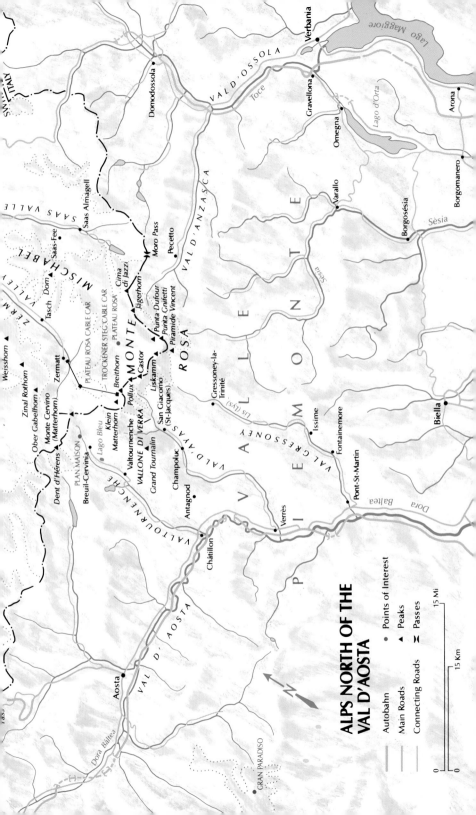

ALPS NORTH OF THE VAL D'AOSTA

Autobahn

Main Roads

Connecting Roads

• Points of Interest

▲ Peaks

✕ Passes

0   15 Mi

0   15 Km

The excursion to the Rifugio Chabod is a popular walk. The trail begins between Eaux Rousses and Pont. From the hut there is a fine view of the crest of the park, with the peaks of the Herbétet (3,778 m/12,395 ft), Becca di Montandayné (3,838 m/12,592 ft), Piccolo Paradiso (3,923 m/12,871 ft), Gran Paradiso (4,061 m/13,323 ft), and Becca di Moncorvè (3,875 m/12,713 ft). The principal glacier seen from this hut is the Ghiacciaio di Laveciau, sweeping down from the Gran Paradiso. The neatly V-shaped moraine in front of the glacier's tongue is a good example of the formations created by retreating glaciers.

A trail south of Pont ascends to the Rifugio Vittorio Emanuele, almost directly below the Gran Paradiso and most often used for climbing it. The view of the mountain from this site, however, is foreshortened. The hut overlooks the Ghiacciaio di Moncorvè and has a good view of La Trésenta (3,609 m/11,841 ft) and the Ciarforon (3,642 m/11,949 ft).

Above the west slope of the Valsavarenche is the long Nivolet plateau, wild and spacious. Several trails climb up to it; the most direct route is from Pont. Near its upper end, at the Col de Nivolet, are several lakes. One- or two-day walks can be taken here, between Dégioz and Noasca. There are overnight accommodations at the Rifugio Città di Chivasso or nearby at the Albergo (Rifugio) Savoia, originally one of King Victor Emmanuel II's hunting retreats. From Dégioz there are also routes to the Val di Cogne (via the Col di Belleface) and the Valnontey (via the Col Lauson). Both routes curve around the base of La Grivola (3,969 m/13,022 ft), the big mountain at the north end of the Gran Paradiso massif.

There is a ski lift near Dégioz and cross-country skiing along the valley.

Val di Cogne

This is the major valley of the park, with the largest selection of accommodations, and it is the most-often visited. One of its tributaries, the Valnontey, is at the base of grand scenery that can be seen on an easy walk. Cogne, the chief village and the only resort in the park, is situated here; nearby is the smaller village of Valnontey, where there are several hotels and the Paradisia alpine garden.

There are several ski lifts and a cable car near Cogne and Epinel. There is cross-country skiing along the valley, as well as a ski jump.

Valnontey. This tributary valley leads straight into the park's most glorious scenery. A long, gentle path follows the Valnontey stream. At the end of the valley is a superb alpine cirque. The great glacier in the center is the suggestively named Ghiacciaio della Tribolazione ("glacier of tribulation"). To the west are the glaciers of Dzasset and Herbétet, to the east the glaciers of Money (pronounced Mo-NAY) and Coupe di Money. Above this fan-shaped spread of ice is a horseshoe crest of peaks: from west to east, the Herbétet, Becca di Montandayné, Piccolo Paradiso, Gran Paradiso, Becca di Moncorvè, and then the Punta Ceresole (3,777 m/12,392 ft), Testa della Tribolazione (3,642 m/11,949 ft), Testa di Valnontey (3,562 m/11,686 ft), Roccia Viva (3,650 m/11,975 ft), and Torre del Gran San Pietro (3,692 m/12,113 ft), among others. What makes this cirque grand is not the particular height of any peak but the breadth of the entire formation.

For the best, most comprehensive views of the cirque, you must hike up the valley slopes on the west or east side. The trail on the west climbs up to the meadows of Herbétet, where there is a natural belvedere from which to admire the spread of glaciers and mountains. From the east side of the valley, you can climb to the meadows at Money for a similarly spectacular view. The hike up to the Rifugio Vittorio Sella, above the west slope of the Valnontey, is very popular; though a little farther from the Gran Paradiso than Herbétet, it enjoys panoramic views of the massif. The Gran Serra (3,552 m/11,654 ft) and the Lauson glacier overlook the hut from the south. West of the hut is the Col Lauson, from which a trail connects to the Valsavarenche.

Vallone di Valeille. This tributary valley, like Valnontey, climbs directly south into the mountains. It is narrow, wild, and uninhabited, with several fine waterfalls. From the village of Lillaz, at the head of this valley, a trail leads up to the moraine at the valley's upper end. Above is the Ghiacciaio di Valeille, enfolded within a crest of rocky peaks. On the west of the glacier is the Torre del Gran San Pietro, in the middle the Ondezana (3,492 m/11,457 ft), and on the east the Punta delle Sengie (3,408 m/11,181 ft), among others.

Valle Soana

The Valle Soana is approached from Pont Canavese, near the southeastern edge of the park. Though the lower Valle Soana only skirts the eastern border of the park, its two upper branches, the Val di Forzo and the Valle di Campiglia, enter the park. Beyond the village of Bosco, the Val di Forzo rises to the northwest. The road ends at the little village of Tressi. Hiking trails continue up to the Col di Bardoney, beneath the Torre Lavina (3,308 m/ 10,853 ft) and the Monveso di Forzo (3,322 m/10,899 ft), the two highest peaks above the valley; there are no glaciers to be seen south of the Col di Bardoney, however. (The upper part of this trail is poorly marked; on the north side of the col, the route descends to the Val di Cogne.) Valprato Soana is the junction for the broad Valle di Campiglia, which leads north into the

A delicate mist sprays the lush greenery by a steep and rushing waterfall on the road northwest of the town of Cogne. Facing page: Small streams lace the Valsavarenche on the hike from Rifugio Chabod.

mountains. Beyond the village of Campiglia Soana the road deteriorates, but trails continue to the long ridge of the Cima di Peradza (2,978 m/9,770 ft) and the Rosa dei Banchi (3,164 m/10,380 ft), the highest point above this valley.

Valle dell'Orco

The long Valle dell'Orco (on some maps, the Valle di Locana) skirts the southern edge of the park, then climbs to high country in its southwestern corner. The valley, wide at first, follows the Orca River beyond Pont Canavese through Locana and Noasca. The road beyond Ceresole Reale, a small resort along the artificial Lago di Ceresole Reale, is open only during the summer. To the south are the Levanna peaks (including the Levanna Occidentale, 3,593 m/11,788 ft, and the Levanna Centrale, 3,619 m/11,873 ft) and glaciers, forming the border with France and the Parc National de la Vanoise. At Lago Serrù, another artificial lake, the road turns north and climbs past Lago Agnel to the Col del Nivolet, a pass from which there are very good views of the Gran Paradiso massif. Below the pass to the north are the Laghi di Nivolet, beyond which cars are prohibited. Hikers may continue along the Nivolet Valley to the Valsavarenche.

The Alps of
Northeastern Italy

Stelvio National Park

This park is centered around the Ortles mountain (3,905 m/12,812 ft) which, with its cluster of nearby peaks and glaciers, makes up the Ortles group. This is the highest Alpine massif east of Switzerland and until this area was ceded to Italy in 1919, the Ortles was the highest peak in the Austrian empire. Part of the great crystalline range extending across southern Austria, the Ortles peaks consist of gneisses and schist, although marble is also present; another zone contains limestone, dolomite, and sandstone. There is no internationally known resort near the Stelvio; the largest resort town is Bormio, west of the park.

The most impressive face of the Ortles group is its northern one; on this side, the line of rugged peaks is guarded by steep glaciers. From the road between the Stelvio Pass and Trafoi, the view extends along the line of many of the Ortles peaks including the Cima Trafoi (Trafoier Eiswand: 3,563 m/ 11,690 ft), Monte Zebrù (3,740 m/12,270 ft), Thurweiser (3,652 m/11,982 ft), and the Ortles itself. A cable car from the Stelvio Pass rises to the Baita Ortles (Ortlerhütte) and Rifugio Piccolo Pirovano in the midst of glaciers; another section of this lift rises to Rifugio Monte Livrio, with additional ski lifts mounting almost to the summit of Cima Tuckett (3,466 m/11,371 ft). There is extensive summer skiing in this area. Despite the grand scenery, the Stelvio Pass itself has been spoiled by development and the presence of many souvenir stands.

The Stelvio Pass road, which nearly skirts the Swiss border, may be reached from Switzerland via the Umbrail Pass. Travelers from Italy have two approaches to the Stelvio: on the west, from Bormio at the northern end of the Valtellina, and from the Val Venosta to the northeast. Travelers coming from the Brenta–Adamello-Presanella region should avoid the Passo di Gávia, where the road is dangerously narrow and poorly paved.

Val del Forno and Val di Cedec

Because of the poor condition of the Passo di Gávia road to the south, Santa Caterina Valfurva should be approached only from Bormio. From Santa Caterina you can head eastward up the jeep road along the Val del Forno;

above to the southeast is the Ghiacciaio dei Forni, the biggest glacier in the Stelvio region. Then continue north up the Val di Cedec to Rifugio Pizzini Frattola, in a splendid location facing Monte Cevedale.

Trafoi and Solda di Dentro

East of the Stelvio Pass, the road descends to the village of Trafoi, at the scenic upper end of the Valle di Trafoi. An almost parallel tributary valley to the east is the Valle di Solda, which rises from Gomagoi to the village of Solda di dentro (Innersulden). This small resort also enjoys an excellent view of the Ortles group, as the Ortles peak is actually midway between the Trafoi and Solda valleys. The villages of Trafoi and Solda are both mountaineering centers, with alpine guides' associations. Solda also offers an excellent view of the Gran Zebrù (Königspitze, 3,851 m/12,635 ft), the region's second highest peak. From Solda di dentro, a cable car rises to the Rifugio Città di Milano (Schaubachhütte) below the Solda glacier, with a superb view of the Gran Zebrù, Monte Zebrù, and the Ortles. From Santa Geltrude (St. Gertraud), a village about 2 km/1.2 mi northwest of Solda di dentro, there is a chair lift and also a path westward to Rifugio K2, on the north slope of the Ortles. From there, a trail extends south to the Rifugio Coston (Hintergrathütte). From this hut you can walk down to the middle station of the cable car between the Rifugio Città di Milano and Solda, returning to Solda by lift or on foot. On the other side of Santa Geltrude, the Rifugio A. Serristori (Zaytalhütte) offers very good views of the Ortles, Monte Zebrù, and the Gran Zebrù, as this hut faces the mountains. A trail climbs northeastward from the village to reach this hut.

Val di Martello

This valley, in the northeastern part of the Ortles region, is unspoiled, with no thicket of ski lifts. Its villages (including Ganda di Martello, or Gand; La Valle, or Thal; and Transacqua, or Ennewasser) are at the lower and middle part of the valley, leaving the upper end of the valley quite undeveloped. There are several mountain inns at Lago Gioveretto (Zufritt-See), an artificial lake near the upper end of the valley. Two km/1.2 mi beyond the lake is another cluster of huts and inns, beyond which is a network of trails. The route south to Rifugio Martello (Martellerhütte), at the edge of the Cevedale glacier, offers a superb view of Cima Cevedale (Zufallspitze, 3,757 m/ 12,326 ft) and the Cima Venezia (Veneziaspitze, 3,396 m/11,142 ft).

Val di Sole and Val di Mare

There are also several southern approaches to the Stelvio massif. From the Val di Sole, which separates the Stelvio from the Adamello-Presanella, the Valle di Péjo cuts northward toward the Stelvio. From the villages of Péjo or Cógolo, you can ascend the Val di Mare to the Rifugio Pian Venezia, and then continue steeply northward to the Rifugio G. Larcher al Cevedale, in wild terrain; to the north is a ring of cliffs topped by glaciers, and to the west is Monte Cevedale.

The Dolomites

Towers and pinnacles characterize the Italian Dolomites, a mountain range unlike any other in the Alps. Due to its chemical composition, dolomitic rock erodes easily, resulting in fantastical forms: there are single peaks that resemble castles, and gigantic blocks that, from a distance, look like cities in the air. The light-colored dolomitic rock also seems to change its hue with the passage of the sun and with every mood of wind and weather: rose or salmon pink after dawn, gray or blue in shadow, lemon yellow at sunset. And while valleys in the Alps are often narrow, in the central Dolomites you can see across great distances to rock masses shaped like buttes and mesas. The effect is somewhat like that in the American Southwest, but in an alpine setting, with forests and green meadows at the base of the mountains.

The geological movement that created the Alps was generally from southeast to northwest. Located in the southeast of the Alps, the Dolomites underwent less thrusting than occurred elsewhere. In contrast to the long linear chains typical of the folded mountain ranges to the north, the Dolomites appear more as isolated, scattered clumps of rock, like gigantic spoonfuls of biscuit dough dropped onto the surface of a pan.

The Dolomites are named for the French geologist Déodat de Dolomieu (1750–1801), who collected and studied samples of this rock. The special element that differentiates dolomite from limestone (calcite) is magnesium; limestone is calcium carbonate—$CaCO_3$—but dolomite is calcium magnesium carbonate—$CaMg(CO_3)_2$. Although both rocks weather easily in moist climates, the magnesium in dolomite makes this rock both harder and more crumbly and thus more susceptible to the processes of weathering and erosion. Dolomite is found also in other parts of the Alps and Europe, as well as in the Western Hemisphere. But it is not the only rock found in the Dolomites: some of the mountains in the region are the more common limestone.

A patch of bloody cranesbill gives way to an uninterrupted carpet of green between the Sasso Lungo and the Passo di Sella in the Dolomites.

The northern part of the Dolomites originally belonged to Austria, and was known as the Südtirol—the South Tyrol. During World War I there was fierce fighting throughout the area, and many marks of the conflict, such as trenches and tunnels, remain. After the war this region was pulled away from the rest of the Austrian Tyrol and given to Italy.

Unlike other alpine areas, these mountains can be seen very well from an automobile, and roads encircle some of the great rock formations. The chief route through the central Dolomites, designated "the Dolomite Road," extends from Bolzano on the Adige River eastward to Cortina d'Ampezzo, reaching its glory at the Passo del Pordoi. A detour here, to drive in a loop around the Sella group, is truly spectacular.

Many Italians come to the Dolomites during August, the Italian vacation month; reservations should be made in advance for this time not only for hotels but also for Italian Alpine Club huts.

Hiking Conditions. In some areas, hiking trails extend across the top of the great dolomitic blocks. These routes are blazed, mostly with numbers painted on the rock, which correspond to those on the hiking maps. Occasionally, upright trail signs also serve as markers. Wandering on top of a vast, open plateau is quite different from the usual alpine hiking, since the landscape has fewer conventional features to identify the route. Hikers therefore should not venture out in heavy cloud or mist. Rainy weather, when the rock becomes slippery, is equally hazardous.

Vie Ferrate/Klettersteig. Besides conventional mountain trails, there are special routes in the Dolomites called *Vie Ferrate* (*Klettersteig* in German), or "iron ways," usually marked on maps by a series of tiny crosses, and indicated on trail signs. Unless accompanied by a licensed guide, hikers should avoid these routes. They are essentially climbing routes with mechanical aids fixed into the rock: metal ladders, cables, pegs, bolts, and steps like giant staples. To use them properly, you must be equipped with a helmet, climbing harness, rope, and carabiners, and you must be an experienced climber. Every year there are accidents and fatalities when people who are either inadequately equipped or trained use the *Vie Ferrate.*

CORTINA D'AMPEZZO

Cortina d'Ampezzo, site of the 1956 Winter Olympics, has become the most fashionable resort in the Dolomites. An urbane town with elegant shops, it can serve as the central base for touring a large number of important mountains. The town, in a broad valley with gentle slopes, is surrounded by giant rock forms that thrust suddenly upward from green meadows and forests.

The broad bands of rock take fantastical shapes—towers, columns, pinnacles, and fingers. The effect is like being in a giant sculpture garden. Three great outcrops of rock overlook Cortina. Northwest of the town is a cluster known as Le Tofane, with three summits, of which the highest point is the Tofana di Mezzo (3,244 m/10,643 ft), a vast citadel of rock; the summit, reached by cable car from Cortina, offers a panoramic view. You can also take a cable car to the Rifugio Falòria (2,123 m/6,965 ft) in the southeast to see the huge massif of the Sorapíss, the second of the outcrops, whose highest point is the Punta Sorapíss (3,205 m/10,515 ft). Northeast of Cortina, behind the long Pomagagnon ridge, is the huge Cristallo massif, whose highest point is 3,221 m/10,568 ft. From Rio Gere, on the road toward the Passo Tre Croci, you can take a cable car to the Rifugio Lorenzi, near the top of the Cristallo. There are trails over the Pomagagnon ridge, connecting Cortina and the Passo Tre Croci; you can take a bus to the pass and walk back toward town.

Cortina is one of Italy's major ski centers, but hiking in the immediate vicinity is fairly limited because many of the routes upon the great rock massifs are difficult or require some passage on a *Via Ferrata*. One easy walk is to nearby little Lago Ghedina, a pretty lake near the foot of the east face of the Tofane.

Passo Falzarego.   A very scenic drive west of Cortina leads to this pass. From here the Tofane is very impressive, a huge slab of pink and gray rock. You can take a cable car up to the Rifugio Lagazuoi for a magnificent panorama, including a close view of the Tofana di Rozes.

South of the road between Cortina and the Passo Falzarego are several interesting formations, including the Nuvolao (2,574 m/8,445 ft), near whose northern edge is a group of five upright slabs like modern sculptures, called the Cinque Torri; a lift brings you close to the base of these curious formations. Along the road to Passo Falzarego is a secondary road to Passo Giau; about 3 km/1.9 mi down this road is the trail head for the Alta Via Dolomiti—trail 437. It leads southeast to Lago Fedèra, a small lake at the foot of the Croda da Lago; you can also hike west on 437 to the Rifugio Cinque Torri, at the base of the five towers.

Parco Naturale Dolomiti di Sesto

Northeast of Cortina is some of the finest mountain scenery in the Dolomites, in and near a group of mountains known as the Dolomites of Sesto (Sexten in German). This is good country for hikers because many of the features in the area are distinct entities, separated from other rock forms, and you can walk around them on fairly safe terrain.

Tre Cime di Lavaredo/Drei Zinnen.   These three huge vertical columns,

Not far from Misurina and Cortina, the small Lago d'Antorno lies below austere, rugged peaks. From Lago di Misurina hikers may continue to the readily accessible

with sheer faces that appear to have been planed by an adze, are one of the most famous formations in the Dolomites. The highest of the three, the Grande, is 2,999 m/9,839 ft. The other two are the Piccolo and Ovest. Although within a wild area, this formation is extraordinarily accessible. From Cortina, you can drive over the Passo Tre Croci past Lago di Misurina, a long lake set between the rock masses of the Cristallo and the Cadini di Misurina. Beyond the lake, a paved and well-maintained toll road climbs to the Rifugio Auronzo. There are scarcely any huts in the entire Alps that you can reach by car, but the Rifugio Auronzo, more like a large hostel than an Alpine Club hut, is a rare exception. From here it is an hour's easy walk, almost on the level, northeast to the Rifugio Lavaredo; the broad trail passes in front of the south faces of the Tre Cime di Lavaredo, like three gigantic sentinels, staring over a vast area. The terrain is strewn with grand rock forms: crags, spires, and broader formations like buttes.

Tre Cime di Lavaredo, most visited and photographed of the Dolomites. The area around the beautiful limestone towers provides excellent hiking.

A popular hiking tour here is to make a circle around the Tre Cime. From the Rifugio Lavaredo you continue north to the little saddle above, the Forcella Lavaredo, and then north on trail 101 to the Rifugio Locatelli, from which you see the Tre Cime from the north. You may then retrace your steps to the Rifugio Lavaredo, or continue to the southwest on 105 to complete the circle, returning to the Rifugio Auronzo.

Croda dei Toni. Another scenic hiking route, 104, continues past the Rifugio Lavaredo east and then north to the tiny Rifugio Pian di Cengia. The scene is dominated by the Croda dei Toni (Zwölferkofel: 3,094 m/10,151 ft) to the southeast. Hikers undertaking a more extensive tour may cross the Passo Fiscalino (Oberbachernjoch), a notch in the rocky ridge between the Pian di Cengia hut and the Croda dei Toni. East of the pass, the trail descends to the Zsigmondy-Comici hut, with more fine views in the heart of the Sesto Dolomites. From there a trail leads north to the Val Sassovecchio (Altensteintal).

Late in the day, visitors to the Drei Zinnen Hütte can watch the sinking sun paint the rocks with vivid alpenglow. Facing page: Larches stand in fall color beneath a natural fortress of stone near Passo Falzarego. Pages 308 and 309: Bathing the rocks in orange-gold, sunrise over the Tre Cime di Lavaredo is as dramatic as sunset, brilliantly revealing the otherworldly landscape of crags and spires.

At the junction, you may turn northeast for the Rifugio al Fondo Valle (Talschlusshütte) and the Val Fiscalina (Fischleintal), or west for the Rifugio Locatelli.

Valle di Landro. The road through the Valle di Landro, which forms the western border of the park, is quite scenic, especially near the Lago di Landro (Dürrensee) at its southern end. From this lake, the view to the west is dominated by the Croda Rossa (Hohe Gaisl: 3,146 m/10,322 ft) and to the south by the Cristallo massif. Several hiking trails enter the park from this valley. From the Hotel Cime di Lavaredo, just north of the Lago di Landro, you can walk east up the Val Rinbon (Rienztal) to the Rifugio Locatelli, with its grand view of the Tre Cime di Lavaredo. Near the northern end of the Valle di Landro is another lake, the Lago di Dobbiaco (Toblachersee). South of this lake is the junction for the trail heading east up the Val dei Baranci (Birkental), which climbs between the Piatta Alta (Hochebenkofel: 2,905 m/9,531 ft) and the Rocca dei Baranci (Haunold: 2,966 m/9,731 ft) to the For-

ALPINE SNOWBELL
Soldanella alpina

The alpine snowbell, a favorite of alpine people, is a herald of spring and can flower before the snow has disappeared. It often breaks through the snow to bloom above the crust.

With only a short season for their biological cycle, some alpine plants are ready to flower even before the snow is gone. Insulation provided by the snow cover keeps the temperature relatively warm under the snow even when the air is very cold; in this case, the plant's dark leaves and stem absorb heat and melt the snow around them, creating warm air pockets.

The deep, slender fringes on the bell-shaped flower's pale lavender petals are distinctive. A long pistil protrudes from the flower. The slender stalk is nearly leafless; round, almost heart-shaped leaves grow in a rosette around the base of the plant. There may be two or three flowers on each plant.

The alpine snowbell prefers a lime-rich soil, and grows between 1,100 and 3,000 m/3,609 and 9,842 ft.

---

cella dei Baranci (Birkenschartl). From this pass you can continue southeast and then north to the Rifugio Tre Scarperi (Dreischusterhütte). The great rock masses of the Dolomites disappear at the northern end of the Valle di Landro as it descends to the Val Pusteria and the little town of Dobbiaco (Toblach).

Val di Sesto. Just east of Dobbiaco is San Càndido (Innichen) at the junction for the Val di Sesto (Sextental), which contours along the northeastern side of the park. From the village of Moso (Moos) in the Val di Sesto, a road leads southward into the park, up the Val Fiscalina (Fischleintal). Near the beginning of the road, at Bagni di Moso (Bad Moos), a lift rises to the meadows at the base of the Croda Rossa di Sesto (Sextener Rotwand: 2,965 m/ 9,728 ft) for good views and hikes around the base of this mountain. At the end of the Val Fiscalina road is Piano Fiscalino, facing a great loop of mighty rock towers. These include a set of mountains with numbers for names: Cima

From a trail east of Rifugio Lavaredo, the view crosses a meadow of striated rock to a wall of dark jagged mountains.

Una (Einser), the Croda dei Toni or Cima Dodici (Zwölferkofel), and Cima Undici (Elfer)—one, twelve, and eleven—so named because the local people could tell the time of day by the position of the sun over these peaks.

Fanes, Sennes, and Braies Natural Park

This area, known as the Braies, is in the northeastern corner of the Dolomites north of Cortina. From the Lago di Braies there is a lovely view of the Croda del Becco (2,810 m/9,219 ft). Access to the lake is from the east, on the secondary road between Carbonin and the Val Pusteria; a branch past San Vito extends to the lake and the edge of the Braies. At the southeastern edge of this group is the Croda Rossa (3,146 m/10,322 ft), whose rock reddens at sunset.

Pelmo

South of Cortina on route 51, the villages of San Vito di Cadore and Borca di Cadore give access to Monte Pelmo (3,168 m/10,393 ft) and the Pelmetto (2,990 m/9,810 ft). The nickname of this great mass of rock, which actually consists of a pair of towers, is "the throne of the gods"; the cleft between them is the bed of a small glacier. The Rifugio Venezia, below the southeast wall of the Pelmo, offers an excellent view. You can reach it from several directions. For a semicircular walk that wraps around the southern side of the Pelmo and leads to the rifugio, take either trail 472 eastward from the Rifugio Staulanza on the Forcella Staulanza, a pass on the road southeast of Selva di Cadore, or take 474 east from Hotel Palafavera, a little farther to the south on the same road. Alternatively, from Zoppè di Cadore, at the southern base of the mountain, you can walk northward to this hut on 471.

Civetta Group

The name of this group means "owl." The Civetta (this is also the name of its highest peak: 3,220 m/10,564 ft) is a cluster consisting of several ridges, giving the appearance from different viewpoints of a long, seamed wall. The Civetta presents impressive breadth; the nearby Pelmo seems to concentrate its force on one great vertical thrust. The Civetta offers rock climbers some of the greatest challenges in the Dolomites; its famous northwest wall has been called "la parete delle pareti"—the wall of walls. There are fine views of the northwest side of the Civetta from the resort village of Alleghe in the Cordevole Valley, southwest of Cortina. From Pescul, southeast of Selva di Cadore, trail 561 leads to Forcella d'Alleghe, below the northeast corner of the Civetta.

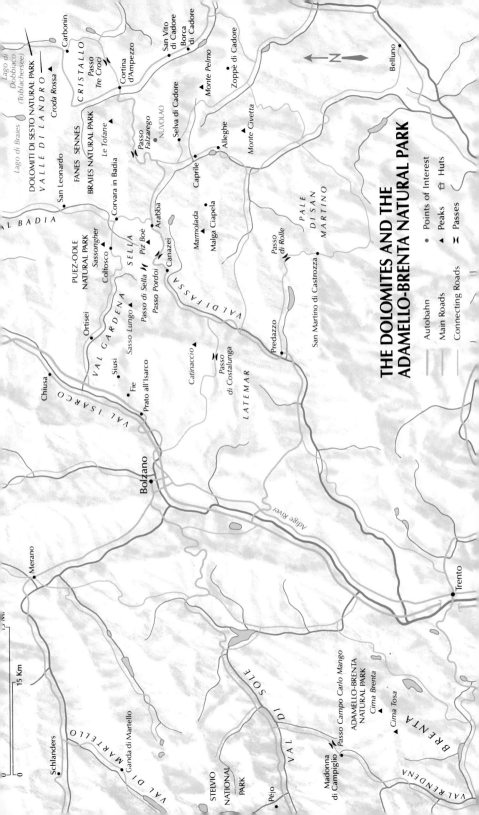

THE DOLOMITES AND THE ADAMELLO-BRENTA NATURAL PARK

- Autobahn
- Main Roads
- Connecting Roads

- • Points of Interest
- ▲ Peaks
- ⌂ Huts
- ✕ Passes

Lago di Dobbiaco (Toblachersee)

Lago di Braies

DOLOMITI DI SESTO NATURAL PARK
VALLE DI LANDRO

Carbonin

CRISTALLO

▲ Croda Rossa

Passo Tre Croci

Cortina d'Ampezzo

San Vito di Cadore

Borca di Cadore

Zoppè di Cadore

▲ Monte Pelmo

FANES SENNES
BRAIES NATURAL PARK

San Leonardo

Le Tofane ▲

NUVOLAO

Passo Falzarego ✕

Selva di Cadore

Corvara in Badia

VAL BADIA

Caprile

Alleghe

▲ Monte Civetta

PUEZ-ODLE NATURAL PARK

Sassongher ▲
Colfosco

SELLA

Piz Boè ▲

Arabba

Marmolada ▲

Malga Ciapela

PALE DI SAN MARTINO

Ortisei

VAL GARDENA

Passo di Sella
Passo Pordoi

Canazei

VAL DI FASSA

Passo di Rolle ✕

Siusi

Sasso Lungo ▲

San Martino di Castrozza

Fie

Catinaccio ▲

Passo di Costalunga ✕

Chiusa

VAL ISARCO

Prato all'Isarco

LATEMAR

Predazzo

Bolzano

Adige River

Merano

VAL DI SOLE

VAL DI MARTELLO

Schlanders

Ganda di Martello

STELVIO NATIONAL PARK

Pèjo

Madonna di Campiglio ✕

Passo Campo Carlo Mango ✕

ADAMELLO-BRENTA NATURAL PARK

Cima Brenta ▲

Cima Tosa ▲

BRENTA

VAL RENDENA

Trento

Belluno

15 Km

N

Small outposts dot the hillside below a magnificent ridge near the Passo di Sella in the Dolomites.

CORVARA IN BADIA

Corvara is the chief resort of the Val Badia, and though it is full of hotels, it is a pleasant village rather than an urbane town like Cortina. From Corvara, the Col Alt lift rises to a large grassy plateau east of the village, where there is a network of trails and several huts; the walk on 23 to the Rifugio Pralongià provides a good view of the Marmolada as well as the Sella group. From Colfosco, a few kilometers west of Corvara, the lift to Pradat brings you just under the tower of the Sassongher (2,665 m/8,743 ft) on the edge of the Puez Odle Natural Park, with a good view across the valley to the Sella group.

Alta Badia

The Alta Badia, west of Cortina, is the name given to the Val Badia and a cluster of its villages, including Corvara in Badia, Colfosco, Pedraces, San Leonardo, La Villa, and San Cassiano. This beautiful valley is in the very heart of the Dolomites, with some of the grandest mountain groups positioned in a virtual ring around it. It is therefore an excellent base for visiting many of the central Dolomites. This is one of the Ladin-speaking valleys of the Dolomites, where the old Rhaetic culture still survives; the language is similar to the Romansch spoken in the Swiss Engadine. There are also German-speaking communities at the northern end of the valley.

Sella Group

This is one of the most impressive formations in all the Dolomites, a rock conglomeration covering an area as big as a city. Its color is light sandy gray with areas that are faintly peach colored. Piz Boè, its highest point, is 3,152 m/10,341 ft.

There are several ways to see the Sella group. The entire mass is surrounded by roads, so you can drive around its periphery. The Dolomite Road passes below the southern wall of the Sella, from Canazei eastward over the Passo Pordoi east to Arabba, but travelers should consider making the entire loop around the Sella group, for there is a different view from each angle. From Canazei, the route northward over the Passo di Sella provides spectacular views of this stone fortress (and of the Sasso Lungo, on the other side of the road). With binoculars, you can watch the acrobatics of the climbers moving delicately up these dizzying, vertical rock walls.

MOUNTAIN HARE
Lepus timidus

This hare is a relic of the glacial period, living only in the Alps—not in the Jura, the mountains of central Europe, or the Pyrenees (though it has been introduced there). It is one of the creatures found in both alpine and arctic environments that change their color seasonally. In summer it is a brownish russet-gray, with a lighter stomach, but in winter it is white. During the transitional seasons its coat has patches of both colors. The very tips of its ears remain black during the winter.

In winter, the thickness of its fur doubles, allowing the hare to survive at 3,000 m/9,842 ft at winter temperatures. In winter, the weight-bearing surface of its paws, especially the hind ones, are covered with long, thick fur, and its big toes can spread themselves widely.

BIRDS OF THE ALPS

Because alpine creatures' dress is generally somber, the wallcreeper *(Tichodroma muraria)* stands out for its splash of color—a bright pink bar along its wings only visible when the bird is in motion. The bird has a unique ability to flutter up steep walls, almost as a butterfly might. It seeks rocks facing south, sprinkled with tufts of flowers that attract the insects on which it feeds.

The ptarmigan *(Lagopus mutus)* changes color seasonally. In the summer its plumage is streaked, a mixture of brown and gray flecked with white, giving it the effect of tweed. During the fall it molts, emerging in November as an almost snow-white bird, though the male has black bands around its eyes, and red wattles. Long feathers grow upon the bird's feet and toes, covering even the bottom of the foot. On steep slopes, the ptarmigan may let itself glide on its stomach.

Above its eyes the male black grouse *(Lyrurus tetrix)* has red caruncles resembling gigantic red eyebrows. During mating season, the

Top left: wallcreeper; top right: ptarmigan; above: black grouse.

caruncles swell so much that they almost touch over the top of its head, creating a distinctive red puff like a tiny cap; during the fall, they shrink greatly. The black grouse performs its celebrated courting dance during the spring, when up to ten birds gather at a traditional site, called a lek, at dawn, raise their wings, and spread out the plumes of their tails showing white feathers below, cooing and emitting shrill cries that can sometimes be heard a mile or two away.

You can also take the Sass Pordoi cable car from Passo Pordoi right to the top of the Sella wall. The panorama is tremendous, including a better, more comprehensive view of the Marmolada than you can obtain on that mountain itself. Huge rock forms rise all around. Below is the green valley; behind you is a plateau of stone, upon which rise mesas of pale gray, yellow, and tan. The effect is like being on an island that is actually a rock fortress in the sky.

To explore the unusual landscape, you can follow hiking route 627 from the Sass Pordoi cable-car terminus to the Rifugio Boè, and then return to the terminus. (Other hiking routes continue along the plateau, but they involve passages on *Vie Ferrate* and thus should be avoided by hikers.) Walking atop the Sella is like being on a stone desert, but the plateau is far from level or featureless. Walls and towers rise like extraordinary apparitions across the barren expanse, and deep gorges cut into the rock. The shapes and colors are slightly reminiscent of what you might see inside a canyon in the American Southwest, except that here you are actually on top of a mountain. To the north, a long line of distant snowcapped mountains is visible, providing a striking contrast between two different manifestations of the Alps: the snow-capped Austrian peaks and the naked Dolomite spires and masses.

Sasso Lungo

This group of stark, sheer towers lies directly west of the Sella group across the Passo di Sella, so that the road between them is a very scenic corridor between gigantic rock forms. Their highest point is 3,181 m/10,436 ft. They overlook the green meadows of Alpe di Siusi to the west.

Puez-Odle Natural Park

The Odle group, the northern part of the Puez-Odle Natural Park, consists of columns and towers rather than massive stone blocks; Odle means "needles" in Ladin. The highest peaks are the Sass Rigais (3,025 m/9,925 ft), Sass de l'Ega (2,915 m/9,564 ft), and the Gran Odla (2,832 m/9,291 ft). There are good views of this group from its northern edge. The nearest approach is via the Val di Funes, which extends eastward from Chiusa (on the autostrada between Bolzano and Bressanone) to the village of Santa Maddalena. From there you can walk eastward on trail 33 to Rifugio Génova, facing the Sass de l'Ega. From Santa Maddalena you can also walk south to Rifugio Brogles, at the foot of the Gran Odla.

The Puez group lies southeast of the Odle group; at its southeastern corner is the Sassongher. Its highest point is Punte del Puez, 2,918 m/9,573 ft. The Puez group can be approached from the Val Gardena to the west, or from the Val Badia to the east. From Ortisei in the Val Gardena, the Seceda lift rises to the western edge of the park, just below the Gran Odla. From Santa Cristina, east of Ortisei, a cable car rises to Col Raiser near two huts, Fermeda and Firenze.

CANAZEI

Canazei is a popular resort near the center of the Dolomites. It is just south of the Sella group and conveniently located for a tour of the Marmolada. It is more compact and densely built than Corvara, with a lively center full of shops.

Marmolada

This is the highest mountain in the Dolomites (3,342 m/10,965 ft), and the only one with an extensive glacier, so that its appearance is different from the other mountains of the region. Its long summit ridge extends in an east–west direction, with the Ghiacciaio della Marmolada dropping away on the mountain's north flank. This northern, snowy side is the Marmolada's most dramatic face, so the best views are from this direction. From Malga Ciapela, east of the mountain, a cable car ascends to the snows of the Marmolada's summit, where there is summer skiing on the glacier. This is not, however, one of the grandest viewpoints in the Dolomites. The view embraces an array of many mountains, but as all are quite distant and lower than the Marmolada, they appear rather flattened out. There is a good view of the mountain and glacier from the road along the northern edge of the mountain, extending between Malga Ciapela past the Lago di Fedaia to Canazei. From Porta Vescovo, on the slope above the Fedaia lake, there is an even finer view: this point can also be reached by cable car from Arabba, a little town south of Corvara. You can also reach the Malga Ciapela from Caprile on the east, which is easily accessible from Corvara and Cortina.

Catinaccio and Latemar

The impressive cluster of the Catinaccio mountains overlooks the west side of the Val di Fassa, south of Canazei. Its tallest peak is the Antermoia (3,002 m/ 9,849 ft). Well-known features are the Torri del Vajolet, seven slender, elegant towers along the southern ridge of the Catinaccio. A small road between Pera di sopra and Mazzin leads up the lower Valle Vajolet to the Rifugio Stella Alpina; from there a trail leads up to the Rifugio Vajolet, from which there is the option of continuing north up the scenic valley to the Rifugio Passo Principe (Grasleitenpasshütte).

South of the road between Vigo di Fassa and the Passo di Costalunga are the fluted pillars of the Latemar group. These formations are reflected in the Lago di Carezza, west of the Passo di Costalunga.

ORTISEI

Ortisei, another popular resort, is larger than Canazei. It is located in the Val Gardena, which extends from the Alta Badia region through the Passo di Gardena and past the Sella group to the Val Isarco, the western border of the Dolomites.

Alpe di Siusi

On the high slope south of the Rio Gardena, the watercourse of the Val Gardena, is Alpe di Siusi, a high, open plateau covered by lovely, undulating meadows and sprinkled with dairy farms. One approach to Alpe di Siusi is by

Coarse rocks and the brown-gold grass of autumn are framed by majestic cloud-topped mountains near the Passo di Sella. Pages 320 and 321: From the top of Passo Falzarego, the view of the Dolomites is tremendous.

cable car from Ortisei to the northern edge of these high meadows. From Prato d'Isarco, northeast of Bolzano, there is a road to Fie and the village of Siusi, from which you can continue eastward to the meadows of Alpe di Siusi. You may wander across this open country on a grid of trails, with views of the jagged Sasso Lungo to the east and of the chunky Sciliar massif to the south.

SAN MARTINO DI CASTROZZA

The Pale di San Martino is the most southern of the great Dolomitic groups, a massive structure crowned with towers, so vast that it rivals the Sella group. The tallest of its many peaks are the Cima della Vezzana (3,192 m/ 10,472 ft) and the Cimon della Pala (3,184 m/10,446 ft)—the latter is known as "the Matterhorn of the Dolomites" because of its elegant pinnacle. Below the western wall of the "Pale," in the Val Cismon, is San Martino di Castrozza, a fashionable resort, less urban than Cortina d'Ampezzo yet more built-up than Corvara. Its situation is very dramatic, as it is built just under the Pale. The great rock mass rises nearly vertically from its base, displaying big sections of blank wall topped with columns and spires.

Pale di San Martino

A two-stage lift from San Martino swings up the wall of the Pale, carrying hikers and climbers as well as those who simply want a view. The top is criss-crossed with blazed hiking routes and also the rather perilous *Vie Ferrate*. The top of the Pale is a great, uneven expanse of stone, not flat, but marked by swells, furrows, and hollows, with columns of rock rising here and there above the general plateau. To sample the scenery upon the "Altipiano delle Pale di San Martino," the central plateau upon the Pale, hikers may walk toward Marucol on 756, or toward the Passo di Pradidali on 707-709, turning back for the lift station when the route becomes difficult.

The meadows of Tognola, facing the Pale from the slope west of San Martino, contrast strikingly with those rocky walls. Tognola is the chief ski area for San Martino, and several hiking trails meander across the open slopes and through the woods, giving fine views of the Pale.

The Passo di Rolle, north of San Martino, connects the Pale with the central area of the Dolomites. As you approach the pass, on the road from Predazzo, you can see the distinctive spire of the Cimon della Pala and other rocky towers atop the Pale di San Martino. From the Passo di Rolle, a small road branches off the main route to San Martino, climbing north and then east, past the Rifugio Capanna Cervino to the Baita Segantini, a hut with a splendid view of the Cimon della Pala. South of the Passo di Rolle are the Laghi di Colbricon, which may be visited either from the pass or from San Martino. From the Malga di Rolle, directly west of the pass, a trail leads southwest to these two little lakes and the Passo del Colbricon, with a good view of the Pale. The trail then continues southeast down the Val Bonetta to the Malga Ces and then San Martino.

ADAMELLO-BRENTA NATURAL PARK

One section of the Dolomites, the Brenta group, lies west of the Adige River, removed from the main dolomitic area to the east. The Val Rendena serves to divide the Brenta Dolomites from the Adamello and Presanella groups. The sedimentary Brenta group in the east comprises sheer-walled blocks of rock, often sculpted by erosion into pillars and fingers pointing to the sky, while the Adamello and Presanella ranges, more characteristically alpine in appearance, have triangular, rugged peaks. The Adamello-Presanella region consists of intrusions of igneous rock, including tonalite, a granite-like rock named for the Passo del Tonale of this region. This igneous rock covers the older sedimentary rock that is the basis of the Dolomites. Despite the visual contrast between the Brenta and the Adamello-Presanella groups, these two different "bedfellows" have been joined within the same park. The line that separates them is the "Linea di Giudicarie," or Giudicarie Fault, which runs through the Val Rendena. Another unusual feature of this park is the presence of a very few brown bears (perhaps fewer than ten); this animal (*Ursus arctos*) is extinct in nearly all other parts of the Alps.

Brenta Dolomites

The major agglomeration of the Brenta group is near the southern edge of the massif. The highest peak in the Brenta is the Cima Tosa (3,159 m/10,364 ft), surrounded by a cluster of rock towers. Almost as high is the nearby Cima Brenta (3,150 m/10,335 ft), amid its own circle of satellite peaks. Between these two is a line of pinnacles connected at the base, known as the Sfulmini chain. Some of the peaks are named Torre (tower), Castello (castle), or Campanile (reflecting a resemblance to the tall, narrow bell towers of Italian cathedrals). On the northern edge of these mountains is the Cima del Grostè (2,901 m/9,518 ft), which overlooks a broad pass, the Passo del Grostè, dividing the southern from the northern Brenta mountains. Just north of this pass is the Pietra Grande (2,937 m/9,633 ft).

Madonna di Campiglio. Along the road forming the western border of the Brenta group is a virtual strip of resort villages, built close together and almost running one into the next. The northernmost and chief of these is Madonna di Campiglio, a large, busy, and very fashionable winter and summer resort that serves as a base for the heart of the Brenta region.

A cable car from Madonna rises to Monte Spinale, a green knob above the town but below the walls of the Brenta group. You can walk east past the little Lago Spinale to the Rifugio Graffer, just below the rocky Brenta plateau.

Another cable car, this one known as the Funivia 5 Laghi, rises from Madonna to Rifugio Pancùgolo, on the slope above Malga Ritorto. A hiking route known as the Giro dei 5 Laghi (Tour of the 5 Lakes) leads from Lago Ritorto around the lakes of Lambin, Serodoli, Gelato (with an optional detour to Nambrone), Nero, and Nambino. From the Rifugio Nambino you can return to Patascoss and then Madonna.

BEAR'S EAR or AURICULA
Primula auricula

Several species of primulas grow in the Alps, many of them pink; this one, however, is a clear yellow. Its light, gray-green leaves are quite large, oblong and fleshy, with lightly scalloped edges. Above this cluster of leaves is a stem bearing up to ten flowers. Each flower emerges from a narrow tube; initially funnel-shaped, the five notched petals spread flat around the center, which is marked with a white ring. This is one of the few scented alpine flowers.

Reaching a height of 5 to 25 cm/ 2 to 10 in, they grow on crags, in rock crevices, and on stony meadows in limestone areas, from 1,600 to 2,500 m/5,249 to 8,202 ft. They flower from May to July.

Facing page: A patch of hogweed (Heracleum spondylium) blooms below snow-capped peaks around the Passo di Costalunga. Nearby is the popular and centrally located resort town of Canazei, and to the west is the Lago di Carezza and the pillar-like rock formations of the Latemar mountains.

Just north of Madonna, a little road climbs from the main road out of Madonna past Patascoss to the Malga Ritorto, a small farm and restaurant with a very good view of the Brenta group across the valley. For a sample of the landscape on this side of the valley you can hike northwest on trail 255 up to Lago Ritorto, which is surrounded on three sides by a crest of low, rocky mountains.

Grostè Cable Car. Directly north of Madonna, on the road to Passo Campo Carlo Magno, is the region's chief lift system, the Grostè cable car, one of the longest in Europe. This rises to within a few hundred meters of the Grostè Pass, for views of the Cima del Grostè and other Brenta summits. From the upper station you can ramble over this high, stone plateau, carved and chiseled into the pillars, crevices, and abstract forms typical of eroded dolomite rock. At many points you can see the layers of this sedimentary rock, inclined in the direction of thrust. The Cima del Grostè, for example, looks like a giant stack of tilted sandwiches. In the distance, to the southwest, you can see the glaciers of the Adamello group, the nondolomitic mountains across the valley, with their more triangular peaks typical of harder, granitic rock.

From the upper Grostè cable-car station, if you walk southeast on route 301 for 20 to 30 minutes, you cross an interesting area of karst, where the rock is eroded into furrows, channels, and deep holes. There is a good view toward the east wall of the Pietra Grande. This route continues to the Passo dela Gaiarda. Another possibility from the upper Grostè terminus is to wander southwest on 316 toward the Rifugio Tuckett.

Adamello-Presanella

In contrast to the dry, barren Brenta mountains, the Adamello region contains an expanse of glaciers that is one of the broadest in Italy. The landscape is alpine and rugged. In the center is Monte Adamello (3,539 m/11,610 ft), the highest point in what is nearly a ring of peaks surrounding the largest glaciers: the Vedretta del Mandrone, Pian di Neve, and Vedretta della Lobbia. The big ridge north of these is the backbone of La Presanella, whose highest peak is Cima Presanella (3,558 m/11,673 ft). Several glaciers extend down the slopes of the Presanella, though none is as large as those in the center of the Adamello.

The Adamello-Presanella region is largely unspoiled, almost virgin territory. There are no major resorts to draw crowds, and very few cable cars, so the only way to see much of the park is by hiking and climbing. Consequently it is much less frequented than the Brenta area. The nearest main roads extend along the sides of this roughly rectangular area.

Val Rendena. Several popular walks near Madonna take you onto the eastern slopes of the granite Presanella massif, a strikingly different terrain from the dolomitic Brenta area across the valley. Water dissolves both common limestone and dolomitic rock, tunneling through the rock to form grooves and channels. Granitic rock is impermeable, however, so it can retain accumulations of water. Thus the western or Adamello-Presanella side of the valley is green and has numerous small lakes, while the Brenta massif on the east is stony, bare, and dry, with scattered chunks and slabs of the pale dolomite rock.

Val di Genova. The Val di Genova forms the dividing line between the Adamello and the Presanella. The valley leads westward from Carisolo, a village directly north of the small resort of Pinzolo on the main road up the Val Rendena. The Cascata di Nardis, a waterfall just west of Carisolo, is a popular attraction. At the upper end of the valley, trail 212, affording views of the Presanella, climbs to the Rifugio Bédole on a grassy terrace. The Mandrone and Lobbia glaciers are above the hut to the south. You can continue up to the Rifugio Mandrone for a superb view of the glaciers.

Passo del Tonale. North of La Presanella, in the Val Vermiglio, a two-stage cable car rises from the Passo del Tonale. It stops at the Passo del Paradiso and then Capanna Presena, at the edge of the Vedretta Presena, a glacier used for summer skiing. The lift station is near the Ristorante Erica, on the south side of the Passo del Tonale, which is on the road along the northern edge of the Presanella. You can also hike from Tonale to the Passo del Paradiso and continue past the Lago del Monticello to Capanna Presena. The hut is on the edge of the glacier, below Cima Presena (3,069 m/10,069 ft).

Lago Venerocolo. From Tèmu, west of the Passo del Tonale, you can walk south up the Valle del Avio, or drive partway up the valley to Malga Caldèa. Trail 11 passes two large artificial lakes, Lago d'Avio and Lago Benedetto, then climbs east to Rifugio Garibaldi, in a very scenic location on the Lago Venerocolo. The view is of the north face of Monte Adamello, with the Venerocolo glacier, the Cima Garibaldi (3,237 m/10,620 ft), and Corno Bianco (3,434 m/11,266 ft).

Parco Nazionale Incisioni Rupestri. South of Edolo in the Val Camónico is Capo di Ponte, the village nearest the Parco Nazionale Incisioni Rupestri. This park preserves an area where numerous symbolic forms were incised onto smooth-sided rock during the Neolithic period, a site similar to that of the Vallée des Merveilles in the Mercantour National Park in southeastern France.

The Julian Alps of Slovenia

T hough much of Yugoslavia is mountainous, only the Julian Alps of Slovenia, in the northwest corner of the country, belong to the chain of the Alps. Slovenia was once part of the Austro-Hungarian empire, and it is often remarked that the region resembles Austria, yet there are differences in landscape and vegetation, and the culture and the flavor of the country have a distinctively Slavic character. It is a region of limestone mountains, especially rich in karst formations, with an abundance of lakes.

For hikers, the easiest approach into the Julian Alps is from the south side; the north side is more rugged. Day trips may be taken, as well as two- or three-day walking tours. Some trails are not especially well marked, and unless you are fluent in Slovenian, skilled at map-reading and route-finding, or very adventurous, it would be advisable to hire a local guide. English-speaking guides are available at moderate cost at several points. One source is Alpinsport, an all-purpose outdoor

Mt. Triglav is at the heart of Yugoslavia's largest national park. According to legend, a goat with golden horns protects the peak.

sports agency in Bohinjsko jezero, which organizes hikers' day trips and longer tours, and also rents kayaks and arranges kayak trips. Contact Dušan Blažin, Bohinj Alpinsport, Ribčev laz 53, YU-64265 Bohinjsko jezero; phone: (38) 64-723-486; telex: 34619. Mountain guides are also available at Kranjska Gora, where there is a climbing school, and at Bovec. For information, contact Turistično Društvo (Tourist Office), Borovška 81, YU-64280 Kranjska Gora; phone: (38) 64-88768. You may also write to Kompas Bovec, Trg golobarskih zrtěv 18, YU-65230 Bovec; phone: (38) 65-86-202. Or you may write to Alpetour, Subicěva 1, YU-61000 Ljubljana; phone: (38) 61-211-118 or 211-358; telex: 31144. There are also many ski-mountaineering routes in the Julian Alps; a guide is essential for these trips, and may be arranged through the above-mentioned agencies.

The best accommodations are found at Bled and in the resort villages around Triglav National Park, particularly in Bohinjsko jezero and Kranjska Gora; as throughout the Alps, there are also huts in the mountains for hikers and climbers.

Addresses: For information on Yugoslavia, contact the Yugoslav National Tourist Office.

In North America, the address is: 630 Fifth Avenue, Suite 280, New York, NY 10111-0021; to request information, (212) 757-2801; for specific questions, (212) 757-2802.

In Great Britain, the tourist office address is: 143 Regent Street, London W1; (44) 1-734-5243 or 1-439-0399.

To join an alpine or hiking association, contact: The Center for Tourist and Economic Promotion, Slovene Chamber of Economy, Trubarjeva 5, 61000 Ljubljana; (38) 61-318-348 (7).

At press time, Slovenia's bid for independence has put the future of the Yugoslav federation in question. Before planning a trip to the Julian Alps, please check with your country's foreign ministry about travel advisories that may be in effect. In the U.S., contact the State Department's travel advisory office, (202) 647-5226. In Great Britain, contact the Foreign Office, (71) 270-3000.

The Julian Alps

YUGOSLAVIA'S LARGEST NATIONAL PARK, with an area of 84,805 hectares/ 209,550 acres, covers nearly the entire region of the Julian Alps. Created in 1981, the Triglav National Park is dominated by Mount Triglav (2,864 m/ 9,396 ft), the highest mountain in Yugoslavia; the country's only remaining glacier is near its summit. The park has associations with Slovenian nationalism. Mount Triglav (its name means "three heads") is considered the symbol of Slovenia, and the regional folk tale attached to the park provides legendary significance. Zlatorog, a golden-horned goat, was guardian of a wonderful garden and a hidden treasure in the mountains. A greedy hunter killed the goat, but from its blood sprang a miraculous flower that restored the animal's life force. Zlatorog destroyed the hunter and also, in his anger, the garden; his treasure remains buried in the mountains. Like this story, which symbolizes nature's revenge when human greed threatens the natural environment, the concept of the park has acquired mythic overtones, associated with the aim of protecting wildlife and restoring the lost paradise.

Since four local men first climbed Mount Triglav in 1778, mountaineering has taken a strong hold in the region, fostered today by the Slovenian Alpine Society. Numerous alpine huts sprinkled throughout the Julian Alps serve climbers and hikers.

The Julian Alps have extensive and unusual areas of karst. This kind of limestone formation occurs when water etches through areas of soluble rock, boring holes, leaving dry channels and furrows, and creating sinks and basins. The Seven Lakes region is rich in many curious karst formations (indeed, the word *karst* has a Slovene derivation). The limestone of the Julian Alps is also quite rich in fossils.

Many alpine animals, including the chamois, are native here; the ibex— which had become extinct in this region, as in many parts of the Alps—has been reintroduced, and colonies of marmots have been established. Alpine flowers are exceptionally interesting and abundant, and wildflower lovers may see several species hard to find elsewhere in the Alps. Several flowers are endemic to these mountains, such as Zois bellflower (*Campanula zoisii*), with its long, blue-violet bells, nearly closed behind a white, star-shaped mouth, and pink hogweed (*Heracleum siifolium*), whose large bursts of bright pink blossoms are much prettier than its name. Although endemic flowers in other parts of the Alps are sometimes rare, or may closely resemble species found elsewhere, these are distinctive and easily seen.

This lovely region saw bitter fighting during both world wars. The Soča River, the former border between Italy and Austria-Hungary, became one of

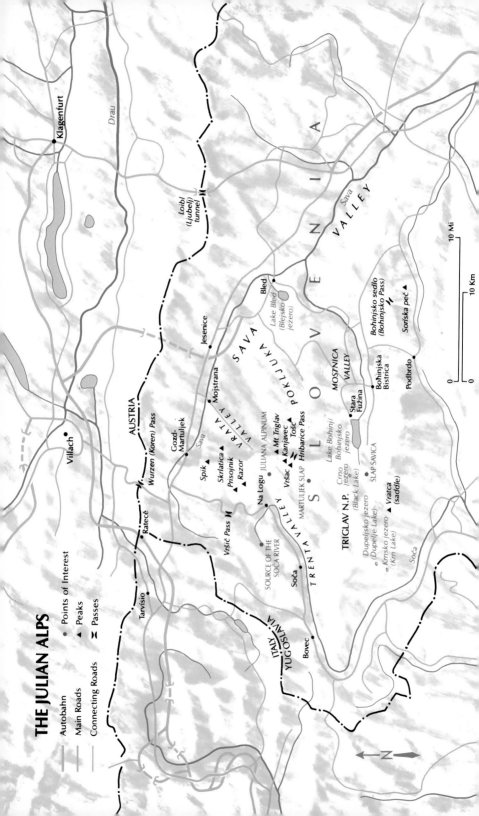

THE JULIAN ALPS

Autobahn
Main Roads
Connecting Roads

• Points of Interest
▲ Peaks
✕ Passes

Klagenfurt

Drau

Loibl (Ljubelj) tunnel

S L O V E N I A

Sava VALLEY

Bled

Lake Bled (Blejsko jezero)

Jesenice

AUSTRIA

Wurzen (Koren) Pass

Gozd-Martuljek

Mojstrana

SAVA POKLJUKA

MOSTNICA VALLEY

Bohinjsko sedlo (Bohinjsko Pass)

Soríska peč ▲

Villach

VRATA VALLEY

Stara Fužina

Bohinjska Bistrica

Podbrdo

Ratecè

Spik ▲
Škrlatica ▲
Prisojnik ▲
Razor ▲

Na Logu

JULIANA ALPINUM

▲ Mt Triglav
▲ Kanjavec
Vršac ▲ Tosc ▲
Hribarice Pass

Lake Bohinj/ Bohinjsko jezero

SLAP SAVICA

Vršič Pass

MARTULJEK SLAP

Črno jezero (Black Lake)

TRIGLAV N.P.

Vratca (saddle)

Tarvisio

SOURCE OF THE SOČA RIVER

Soča

TRENTA VALLEY

Dupeljsko jezero (Dupelje Lake)

Krnsko jezero (Krn Lake)

Soča

ITALY
YUGOSLAVIA

Bovec

10 Mi

10 Km

N

The road over the Vršič Pass, west of Mt. Triglav, nestles between rock walls before winding through a mountain valley. This pass route provides spectacular views as it descends into the Trenta Valley.

the bloodiest fronts during World War I. The Germans invaded the region during World War II, encountering fierce resistance from the local people. The countryside is full of monuments to the tragic events of this time.

From Austria, there are entry points south of Villach at the Wurzen (Koren) Pass, which descends to the Upper Sava Valley, and farther east, south of Klagenfurt through the Loibl (Ljubelj) tunnel. A new tunnel, projected for 1992, will connect Villach with Jesenice. The main approach from Italy is via Tarvísio to Rateče.

Several resorts are located on the periphery of the park, most notably to the east and north. The plateau above the massif is crisscrossed with hiking trails. An auto tour of the area could begin either from Bled or Bohinjsko jezero, a lake within the park. It is possible to make a complete driving circuit around the park, although the last segment of the trip, between Podbrdo and Bohinjska Bistrica in the southwest, is poorly marked.

Bled

Bled is the only resort in Slovenia that is internationally known, with first-class hotels among its accommodations. It is east of the park, on the shore of Lake Bled, surrounded by wooded hills. In the center of the lake a baroque church stands on a tiny island that you can visit by boat. The other hallmark of the lake is the cliff on its western shore where an eleventh-century castle perches dramatically on the height; from here there are good views of the Julian Alps to the west. Bled boasts an 18-hole golf course, as well as swimming, boating, and skating in winter. The main headquarters of Triglav National Park is also here.

Lake Bohinj/Bohinjsko Jezero

Although not nearly as well known outside of Yugoslavia as Lake Bled, this larger lake is more scenic, with a backdrop of steep, rugged mountain walls. Lake Bohinj is at the foot of the Julian Alps, within the boundary of the national park, and is the starting point for many hikes. The Yugoslavs have preserved Lake Bohinj in something close to its natural state by permitting almost no development along the shoreline. The few hotels near the lake are mostly tucked away in the trees. While the lake is used for boating and swimming, there are no docks (you just pull your canoe or kayak to the water's edge and paddle away), and the grassy banks make a simple beach. The most visible structure at the head of the lake is the little Gothic church of St. John, whose interior is decorated with frescoes, of which the oldest date from the fourteenth century.

At the western end of the lake is Slap Savica, a waterfall that emerges from a tunnel in the mountain wall—the source of the River Sava, which flows into the Danube. From the southwestern corner of the lake, a cable car ascends to the Vogel ski area on a terrace overlooking the lake, with a fine view of the Julian Alps including Mount Triglav. This is the highest ski center in the Triglav area, with a hotel near the upper cable-car station.

Stara Fužina. Apart from the sprinkling of hotels and shops near Bohinjsko jezero, this village, about 1 km/0.6 mi from the lake, is the only nearby settlement. It is unlike any other village found today near an important alpine location. Compared with Stara Fužina, even unspoiled villages look like resorts. To walk through its winding lanes is like stepping back into another age: houses, barns, and stables are jumbled together amid little gardens of vegetables and flowers, and every yard has an open-sided hay rack.

Triglav Lakes Valley. This is considered the heart of the park. Seven lakes of differing colors—one blue, another green, another almost black—are strung in an arc high on the plateau northwest of Bohinjsko jezero. To see all the lakes requires a two- or three-day trip. The Crno jezero (Black Lake) is the southernmost lake, closest to Bohinjsko jezero. Continuing northward along the trail, the next lake is Dvojno jezero (Double Lake); in early summer when the water level is high, its two parts are connected, forming one lake. The Koča pri Sedmerih triglavskih jezerih (Triglav Lake Lodge—essentially, an alpine club hut) is next to this lake; on the opposite side are some karst sinkholes, in which you may hear the sound of gurgling water.

The next lake to the north is Veliko jezero (Great Lake), the largest of the seven. North and slightly east is Zeleno jezero (Green Lake), the most shallow of the group, tinged green by algae; alpine newts (*Triturus alpestris*) may be seen in this lake. It is followed by Rjavo jezero (Brown Lake) and its neighbor, the very small Mlaka v Laštah (Laste Pond), which sometimes dries up in summer; nearby is the Zasavska Koča na Prehodavcih (Zasavska hut). The last lake is Jezero pod Vršacem (Lake below Vršac), which lies between two peaks—Vršac (2,194 m/7,198 ft) and Kanjavec (2,568 m/8,425 ft). This is the highest of the Triglav lakes.

The Triglav Lakes Valley may be reached from the western end of Bohinjsko jezero (you can take a taxi or the path along the lakeshore). Near the Savica waterfall, a trail climbs steeply up through woods to reach Crno jezero and the plateau.

Velska Dolina. A tour of two to three days can begin at Crno jezero, continuing to the Triglav Lake Lodge or the Zasavska hut for an overnight stay. From the latter, hikers can continue eastward to Hribarice Pass (with a good view of Kanjavec). The trail descends eastward through the Velska Dolina (valley) to the basin of Velo polje and the Vodnikova koča (Vodnikov hut), another possibility for an overnight stay. South of this hut, at Na zagonu, a trail leads east around Tošc (2,275 m/7,464 ft), then turns southward toward Koča na Uskovnici (Uskovnici hut). Instead of continuing to this hut, however, you can take the trail that intersects to the west. This leads southward to Planinski dom bohinjskih prvoborcev (the Mountain Lodge of Bohinj veterans). From there you can descend by the Mostnica Valley through the Mostnica gorge, spanned by the Devil's Bridge, to Stara Fužina and then to Bohinjsko jezero.

Pokljuka. To the north of the stretch between Stara Fužina and Bled is the Pokljuka plateau, in which several peat bogs are set amid a forest of hand-

Pages 336 and 337: Tranquil and unspoiled Lake Bohinj, framed by the Julian Alps, offers swimming and boating opportunities.

some spruce. The location of these marshy meadows is unusual in that most peat bogs in Europe are found much farther north. On the Pokljuka bogs are found wild cranberry (*Vaccinium oxycoccus*), bog whortleberry (*Vaccinium uliginosum*), and several species of sedge and mosses, including peat moss (*Sphagnum*) and few-flowered sedge (*Carex pauciflora*).

Mojstrana and Vrata

The road along the northern side of the park passes through Jesenice, the only industrial town on the route, to reach Mojstrana, an old village on the banks of the Sava and Bistrica rivers, now a small, quiet resort. From Mojstrana, a gravel road, about 13 km/8.1 mi long, leads southwest up the wooded Vrata Valley, approaching the north face of Mount Triglav. About 5 km/3 mi up this valley on the western side are the Upper and Lower Peričnik waterfalls. The road passes Aljažev dom, a hut for climbers and hikers bound for Mount Triglav. A little farther, at the road's end, is an arresting monument in the form of a huge carabiner clipped to a piton (two items of climbing equipment); it memorializes the partisans and mountaineers killed in this region between 1941 and 1945.

From the end of the road, there is a grand view of a huge, U-shaped wall—the north face of Mount Triglav, a tremendous span of rock 1,000 m/ 3,280 ft high and 4 km/2.5 mi wide. The pale gray limestone of this rampart is printed with an intricate texture of folds and fluting. Above, the summit rears its head, streaked with snow. This immense wall is a testing ground for expert rock climbers.

West of Mojstrana is Gozd-Martuljek, facing the peaks of Spik (2,472 m/ 8,110 ft) and Skrlatica (2,738 m/8,983 ft). At the foot of Mount Spik are the Martuljek waterfalls.

Kranjska Gora

This attractive village is on the northern rim of the park, west of Mojstrana. It is a real resort, with several hotels, restaurants, and shops, yet on a small scale, and a ski center in winter—one of the best-known in Yugoslavia, with several lifts; the skiing is good for beginners and intermediates. From a small lake south of the village, there is a fine view of Mounts Prisojnik (2,547 m/ 8,356 ft) and Razor (2,601 m/8,533 ft).

Krnica Valley. To hike into the mountains from Kranjska Gora you can drive south up this valley and park at the Hotel Erika. Follow the path south to Koča v Krnici (Krnica hut), and continue to Kriška stena, a very fine cirque below the wall of Križ (2,410 m/7,907 ft). To the west is Razor, to the northeast, Spik and Skrlatica.

Vršič Pass. From Kranjska Gora, a road climbs steeply southwest to the Vršič Pass, the link to the Trenta Valley (one of the most scenic points on any auto tour of the region). This road was built by Russian prisoners of war during World War I, along the old border between Italy and the Austro-Hungarian empire. On the way up to the pass from Kranjska Gora there is a small Russian chapel made of wood shingles, both charming and poignant, built in memory of the hundreds of prisoners buried by a snow avalanche in the winter of 1915–16. This route runs between great walls of rock thrust up on every side. The pass yields close and impressive views of the huge, pale gray crags and towers of the northwestern Julian Alps, especially of Prisojnik and Razor, with dizzying views down to the Trenta Valley.

Trenta Valley

The road from the Vršič Pass descends to the Trenta Valley. The source of the Soča River, which flows into the Adriatic, is on the south side of the pass: it can be reached by taking the road to the right (northwest) at the first junction; a gravel path leads partway along the stream, but to see the source you have to scramble over rocks where there is no external protection. Below the rocks is a deep, almost vertical channel in the base of the mountain, at the bottom of which is a clear, blue-green pool. The water reemerges farther down as the Soča, a pretty, light blue river favored by kayaking enthusiasts. The main road continues on the left (south) of the junction. It passes the Alpinum Juliana, a botanical garden of flowers found in the Julian Alps. A little farther down the valley is Na Logu, a pretty hamlet surrounded by mountains. (A new national park information center is planned for Na Logu.) The road continues southwest through the village of Soča.

Krn Lakes. These lakes, in the southwestern region of the park, may be approached from Soča in the Trenta Valley. A trail heads up the Lepena Valley to the Dom dr. Klementa Juga (Dr. Klement Jug lodge); from this hut you can take a trail southeast to the Krn lakes. It leads first to Dupeljsko jezero (Duplje Lake), next to the Koča pri Krnskih jezerih (Lodge at the Krn Lakes), and then to Krnsko jezero (Krn Lake) below the summit of Krn (2,245 m/ 7,366 ft), the highest peak in the southwest of the park. From the Krn Lakes lodge, you can continue eastward over the Vratca saddle to the Koča pod Bogatinom (Bogatin hut), and then to Crno jezero, the most southern of the Triglav seven lakes.

Zadnjica Valley. The Zadnjica Valley, in the north central area of the park, climbs into very scenic country near some of its greatest mountains. Most notably, the valley offers a view of the west face of Triglav, 2,000 m/

EUROPEAN CYCLAMEN
Cyclamen europaeum

The intensely sweet fragrance of the European cyclamen makes it a rarity among the generally unscented alpine flowers. Though this very pretty flower hangs downward from its short stalk, its pale mauve petals fold back and stand erect, giving it an upside-down look. The leaves, very broad and heart-shaped, are clustered at the base of the plant. They are dark green, marbled with a paler green, on their upper surface, but reddish underneath. This small plant, 5 to 15 cm/2 to 6 in high, grows in lime-rich soils up to 2,000 m/ 6,562 ft, in wooded areas (often among deciduous trees), thickets, or among shrubs, flowering from June to August. It is rather rare, but can most frequently be seen in southern Alpine areas such as southeastern France, the Swiss Ticino, and Yugoslavia's Julian Alps.

6,560 ft from floor to summit—the greatest altitude differential in the Julian Alps. It also affords a view of the steep wall of Kanjavec. From Koča Zlatorog (Zlatorog hut) at Na Logu in the Trenta Valley, the way leads eastward up the Zadnjica Valley. To make a loop trip and return to Na Logu, take the trail southwest at the first junction to Trebiški Dol; continue from there on the trail southwest and then northwest to the Trenta Valley.

The Western Edge of Mount Triglav Park

Although the stretch of road between Podbrdo and Bohinjska Bistrica is difficult to navigate, it is possible to complete a circle around the park by following this route. From Soča, in the Trenta Valley, the road around the park continues to Bovec, a modest resort. The mountains on the west of the park are lower, less rugged and rocky. Approaching the Italian border, the villages on this side of the park have a northern Italian appearance, with houses that have plaster walls and red-tiled roofs. As the road turns around the southwest corner of the park, however, past the Most na Soči reservoir, the landscape becomes more rugged and very hilly, and the road must twist continuously. The villages look Slovenian again, though Podbrdo, with a small factory, is less appealing. To return from there to Bohinj, you must drive past Soriška and over the Bohinjsko sedlo (pass), where the road is not well marked, to reach Bohinjska Bistrica.

Near Mt. Triglav, fall colors at the tree line highlight the beauty of Zeleno jezero (Green Lake), the fourth of seven lakes flowing one into another down the mountainside.

Index

Chamois

The type in this book was set in Century Expanded 701b and Futura Book,
input on the Macintosh IIsi in QuarkXpress 3.0,
and output on the Mergenthaler Linotron 202
at Graphic Arts Composition, Inc., Philadelphia, Pennsylvania, USA.

The book was printed and bound by
Dai Nippon Printing Company, Ltd., Tokyo, Japan.